Think Outside the Box:

The CIA of Blended Learning and 10+ Designs for Secondary Schools

KIM LOOMIS

Published by: i3DigitalPD, LLC
Las Vegas, NV
http://i3digitalpd.com

First Printing: October 2017

DEDICATION

This book is dedicated to my two daughters, Jolie and Jocelyn, who motivate and inspire me to give my best to others every day. In my teacher trainings, I tell participants, "When you leave (e.g. retire), don't just leave. Leave a legacy." This means, pass on your knowledge and wisdom. Always remember these words: have a good heart, honor your family, and use your internal voices. You are my legacy.

CONTENTS

ACKNOWLEDGMENTS

"If I have seen further it is by standing on the shoulders of giants."
Sir Isaac Newton

This book was born out of love and passion for getting digital content into the hands of every learner. To not let it be reserved for the select few, or a special population, but creating classrooms that embrace digital curriculum as a partner in educating today's youth. My eyes were first opened nearly twenty years ago when Jhone Ebert, today the Senior Deputy Commissioner for Education Policy in New York State Education Department asked me to join her in a small Cyber Schoolhouse project in Clark County School District. I cannot thank her enough for showing me a new world and all its possibilities (see video on page 21). She is a wonder woman, whose heart is centered on children. Jhone will forever be my innovative leader mentor.

It was through the research and sharing by the Christensen Institute, the International Association for K-12 Online Learning (iNACOL), The Learning Accelerator (TLA), and Evergreen Education Group that forged a path that others like myself have been able to grow and expand upon. Many thanks to them for all they have done and continue to do in providing high quality resources for policy makers, district administrators, and classroom teachers looking to embrace digital curriculum in their states, districts, schools, and classrooms. I cherish the many collaborative conversations with peers as we attempted to make meaning of the new learning environments via the numerous whitepapers, reports, and publications from these torchbearers. Thank you, Allison Powell, former iNACOL vice president, and John Watson, CEO of Evergreen Education Group, for the many deep heart-to-heart chats about a field we love most.

Clark County School District building administrators have made me reflect, grow, and envision more than I ever thought possible. Vendor partners too. Thank you for asking the tough questions. For making me **think outside the box**. Together we built amazing program designs. This book is filled with your stories. If it wasn't for you, there would be no book. Thank you for allowing me to compile and catalog your deployment designs to share with others. It was vendor partners, Jason Mitchell who said, "Kim, you should write a book" with Nora Ocariza and Elaine Crawley who second and third the idea that inspired me to put pen to paper.

i

To the K-12 Online and Blended Learning and BlendED teams, thank you for putting up with my passion and desire to do and be more. Together we helped hundreds of schools and thousands of classroom teachers build high quality digital learning environments, via professional development, district-develop digital content, digital tools and systems, plus side-by-side consultation. Much thanks to Neal Shebeck for allowing me to think outside the box and push tech innovation. You have never let me down. A special thank you to Tricia McDermott who read every word before publishing. Lucas Leavitt, many thanks for our frenzy high energy out of the box discussion. You guys are the best!

My rock through all this was my family: Jaini, Jolie, and Jocelyn. Thank you for all your love and support. My heart belongs to you three. Yet, as you know, I also have a burning fire to grow digital learning. So much so, I can't stop talking about it - in the car, at the dinner table, even while taking family walks. Thanks for putting up with my crazed obsession. I love you.

My final thanks is reserved for you, the reader. It is your commitment to grow professionally through the process of reading, reflecting, and refining your work that our students, tomorrow's future, benefits from. I praise you for being a continued lifelong learner. I hope this book compels you to **think outside the box**.

Icons by Zlatko Najdenovski from www.flaticon.com
and others via Icons8.com

INTRODUCTION

Too often schools or districts purchase digital courseware for a singular purpose, typically as a credit recovery solution. One box, one solution. However, digital courseware can solve several problems and create numerous opportunities. Having access to digital content creates scenarios that you may have not even considered. Thinking outside the box allows us to see beyond the most obvious. Thinking outside the box opens doors to new prospects. Thinking outside the box forces us to be innovative. That is why this book is titled **think outside the box**. Boxes come in all sizes; from the student information system in your district, to the four walls of a classroom, or even the socio-economic classification one was raised in. It's a reminder to all of us that boxes do <u>not</u> define our limitations.

I was born to a poor family in central California, with parents who dropped out of high school in grade ten to get married. My mother was pregnant with my older brother. My parents started adulthood at sixteen years old, no high school diploma, and little to offer an employer. This drove me to want more. I always knew that education was the way out. I remember a time in second grade when I was misbehaving and causing problems in school and at home. My mother, a waitress, and father, a truck driver, were going through a divorce. My mother was so upset with me after an altercation at school. Back then principals spanked misbehaving students and I surely got one, with my mother's consent. When she picked me up from the school office, she could not even look at me. She would not speak to me. She was a wise woman and asked a friend to intercede. The three of us sat at the kitchen table discussing my attitude and actions. At one point, the friend asked me, "Kim, what do you want to be when you grow up?" I responded, "I want to be a teacher." My mother quickly stood up, slammed her fist on the table, and shouted, "Teachers don't act like this!"

That night, a dream was born. I never wavered from wanting to be a teacher. While going through grade school, I would ask myself if this grade level or subject matter was something I might want to teach. Finally, in my senior year, while sitting in a Calculus class, I realized that math came easy to me and it was fun, so... teaching high school mathematics would be my future.

I taught high school math for ten years. Professional development and personal growth strove me to be *more* and offer *more* to my students. I was on numerous textbook adoption committees, helped write Nevada state standards and proficiency exams, conducted countless teacher workshops, and spoke at national conferences.

Later I turned that passion to teacher training, knowing that I could impact more young students through the lives of their teachers that I influenced. My path has been filled with helping educators to grow and expand opportunities for their students. I've been a teacher trainer, school administrator, curriculum coordinator, instructional design manager, headed high school reform and innovative projects, and now lead Nevada's Clark County School District's K-12 digital learning initiative.

Passion for Digital Learning

I fell in love with online and blended learning in 2000, when I taught an online credit recovery course to eighth grade math students. I was transitioning to a teacher training job that summer and knew that if I could build an online course and students could learn online, then adults could do so too. Since then, digital learning for both students and adults has been my love and passion, by embracing digital learning to expand innovation in classrooms and via professional development.

Nevada's Clark County School District is the fifth largest in the nation with over 320,000 students in more than 350 schools. It was also one of the earliest adopter of a virtual high school and I was there in the beginning, middle, and even today I continue to work with the Nevada Learning Academy at Clark County School District (CCSD).

My passion for online and blended learning came to a head in 2011. It was a time when the Clark County's superintendent was a board member of the International Association for K-12 Online Learning (iNACOL) and made an audacious goal of 100,000 students in an online or blended learning environment in the next five years. The 100,000 goal was instrumental to the growth of online and blended learning in Clark County.

Let's talk numbers. If the district (at that time) had a little over 300,000 students, then the 100,000 goal was one-third of the student population. There was no way one program or one school, like the virtual high school - even with concurrent enrollment, was going to carry the burden. So, if one-third of the student body was to engage in an online or blended learning environment, then one-third of the teachers would have to be ready to teach in this environment with digital content and tools readily available to them. This became the three pillars of my job as the newly appointed K-12 Online and Blended Learning Director. And our success:

1. Professional Development: Teacher training was a must! 100,000 students were over one-third of the students in Clark County, which meant that one-third of the teachers would need training in pedagogy and philosophy of digital learning.

2. Digital Learning Environment: A digital learning environment was needed. Teachers would need a virtual classroom setting in the form of a district enterprise learning management system. One that every teacher had access to and training on how to create quality online lessons, based on the components of an effective lesson. But you and I know that there is not enough time in the day to build digital content. So getting digital content into teachers hands, ready for deployment, was essential.

3. Digital Content: Get digital content into classrooms. You may remember 2011 was also the same year Common Core Standards were hitting the national forefront. Clark County's virtual high school needed to revamp their online content, so we decided that any newly developed or revised content would be available to all teachers. Over the years, we have created a catalog of over fifty semester district-developed digital courses for grades six through twelve.

Size matters. Clark County is a huge train. Over 350 schools long. It's hard to turn a train, much less one with hundreds of cars. It was going to take time to meet the goal. The size of Clark County also made it a great "research lab" with numerous schools, classrooms, and courageous leaders. Imagine all the data that could be collected, programs that could be piloted and refined, or much less all the trials and errors made along the way. It has been my pleasure to partner with central office staff, classroom teachers, and school administrators to grow digital learning. In this book, you will hear many of their stories.

Growing Digital Learning

Vendor courseware is typically the first step into the digital learning arena. Like most large districts, Clark County had a high percentage of dropouts that aligned with a low graduation rate. Digital learning via vendor courseware was a quick fix. It opened the door to quick credit recovery. In 2009, while working as the high school reform coordinator, I was on the team that brought in a large vendor contract for virtual credit recovery.

Buying the vendor courseware was the easy part. It's all the planning and policies, like course deployment and coding, that had to be thought through. This also included ensuring eligibility from the National Collegiate Athletic Association (NCAA) non-traditional courses. Over the years, I've had numerous opportunities to work with NCAA for Clark County schools. When a new student information system was purchased, I worked with central office staff to ensure that we established a course coding system that would not only meet NCAA requirements but also created quantitative data to measure progress toward the 100,000 goal.

Vendor courseware contracts and deployment are usually an easy adoption for comprehensive traditional brick-and-mortar schools to start their digital learning endeavors. Over the years, I've managed several vendor contracts and deployments, from systems set-up to writing policies and procedures, as well as helping school design digital learning programs. For many schools the first step into vendor courseware is with credit recovery in mind. Too often that is where the thinking stops.

I challenge schools to look beyond credit recovery. To **think outside the box**. Working side-by-side with school administrators at over one hundred secondary schools in Clark County, I've been able to identify ten designs for deploying digital courseware. These ten innovative digital learning designs not only look beyond credit recovery, they challenge or disrupt traditional schooling, setting the foundations of creative and engaging learning environments that students and parents are crying for. See Part two in the book for the ten digital learning designs.

For the record, we made the 100,000 student goal in December 2015. Six months early!

Creating District Courses

As I was saying, to reach the goal we needed high quality digital content available to teachers so they could deploy a variety of online and blended learning environments. We secured vendor contracts, but also knew that in-house district-developed digital assets would reduce the reliance and cost of vendor contracts. Especially if blended was going to be the future of education.

Curriculum and instructional design has always held a soft spot in my heart, so we created a team of course designers for the new district-developed courses that could be deployed in the district enterprise learning management system. From my early days in creating an eighth-grade recovery math course, I knew that using a third-party authoring system makes content portable. Great tip from Julie Young, formerly at Florida Virtual. Thank goodness too, because in the early 2000's we went through several learning management systems. Smack dab in the middle of the five-year goal of 100,000 students, a new learning management system was taking over in many of the Nevada's higher education facilities and Clark County jumped on. Today, every teacher has access to the district's enterprise Canvas™ learning management system that is integrated with the student information system for ease of student enrollment.

Clark County has a strong curriculum and instruction division that unwraps standards and benchmarks curriculum content into semester-based courses. Using these resources, we journeyed into the development of secondary digital courses. Over the years, my team of four dedicated full-time designers, one in each of the core areas, have built a full catalog of secondary, grades six through twelve, district-developed digital courses that all CCSD teachers can access.

The full district-developed digital courses with teacher resources, discussion questions, student assignments, and exams - along with answer keys and grading rubrics, can be deployed in the Canvas™ learning management system. Since we used a third-party authoring tool, weblinks to digital content are made available to teachers within the district Curriculum Engine that teachers use to plan and calendar lessons. This allowed teachers who use Google® Classroom to easily distribute the digital content to students as well.

Over the years the course development and design process has grown. We've made mistakes and learned from failures. But I'm proud to say that my designers have been honored by SoftChalk™, the third-party authoring tool, with awards in the 2016 and 2017 annual design contests. Having a team, working with templates, with a strong development, design, and review process has kept us learning and growing each and every year.

Teacher Professional Development

Of the three pillars to our success, teacher professional development was the most needed and the first endeavor we tackled. Building secondary semester-based courses takes time, so this gave us the opportunity to design a professional development program that required teachers to become digital learners in the district enterprise learning management system. Our belief has always been, *"it is difficult to be a teacher in an environment that you yourself were never a student of,"* thus it was important to build a program with online courses for adult learners.

To ensure that everyone had a standardized definition of what blended learning is and how to create quality digital learning environments, the national research from the Christensen Institute and the International Association for K-12 Online Learning (iNACOL) was used. A two-tier professional development program that focused on philosophy and pedagogy first was established. Once participants understood what is blended, why to blend, and how to blend, gained in the courses in the first tier, then they could enroll into professional development courses on tools of blended, like utilizing a learning management system, video production, and elements of designing online digital content.

The two courses in the first tier were kept affordable, only $15 for enrollment. This opened the door for educators to become an online student in the local learning management system rather inexpensively. The tools courses run the full pricing of $75 each. As the online and blended learning industry expanded, the professional development courses were revised and new digital learning courses were added to the catalog. Putting the foundational pedagogy and philosophy professional development first and keeping them inexpensive created an easy path to start a teacher's journey into digital learning.

Changing the Classroom

In 2007, I oversaw a multi-million-dollar grant in high school reform where eight Clark County schools were attempting to transform the landscape of the high school experience. It was a time when we were looking at small learning communities and ways to bring rigor and relevance to the curriculum, while capturing kid's hearts. Lots of big money was being thrown around, but the classroom itself did not change.

Students were still listening to adults preach to the middle. Students continued to drop out. Achievement gaps continued to grow. Frustrations continued to climb on the part of administrators, teachers, students, and parents. The nation was failing, and I was part of it. No matter how much money was thrown at these schools, nothing was changing. We were spinning our wheels and going nowhere.

This was also the time online and blended learning was taking root in new charter schools. Not only were public schools losing students to charter schools, but innovative teachers and administrators were jumping ship to build new engaging technology driven learning environments in visionary charters. KIPP™ and Rocketship™ laid foundations for elementary blended learning. Vendors like K12™ and Connections™ Academy took their courseware and created online and blended learning schools nationwide.

The lack of success in high school reform, without changing how teachers instructed and how students learned was a huge failure. Yet, it was the tipping point for digital learning environments to step in and change the role of both teachers and students.

I remember being at a high school where I had once taught math years ago, meeting with their staff. We were talking about the potential of digital learning. Teachers were having difficulty grasping the idea. I asked a math teacher, *"Would it bother you if a student mastered Algebra without you?"* You should have seen the shock and awe on their faces, when I said, *"That's the power of digital learning. Some students will need you less, providing time to service those that need you most."* I'm proud to say that this school is one of the most innovative schools in Clark County with numerous deployment designs of digital courseware; from online courses for original credit, blended classrooms, unit recovery, and of course, credit recovery. They have a strong leader with a vision, who is willing to **think outside the box**.

That's the power of digital content. Students taking ownership of their own learning, and teachers spending time with the students who need them most. No longer teaching to the middle, but guiding, coaching, and meeting individual student needs. Isn't that why we all became educators in the first place? Because we care. We want our students to succeed. We want them to learn the skills to excel as adults. Qualities such as self-discipline, perseverance, and time management are built when using digital learning. These are also the foundations to college, career, and citizenship.

The Future of Digital Learning

Innovative school models, new learning environments, re-thinking staffing, and how student learn are all exciting. The growth of digital learning, both on the side of educational technology and online courseware have opened opportunities that engage students and meet individual needs. Technology continues to grow in hardware and software capabilities. I've seen the growth of digital learning from *attempting* to draw a select few students to a fully online school environment, to today's classroom where students have technology and online curriculum at their fingertips in traditional comprehensive neighborhood schools. It's truly exciting times.

Yet, my frustrations stem from the mystical and mythical belief that technology is magic. And magic means easy - right? I fight mindsets of central office and school administrator who *"bought it and forgot it"* when it comes to digital curriculum. They don't cast a vision, document paths to success, or monitor teachers or student usage data.

Frustration also comes in the mindset of *"set it and forget it."* Especially in secondary schools who assign digital courseware and leave students unsupported and floundering. Then they act surprised when students fail to complete courses.

Not only will schools of the future have to **think outside the box**, they must think differently about the relationships of curriculum, instruction, and assessment (CIA). In blended and personalized learning, that's:

Digital **C**urriculum

Guided **I**nstruction

Authentic **A**ssessment

More about the CIA of blended learning, ten deployment designs, and changing mindsets can all be found in this book. With nearly two decades in the online and blended learning arena, I've seen the growth and potential of technology to transform the classroom. My passion runs deep and I love sharing it with others. In these pages, I hope to provide readers with options and opportunities to **think outside the box**.

Speaking about passion, let me say that this book was written from the heart. Thus, I may not have followed all the grammar rules. For when the heart speaks its intense fervor, zeal, and frenzy. You may have noticed just by reading this introduction that I speak in an informal tone. Sentences may start with *and* or *but*. And some sentences will end with prepositions. I hope that I have not offended readers, as I have written from my heart, in a conversational style between friends who seek to learn and grow from one another.

I have had the fortune to be in the middle of an educational revolution, in the nation's fifth largest public school district that provided me ample opportunity to see the cautious beginnings, the messy middle with numerous trials and errors, to the flourishing fruits of our efforts. Unlike other authors who share a single school or classroom experience, or the researchers who compiled examples of fine-tuned exemplars, this book was written from a practitioner's first-hand experience of nearly one-hundred schools. I've been in the weeds seeing many failures and success stories. I have experiences with hardware and software purchases, crafting a plan for developing digital content aligned to strict benchmarks and standards, establishing professional development to change teacher mindsets, and handling messy phone calls from parents and the National Collegiate Athletic Association not from just one school but many. I've worked with building administrators, classroom teachers, and central office staff to craft plans for establishing digital learning environments. For the past two decades, my job has been to **think outside the box** and help others create innovative learning environments. I've loved every minute of it and being a good teacher, I want to share my enthusiasm and obsessive energy with others.

Like this book, i3DigitalPD.com was created so that I can share my passion beyond the *box* of Clark County. I truly enjoy working with schools and districts who are ready to **think outside the box** when it comes to digital learning. I hope that one day we will meet and I can hear your dreams and desires and together we can make them come true for your students. Our future.

Think Outside the Box

PART 1
FOUNDATIONS OF BLENDED

I've had nearly two decades in the online and blended learning arena. I've seen full online learning programs change with the times, by adding face-to-face support for their learners and adopting a blended enriched virtual model. Better yet, I've seen traditional institutions embraced digital courseware so that students don't have to leave their neighborhood schools to recovery credits. Most kept the highly qualified core teacher and student distance, using a virtual lab setting in what could be called an a la carte model. Credit recovery was one of the first steps to blended learning in the public sector, while charter schools flourished and began using digital courseware in new and innovative classrooms. It was from charters and small public-sector experiments with digital curriculum that researchers like the Christensen Institute were able to define blended learning and classify models. The North American Council for Online Learning (NACOL) which began as a venue for virtual schools to collaborate, added international and K-12 to become the International Association for K-12 Online Learning (iNACOL), a leading voice in online, blended, and competency education.

These early beginnings show how blended learning laid their roots into today's classrooms. It was a time when we began to realize that the world was changing. That technology was becoming a norm in our lives. Society began calling for changes in education as proficiency gaps continued, dropout numbers increased, and graduation rates declined. Would having technology in the classroom become a knight in shining armor? It's not devices in the classroom, but *how* we use them that matters. We must go beyond substitution. If we are only using devices as fancy notebooks, or student agendas, and teachers are still lecturing, but now students can view the presentation at their desk on a laptop, teachers still control the environment, the curriculum, and the pace of student learning. Classroom pedagogy did not change. Pupils are still restricted to the teacher's calendared lesson plans and delivery timeframe.

I believe the power of technology lies in digital curriculum. It has the potential to open the doors to a brighter future, help fill gaps, and provide more time for deeper learning. It puts the student in the driver's seat, one that is personalized for their individual needs by allowing them to rewind, replay, and own their learning. Teachers are afforded more time to differentiate with immediate data to rectify and stretch student learning in the moment. Yet, the question lies in how do we prepare staff for the change in pedagogy. Blended learning requires teachers to share the stage with digital courseware and empowers students to take ownership in their own learning. In this section we tackle this change process.

This Part of the Book

Each chapter in this part of the book will help you understand the infrastructure of blended learning, from when and where it started, to the various models, and the changes that must take place for adopting blended as a strategy for personalizing learning. It is filled with numerous videos to help you visualize the different blended learning models, while you consider embracing digital programs. As with any transformation, the change process will be rocky, especially when trying to move someone's cheese. They key will be to focus on the change in pedagogy.

CIA of Blended

In the blended learning classroom, teachers will need to think differently about the relationships of curriculum, instruction, and assessment (CIA). However, in the blended arena there are distinct qualifiers to the CIA:

    C = *Digital* **C**urriculum,

    I = *Guided* **I**nstruction,

    A = *Authentic* **A**ssessment.

Understanding and implementing the CIA of blended learning is all-important in transitioning to a balanced approach between computer *digital* **c**urriculum, teacher *guided* **i**nstruction, and learner *authentic* **a**ssessment. You will undoubtedly want to share the CIA infographic found in this chapter when planning your program and deploying professional development with staff.

Cost of Change

When making changes, there is always a cost. Moving from the familiar to an unknown is difficult. One of my favorite terms is to "go slow, to go fast." Ensure that as you adopt blended learning models and pedagogy to leave plenty of time for making the change. Know that the transition phase will be messy, possibly disorganized, and highly emotional. Cast a clear vision. Support it with professional development. Help your staff to shift their mindset.

Mindsets

Asking staff to embrace new instructional strategies will require a growth mindset. One that is willing to take risks and learn from failures. iNACOL has conducted research to identify the mindset shifts that must take place in a blended classroom. Much of the skills are the same as those needed in a traditional classroom, yet like the CIA have a few distinct qualifiers. Helping your staff determine the type of mindset shifts needed will be imperative. Depending on your model, staff will need to adopt one, or more, of four mindsets:

1. Online
2. Blended
3. Innovator
4. Designer

Be sure to check out the infographic in this chapter about the cost of change for each of these mindsets.

Read On

This part of the book is paramount in laying the foundation for digital learning adoption. Throughout the remainder of the book, we will continue to reference mindsets and CIA of blended learning. As you read this section start to think about the professional development needs of your staff. Administrators must ensure teachers have a clear and stable base grounded in the underpinnings of blended so that they can create quality and successful digital learning environments in a classroom centered around the student. One that releases ownership of the learning to the pupils. The last three chapters in this section is designed to help teachers understand their role in establishing a blended learning instructional model that differentiates to meet individual student needs. Look for sample lesson planning suggestions. Enjoy the read.

CHAPTER 1
MAKING THE DIGITAL TRANSFORMATION

"...according to our projections, 50 percent of all high school courses will be taken online by 2019—the vast majority of them in blended-learning school environments with teachers, which will fundamentally move learning beyond the four walls and traditional arrangement of today's all-too-familiar classroom."

Clayton M. Christensen and Michael B. Horn[1]

Day-to-day use of technology leads the world today. When we forget our phones at home, we feel out of sorts, less connected, and typically turn around and go back home to get them. Technology has transformed our lives in so many ways, from automobile advancements - who needs a key anymore, to the food in our refrigerators where you can peek inside from your phone on your drive home to check if you have enough milk. We even look to technology to help us learn, with "Do It Yourself" (DIY) videos at our fingertips.

Technology can be a powerful tool for the classroom, but like any tool in a toolbox, just having a tool is not enough. Teachers have many tools to choose from in their toolboxes. Teachers and leaders must understand *how* and *when* technology is the best tool for learning. Having devices in a classroom is not enough, if the teacher doesn't know *when* it is appropriate to embed it into the lesson, or *how* to access and use the data from the digital content to support the learning. It's not enough to just have the devices and software, if there is not a pedagogical shift in instruction.

This book is designed to help leaders and teachers to understand *how* technology and digital content can reinvent our approaches to learning and *when* to maximize their use to establish learning experiences that meet the needs of today's learners.

Let's start with a story. It was Christmas in 2007 and I was back home visiting the family when my nephew, Jacob (a high school freshman), and I were having a conversation about school. At that time I was the high school reform coordinator for Nevada's Clark County School District, doing some innovative school redesign. Working with big money in small learning communities grants we were attempting to create freshmen academies, capture kid's hearts, and bring forth rigor and relevance to the curriculum. I shared some of the movements being made at eight of our local high schools. Jacob was so angry about his learning experiences, his teachers 'on-stage' learning approach and the low-quality regurgitation of materials for homework assignments. He said, "I'm not like my sister (a senior) who can sit in class, smile, and play the game." To him, and many other students in our classrooms today, school had become a game. A game they no longer wanted to partake in. It was an enjoyable conversation that ended with a sad compliment, when he said, "Why is it that you're an adult and you are the only person who really gets what I'm talking about."

I would love to say that my nephew figured out the game and won. Jacob did graduate from high school and even went to college, but found the same unstimulating game waiting for him there. After one year he dropped out. Jacob has tried many times over to go back and each time he was disappointed with the learning environment. His sister on the other hand, who was very good at the game of listening, smiling, and regurgitation, obtained a Master's degree at the University of Southern California (USC). This parallels today's statistics showing that females are outpacing males in college enrollment, across ethnicities.[2] If you ask me, this demonstrates more of a compliance issue, rather than a gender problem.

As advancements in technology have led other industries to make changes for the good of the customer, safety in cars and conveniences in refrigerators, why is it that our customers, our students are stuck in many of the same old factory, unappealing classrooms of yesteryear? Don't get me wrong, there are many small pockets of change. Schools and classrooms that have embraced technology and digital content. Most of the early adopters were charter school programs with the freedom to build a new - new structures, new practices, and new teaching strategies. They had more opportunities to re-invent the classroom than our larger public schools strapped by tradition, old buildings, existing staff, unions, and legislation. Parents took their kids and ran, fleeing in droves to these new and different learning opportunities. Wanting more for the next generation. Remember the 2010 movie *Waiting for Superman*,[3] a documentary criticizing public education as parents attempted to gain access to charter schools for their children.

The question is, "How do we grow these types of innovations to reimagine learning for all students in all schools?"

Cornerstone Charter Schools, in Detroit Michigan, has three K-8 schools and a high school. They use personal learning as a methodology and blended learning as a strategy to reach their goals. Cornerstone utilizes several digital content providers plus a learning management system to meet the various needs of students.

- Video (4:13) - See QR code or the Internet Web address below: https://www.youtube.com/embed/UQ-LYOthoQ4

Growth of Online Learning

Distance education is not a new idea, it has been around since the time of U.S. Postal Services with correspondence courses, then moved to televised video courses. In the 1960's the University of Illinois created PLATO (Programmed Logic for Automatic Teaching Operations) which started as an intranet computer assisted instruction system. PLATO was an early learning platform that spanned four decades with tools such as online forums, message boards, online testing, email, instant messaging, and remote screen sharing.[4] In the 1990, as personal computers arrived on the scene, other online learning platforms were introduced. WebCT™ (1997), CourseInfo™ (later to be known as Blackboard™) and Moodle ™ (an open source) introduced their own online learning platforms that opened doors to virtual learning classrooms. I taught in all three of these platforms over the decades, as well as using Microsoft's Outlook® as an adjunct instructor at the University of Phoenix (the first collegiate institution to offer fully online programs[5]) to post lectures, assignments and discussions, as I too was testing the capabilities of online learning for K-12 and adult learners, in the late 1990's and early 2000's.

Those of us that have been in the field of K-12 online and blended learning the last two decades recall seeing it grow as technology advanced and opportunities increased for online distance education. With the rise of the internet and the introduction of tools to create virtual learning experiences, online schools advanced upon the American education experience. Utah's Electron High School transitioned from solely correspondence courses to offering online courses in the mid 1990's. About the same time state-funded Florida Virtual School (1997) and the Virtual High School (1997), a federally-funded national collaborative program, opened their doors to secondary students. State virtual schools became early pioneers providing options to K-12 schools as supplements to the traditional school setting, including Michigan Virtual School (1998), Kentucky Virtual High School (2000-closed 2012), Idaho Digital Learning (2002), and Texas Virtual School Network (2007), which all started by focusing primarily on high school students. In 2000, Nevada's Clark County School District jumped into the field with a small Cyber School program targeting specific subject areas: Health, English 9, Math 8, and Advanced Placement (AP) Microeconomics and Macroeconomics. I had the pleasure to work with the eighth-grade math students within an online classroom, mixed with weekly synchronous webinars.

In the late 1990's and early 2000's online education was just beginning to blossom. You may ask, why would Clark County start with such a diverse catalog of courses: Health, English 9, Math 8, and AP Microeconomics and Macroeconomics. It reflected how online planted its simple roots. Online learning started as an alternative for special populations, with limited and/or possibly no alternatives. In Nevada, Health is a required course for high school graduation. Typically, Health is taken in ninth grade. Many students move into Clark County from other states as upper classmen and already needed a full schedule of required courses. Nor did they want to sit in a class with a bunch of freshmen. Online Health was an excellent alternative for both the student, as well as schools, who could not create a period of Health for one, two, or a handful of upperclassmen students. It was a good economical choice. As too was the AP Microeconomics and Macroeconomics course. With only one teacher in a large district that was certified to teach such a specialty area, only one school was benefitting from the instructor's unique skill set. By creating an online AP course, all students in the district could be offered this advanced course. Math 8 and English 9 were needed for credit recovery, again an excellent choice for schools that could not afford to offer recovery options in a traditional school day with so few students needing the service. Online learning grew out of providing choices where few existed; advanced courses, credit recovery, alternative education, and by adding courses offerings in small or rural schools.

Online learning also grew from parents attempting to homeschool or support homebound children. Online content provided guidance and learning opportunities that were not available in paper-and-packet learning. As technology expanded communication tools for synchronous real-time online learning for tutoring options with a content specialist (e.g. teacher) for one-on-one or one-to-many webinars became available. Today simple and free tools like Skype™ and Google® Hangouts are available.

Choice is what brought most students to online learning. Where there was no previous alternative, online learning could fill the gap. Teachers from afar could service students at a distance. Students now had a choice where none was present beforehand. But with distance, came new concerns, such as student's lack of time management skills and low course completion rates.

Benefits of Online Learning

In these early days of online learning the courses were 'rough' to say the least. Creating an online lesson is different than standing and delivering. Over time the technology tools grew, as too did our knowledge of what worked with students. Even some of the early pioneers in vendor products grew from flat posted text PDF's and video lectures to interactives and engaging activities.

Online learning has expanded beyond its roots of distance learning. In today's online classroom, lesson materials -- articles, graphs, videos, practice questions, interactive manipulations, discussion boards, and assessments -- are available online any time. Students can view and review as many times as needed. Data is generated quickly and available to the course instructor immediately to access and analyze. Need for remediation and intervention can be spotted easily and early using the data.

With the ability to serve students from a distance, online courses opened opportunities in areas of teacher shortage or credential limitations allow students to take courses that were not readily available in their brick-and-mortar schools. Distance does not mean far. Online teachers are just a text or email away. Time is not locked into a 50-minute class period or the five days in a workweek.

The online classroom also gives every student a front row seat. Students are encouraged to email, text, or instant message, their teacher directly, even call on the phone or set-up a web conference for a one-on-one discussion if they need added assistance. This environment allows for individualized instruction set at a pace, place, and path specific to student needs.

Edutopia produced a video on the advantages of online learning in 2010 that demonstrated how schools and districts around the country were benefiting from online learning's flexible scheduling, personalized learning, and expanded course offerings despite budget cuts.

- Video (5:32) - See QR code or the Internet Web address below:
  https://www.youtube.com/embed/XhzIYo2e5kY

Supporting Organizations

As the online learning movement grew, these early leaders sought interaction and communication among their virtual school peers and colleagues. In response to their need for a national organization, the North American Council for Online Learning (NACOL) was created in 2003. Later the organization expanded to an international reach and became the International Association for K-12 Online

Learning (iNACOL). Working collaboratively with experts in the field, iNACOL publishes reports and related resources on key topics in online learning. One of those experts includes John Watson's Evergreen Education Group, a private consulting and advisory firm, who began publishing an annual *Keeping Pace with K-12 Digital Learning* report reviewing policies and practices in the field in 2004. I had the pleasure to work with John as Clark County's endeavors debuted in this very first publication.

iNACOL and Evergreen Education Group partnered to publish *Promising Practices in Online Learning,* a six-part white paper series exploring some of the key issues in online learning. In January 2008, a *Promising Practice* white paper titled: Blended Learning: The Convergence of Online and Face-to-Face Education was released, where the new term "blended learning" was first introduced.

Defining Blended Learning

Through Evergreen Education Group's extensive annual research, they began to see stagnation in fully online programs. In the 2008, the iNACOL *Blended Learning Promising Practice* white paper claimed that students seeking a fully distance-education environment will remain relatively low, but that the advent of a new practice which combined online and face-to-face learning was growing. Some schools had coined this as "blended" or "hybrid" learning. The white paper predicted the growth of this new pedagogical approach as the model of the future:

> *Blended learning, combining the best of the online and a face-to-face education, is likely to emerge as the predominant teaching model of the future.*
> The Convergence of Online and face-to-Face Education (2008)[6]

At this same time, Clayton M. Christensen, author of *Innovator's Dilemma,* published *Disruptive Class: How Disruptive Innovation Will Change the Way the World Learns* (copyright 2008) with Michael B. Horn, and Curtis W. Johnson. The timing could not have been better as the growth of blended learning was on the rise. More states were adopting legislation for charter schools, who were exempt from certain state and local rules and regulations, offering more flexibility and autonomy. Many charters were capitalizing on technology and opened their doors with a new look to the classroom that embraced virtual learning opportunities. It was also a time when the internet provided openly available resources like Khan Academy™.

States like Florida, Alabama, and Michigan had added laws on the books requiring students to take an online course for high school graduation, and others like Idaho and Virginia were also considering laws, or highly recommending an online experience for students.[7] Still others were leery of the technology boom and how it might change the classroom and stood still watching and waiting. A new phenomenon, a blend of classroom and online learning experiences was growing. It was in 2008 when Christensen and Horn predicted that "the data suggest that in about six years 10 percent of all courses will be computer-based, and by 2019 about 50 percent of courses will be delivered online."[8] With a new classroom innovation on the cusp, they began researching the field extensively and started writing white papers on blended learning.

In January 2011, the Christensen Institute (formerly called Innosight Institute) penned their first white paper on blended learning: *The Rise of K-12 Blended Learning,* that demonstrated how online learning was sweeping across America and it was no longer just a distance education option, but growing within, not outside of, the face-to-face classroom. In this document a formal definition of blended learning was presented:

> Blended learning is any time a student learns at least in part at a supervised brick-and-mortar location away from home <u>and</u> at least in part through online delivery with some element of student control over time, place, path, and/or pace.[9]

The paper also classified blended learning into six models, which were presented in depth in the second white paper: *The Rise of K-12 Blended Learning: Profiles of Emerging Models* in May 2011. We'll explore these more in chapter two.

With a definition for blended learning, schools began to self-evaluate technology implementations. Many were hung up on the student control elements of time, place, path, and/or pace. Notice the "and/or" between the terms. Student do not have to have complete control over all elements.

Many virtual schools opened doors to freedoms of time and place, but others kept the pace calendared to the 18-week semester with assignment due dates. By doing so they stayed within the school calendar year, keeping parents and students in familiar territory. They provided student control of *when* they worked on courses, as long as they met specific due dates. Time management is difficult for most of the population, imagine what the freedom of pace does to teens. Think about the last time you asked your son or daughter to take out the garbage or to wash the dishes. Did they jump right up and do it? Or did you have to ask many times before they completed the task? When schools manage pace, students are much more successful.

Too much student control is not good for every learner. When given the opportunity to control their own pace, adults thought that students would advance quickly through courses. Let's think about this for a moment, if a kid dislikes a subject why would he want to do more of it, hours on end, each day to finish the course quickly? There are a few elite students who could pace themselves and finish quickly, but for the vast majority this is not the case. Students are good at procrastination when given a choice. Well, aren't we all? Schools learned quickly that it was too easy for students to be enrolled in courses for a full 18-weeks and have very little progress without pacing the content for them by calendaring due dates. Online courses do not mean automated learning. Adult supervision cannot be left behind when technology is introduced if we wanted students to succeed.

Digital Age

Technology is everywhere. We live in a world that is advancing quickly when it comes to technology and our classrooms cannot be left behind. Schools are adding mobile devices as quickly as they can find a budget for them. One-to-one schools are becoming part of the norm.

Many of today's schools are tech-rich. The internet is at our students' fingertips. Cloud-based applications, such as Google® Suite, are finding their way into our classrooms. Rather than photocopying worksheets, teachers are generating them as online documents and students are submitting them electronically. Teacher slides are not only being projected on large screens, but students can also view them on their own devices and follow along. Technology has even allowed quick online polling features, such that teachers can pose a question to the class and every student answers, rather than calling upon a single student to orally respond. Technology has become a new tool in the toolbox, substituting old tools and strategies with new innovative ways to meet the same instructional practices.

Tech integration has provided new avenues to old practices. With access to the internet, summative assessment such as student projects can require in depth analysis of multiple resources. Student projects can entail technology production tools where students craft videos, digital storyboards, infomercials, online blogs, and more. Rather than creating a poster board, students can share digital presentations. Rather than crafting a literary analysis that only the teacher once read and graded, it can be posted for the whole class to read on a discussion board, or on a class website for grandparents in another city or state can view as well. Daily access to technology is changing assignments and practices, but is it changing the classroom itself?

Tech-rich classrooms is key to our students' future. Not a day goes by that you and I don't use technology in our work and daily lives. Today's students must have technology at their fingertips to know and understand the world before them. Technology can be a powerful tool. It helps reduce long standing equity and accessibility gaps. It can be used to adapt learning experiences to meet the needs of all learners in preparation for the future that lies before them. Getting technology into the hands of students is vastly important. However, tech-rich learning environments in and of itself falls short of blended learning, where online digital content and face-to-face traditional teaching methods merge.

Blended Learning Redefined

The Christensen Institute continued to follow the blended learning trend over the years, conducting research and collecting data on how digital content was being utilized in the classrooms. Today, the Christensen Institute, through its research and analysis of educational practices, has provided a nationally shared definition of blended learning which helps us to understand the current disruptive innovation in education. In their May 2013 whitepaper, *Is K-12 Blended Learning Disruptive*, the definition was revised to include three parts:

Blended learning is a **formal education** in which a student learns:
1) at least in part through **online delivery** with some element of **student control** over *time, place, path,* and/or *pace*;
2) at least in part at a **supervised brick-and-mortar location** away from home;
3) and the modalities along each student's learning path within a course or subject are connected to provide an **integrated learning experience.**[10]

Let's break this down into its components:
- **Formal education program**: distinguishes blended learning from informal online learning such as students playing educational video games on their own and the traditional classroom with technology-rich instruction (e.g. smart boards and clickers).
- **Online delivery of content and instruction:** educating through activities and digital content that impart knowledge or skill - distinguishing online learning from just using the internet for tools, games, and research options.
- **Student control over time, place, path, and/or pace:** learning is no longer restricted to the school day, the walls of the classroom, pacing of the entire classroom population, or teacher's pedagogical approach - interactive and adaptive software customizes to meet individual student needs.
- **Supervised...away from home:** distinguishes blended learning from full-time online learning, yet opens door for students to experience online courses as part of their brick-and-mortar school day.

- **Learning path modalities are integrated:** When a learning takes place partly online and partly through other instructional modality (e.g. face-to-face direct instruction, small-group interaction, one-on-one tutoring) the instruction is connected, topics relate and move together when student leave/change modalities.

The addition of the integrated learning paths from the original definition added validity to what is truly blended learning and not just supplementation or a tech-rich learning environment. Blended meant the meshing of two objects, but some classrooms were adding technology software application without truly changing the learning environment, by moving what was once worksheets to software applications. If teachers were not using the data from the online learning session to drive instruction, identifying student strengths and weaknesses, to adapt the face-to-face learning instruction based on data analysis, then blending was not occurring. They were two separate learning modalities standing side-by-side.

This blending of two modalities, online and face-to-face instruction, requires a shift in teachers instructional planning. It involves data analysis on a regular basis and necessitates understanding of when it would be okay for the technology to teach concepts, allowing instructors to guide and support students with intervention. Blending is taking the teacher off the stage. They no longer had to deliver all the instruction. Technology software applications could lift some of the burden. This calls for a mind shift for both students and teachers.

In the next chapter we will look at some blended learning models that meet these elements. We'll see examples of the growing trend that morphs online and face-to-face learning to create a new blended classroom filled with technology and new roles for students and teachers alike.

NEXT STEPS

Questions to Consider

1. What are the best elements of online learning? What are the best elements of the traditional face-to-face classroom?
2. What drove the development of online learning environments?
3. Being just a few years away from 2019, consider what it would take to move America's schools closer to the prediction of about 50 percent of courses to be delivered online?

Actions

1. Identify technology ready staff members.
2. Browse the National Education Technology Plan. Found at:
   https://tech.ed.gov/netp/

Notes

1. Christensen, C. M. & Horn, M. B. (2011, October 11). *The Rise of Online Education.* Web Article. Retrieved June 5, 2016 from: https://www.washingtonpost.com/national/on-innovations/the-rise-of-online-education/2011/09/14/gIQA8e2AdL_story.html
2. Lopez, M. H. & Gonzalez-Barrara, A. (2014, March 06). *Women's College Enrollment Gains Leave Men Behind.* Web Article. Retrieved June 1, 2016 from: http://www.pewresearch.org/fact-tank/2014/03/06/womens-college-enrollment-gains-leave-men-behind/
3. Guggenheim, D. (2010). *Waiting for Superman.* Documentary. Retrieved June 5, 2016 from: https://vimeo.com/69353438
4. *Online Learning Timeline.* Website. Retrieved June 5, 2016 from: http://www.innovativelearning.com/online_learning/timeline.html
5. *The History of Online Schooling.* Website. Retrieved June 5, 2016 from: http://www.onlineschools.org/visual-academy/history-of-online-schooling/
6. Watson, J. (2008, January). *Blended Learning: The Convergence of Online and Face-to-Face Education.* Publication. International Association for K-12 Online Learning.
7. Sheehy, K. (2012, October 24). *States, Districts Require Online Ed for High School Graduation.* Blog. Retrieved June 5, 2016 from: http://www.usnews.com/education/blogs/high-school-notes/2012/10/24/states-districts-require-online-ed-for-high-school-graduation
8. Christensen, C. M., & Horn, M. B. (2008, May 05) *How Do We Transform Our Schools?.* Web Article. Retrieved June 5, 2016 from: http://educationnext.org/how-do-we-transform-our-schools/
9. Staker, H. (2011, May) *The Rise of K-12 Blended Learning.* Publication. Innosight Institute.
10. Christensen, C. M., Horn, M. B. & Staker, H. (2013, May). *Is K-12 Blended Learning Disruptive? An introduction to a theory of hybrids.* Publication. The Clayton Christensen Institute for Disruptive Innovation.

CHAPTER 2
ADOPTING A BLENDED MODEL

"We predict that hybrid schools, which combine existing schools with new classroom models, will be the dominant model of schooling in the United States in the future. But within secondary schools, the disruptive models of blended learning will substantially replace traditional classrooms over the long term."

Is K–12 Blended Learning Disruptive?
An Introduction of the Theory of Hybrids (2013)[1]

When you think of the words "blended learning" what image comes to mind? I ask this because blended learning is not just one thing. It's like the words, "vehicle" or "home." You have a mental image of a vehicle and a home, but your mental image is probably not the same as the person next to you. Vehicles and homes come in many different shapes, sizes, colors, and prices. A pickup truck, compact automobile, and luxury sports car are all very different vehicles. As are a two-story, ranch, and apartment homes. Sadly, for some of our students their vehicle is home.

Blended learning, like vehicles and homes, comes in many different formats. Some are just a few small steps outside the traditional setting, others are very large leaps away from what one would consider a traditional classroom. And like the varying prices of vehicles and homes, the price or mind shift change in pedagogy and structures of the blended classroom or school can be low or steep. Blended learning is not just one thing. It's underpinning, like the four wheels of a vehicle or the foundation of a home are described in the definition: *combining online digital curriculum with traditional classroom instructional methods*, but each deployment model, just like vehicles and homes, will look and feel very different when filled with students and teachers.

> Blended learning comes in many different formats. Some are just a few small steps outside the traditional setting, others are very large leaps.

Like the varying prices of vehicles and home there is a cost, or "purchase" price of the adoption of each type of blended learning model. As you consider blended learning adoption, think about what structural changes your classroom, school, or district would have to make to buy into its adoption. The cost of adoption is truly the **change process** and change is often not easy to make. Students and parents are clamoring for change in education, but are you and your staff ready and at what cost? Are they ready for small steps or large leaps, or maybe somewhere in between? There are several models to choose from. I'm sure you will find one within your price range, or change process tolerance.

As the leader of a district, school, or classroom it will be up to you to set the underpinning principles of blended learning you have selected to put into place. To document policies and procedures for others to understand. You will cast the vision, set the tone, and determine expectations for adults and students in the building or classrooms. And how much change is needed will depend on the deployment model you choose to adopt. Consider all options. Know your own budget and how much **change tolerance** you, your staff, and students are willing to make when picking a deployment model. It could range from a simple station or lab rotation, to a whole new look, disrupting the traditional classroom to a flex or enriched virtual model. No matter the blended learning model you select, just like any good vehicle or home, once you determine a model to your liking you will customize it and make it your own.

Models of Blended Learning

When selecting a model, know your own budget and how much change you and your staff are willing to make. Understand that professional development, policies and procedures, and support systems must be put in place to ensure that everyone has the same vision and understanding of the future model of their classrooms.

Model selection is just the start. Over time you will tailor it and make it your own. Let's look at the foundation of the four model, as identified by research from the Christensen Institute[1]. Some models, like rotations, build upon the current traditional classroom with sustaining enhancements. Making these slight changes are typically easier to tolerate, thus have been coined as hybrids, mixing the old traditional practices with the technology instruction. Others are poised to disrupt, or transform the classroom. The Flex, A La Carte, and Enriched Virtual will definitely disrupt classrooms and schools as we currently know them, especially at the secondary level.

Rotation Models

Elementary teachers have used a rotation model for years, with different learning stations where students rotate on a fixed schedule or at the teacher's discretion between learning modalities. Adding digital learning as a station is a comfortable fit to the mix. With software products like Dreambox™ and iReady™, teachers no longer have to run off papers to create a skills-based practice station. The software can deliver concepts, have students practice, and generate data to demonstrate student mastery. The adaptive nature of such software products allows for an individualized learning approach and helps aid the classroom teacher.

Classroom sets of devices, or just a handful, provide opportunities for stations where students can engage with digital content. I have seen a well ran kindergarten classroom with students actively learning the foundations for literacy with Smarty Ants™ at stations with mobile devices. At the same school, fifth grade students rotated from the teacher's direct instruction in math to ST Math™ software utilization in a lab. The lovable characters in these game-based software engages students and keeps their attention. Students tend to like 'playing' on the computer when they are challenged to level up or have a new world to explore, even if it means doing a few problems along the way.

However, having a technology station or sending students to the lab in a rotation model is not enough to say you have incorporated blended learning. Blended means combining face-to-face and digital learning modalities, not having two separate learning techniques standing side-by-side. The power of learning online is the data teachers get about students understanding. What good is the digital instruction if teachers are not utilizing the student data to make instructional decisions? The power of technology is the not only providing instruction, but also generating statistics about individual student gains and gaps. Data from the software must be analyzed and used to determine next steps for the individual learner or the class as a whole. Like the definition of blended learning states; the modalities along each student's learning path within a course or subject are connected to provide an integrated learning experience.[1]

Software can only provide low level Depths of Knowledge (DoK); recall and reproduction, skills and concepts. The teacher must provide instruction and opportunities that will increase rigor that leads to higher DoK levels. Through guided instruction, teachers must require students to analyze, evaluate, and extend their learning through critical thinking and creation. By using software to help students master skills, teachers can use the data to determine when students can 'take it to the next level,' possibly via authentic assessments.

Station and Lab Rotations

Rotation models include an easy to adopt **station rotation** or a **lab rotation** where students may be removed from the classroom and attend to digital content possibly with another adult (e.g. lab aide) in the room. A homework model, called a **flipped classroom**, asks students to engage with digital content as a homework assignment. Flipping may include playlist, videos, and/or discussions. All these rotation hybrid models typically moves the entire classroom at the pace and control of the teacher.

The **Knowledge is Power Program (KIPP) Empower Academy** is part of the larger national KIPP charter network found across the nation. They utilize a **station rotation** blended learning model to deliver high quality instruction to K-2 students in all core areas including reading, writing, math, and science. Their model rotates students among three configurations from teacher led, small group, and digital learning.[4]
- Video (9:57) - See QR code or the Internet Web address below: https://www.youtube.com/embed/ZvFOHRUG70g

---

Arthur Ashe Charter School is part of the First Line charter network. They utilize a **lab rotation** blended learning model that incorporates face-to-face instruction with digital curriculum. Students rotate between their traditional classrooms and a computer lab, where they engage with several different digital learning software programs. Students in grades K-3 spend approximately 60 minutes per day in the lab; students in grades 4-8 spend up to 100 minutes per day in the lab. Two lab coaches oversee the two computer labs, filled with 40 to 60 students at any one time.[5]
- Video (6:16) - See QR code or the Internet Web address below: https://www.youtube.com/embed/5mqih8pl264?

The one thing that most vendor product digital content does <u>not</u> lack is data. Matter of fact it has so much data that it may be difficult to figure out what data should be focused upon. Many of today's platforms have student and teacher dash boards that help us to see individual progress in a 'big picture' format. Que colors like red, yellow, and green make it very easy to find students' lack of understanding, mastery, acceleration, or slow progress. How teachers use this data to change classroom instruction is the underpinning foundation of blended learning.

Flipped Classroom

To make time in the classroom for deeper discussion, scientific explorations, and higher order thinking skills, many teachers have turned to 'flipping their classrooms,' where students first exposure to new material is outside the classroom, usually via videos and internet resources. They are turning the traditional model on its head, by asking students to obtain knowledge outside of class, and focusing on deeper depths of knowledge in class.[2] The Khan Academy™ and Crash Course™ videos have helped many teachers flip their classrooms. Technology makes it easy to record lectures.

Clintondale High School is a public school just outside Detroit, Michigan. The entire school has embraced the **flipped classroom** blended learning model. Students attend to their teacher's lectures as homework. Students can rewind and watch lessons as many times as necessary to fully grasp concepts. While in class, the teacher can work one-on-one, and small- or whole-group.[3]
  • Video (7:42) - See QR code or the Internet Web address below: https://www.youtube.com/embed/G_p63W_2F_4

Too often we see teachers adopt technology in a rotation model, but only as a supplement, when it should help drive instruction. Digital content is like having a teacher's aide in the classroom, helping to tutor, coach, and motivate students. It's like each and every student has their very own teacher's aide. The classroom instruction must change when digital curriculum provides individualized attention. Digital learning cannot be an *extra* activity. Teacher should <u>not</u> be planning 'around' it, but rather *with* it. Using data to drive instruction is the cornerstone of the individual rotation.

Individual Rotation

A disruptive, **individual rotation** model allows the digital curriculum to adjust and create a personalized path for each student. Students move through the content having control over path and pace. This model requires students to be more self-directive and self-motivated. Thus, this model tends to be adopted with older students at middle and high school levels. The individual rotation blended learning model is *disruptive*, taking very large leaps from today's traditional classroom. It provides a more personalized approach to learning.

> **Teach to One: Math** is New Classrooms software solution designed for middle schools to create an **individualized rotation** model. As of August 2016, over 13,000 students at 40 schools in 10 states were using the software program.[6] It incorporates a computer algorithm to deliver a unique lesson plan for the day to each individual student. Students experience learning in a variety of ways, including live teacher-led instruction, student collaboration, software, or virtual tutors/instructors. Unique activity schedules, displayed on large monitors, are generated day-to-day based on each student's data from the day before, to ensure that students receive the most personalized instruction as possible.
> - Video (5:11) - See QR code or the Internet Web address below:
>   https://player.vimeo.com/video/105579982

Secondary vendor courseware is ideal for individual rotation models, allowing students to move at their own pace through a standards-based digital curriculum. Since each student will be at different places at any given time, the teacher's role becomes one of analyzing student data and guiding instruction at the individual student level. Teachers can pull aside individuals or small groups of students for guided instruction when deficits are recognized.

Flex Model

In the **flex model** digital courseware is the backbone of student learning. It is *disruptive* in that it has no need for age-based cohorts because all students are moving through courses at their own pace and on their own schedules. Flex labs are relatively simple to implement and easy to duplicate because they depend on vendors' products for content and instruction rather than upon the calendar and schedule of a highly qualified face-to-face teacher. That is not to say that the teacher should step aside, the opposite is true. Teachers need to closely watch and guide students' progress in a Flex model.

Flex models tend to have large rooms with lots of students with teachers in the room. Some schools also incorporate non-licensed coaches in the room as well. Courseware allows students to move on an individually customized, fluid schedule among learning modalities. Teachers, or other adult coaches in the lab provide face-to-face support on a flexible and adaptive as-needed basis through activities such as small-group instruction, group projects, and individual tutoring.

Some flex implementations have substantial face-to-face support, while others have minimal support. For example, some flex models may have daily or weekly face-to-face time with teachers who supplement the online learning, whereas others may provide little face-to-face enrichment. Still others may have different staffing combinations and instructional requirements. Much like the individual rotation model, often a flex model is set up in a large open area, that allows for various instruction needs, such as breakout rooms for small-group instruction, collaboration areas for group projects, or round tables and/or desks for individual tutoring or proctored exams.

The **San Francisco Flex Academy** opened in 2010 as a small public charter high school in downtown San Francisco and now is part of a growing network of **flex academies** designed by for-profit education company K12®.[7] Students attend school five days a week from 8:00 a.m. to 3:00 p.m. for a full day of instruction, where students have the flexibility to work independently through online learning vendor courseware at their own pace, in addition to face-to-face classroom instruction with high qualified teachers. The online courses deliver the curriculum and instruction, while face-to-face teachers use a data dashboard to identify and offer targeted interventions and supplementation throughout the day for all core courses. Students meet daily with academic advisor and twice weekly with each core subject area teachers in a small group instructional setting

- Video (2:13) - See QR code or the Internet Web address below: https://www.youtube.com/embed/oDvssKlTsLQ

The strength of the flex academy is the ability of students to work on different courses, even different semesters, at their own pace. In Clark County, flex academies come in different shapes and sizes. At a middle school site, they took down a wall between two large classrooms and brought in cubical style seating. Four teachers, one in each subject area circulate the room, guiding and supporting students working in their online courses. Teachers conduct pull out instructional session in another classroom down the hall. Face-to-face instruction includes science labs, hands-on math investigations, explorations of character, plot, and themes of assigned novels. A high school flex academy had students working on a full catalog of online courses in a large room with various seating arrangements. Computer stations were set up for proctored exams, but seating throughout the room varied from short and tall tables, bar seating along windows, and even lounge type seating in couches, bean bags, and gaming chairs for students on laptops. Teachers in core subject areas conduct one-on-one or small group sessions throughout the room.

In a flex model, with teachers in the same room as the students, the movement between online instruction and teacher led instruction is fluid and on an as needed basis. At the secondary level full courseware can present the vast majority of instruction, thus the role of the teacher changes. They must use the data from the learning management system to identify student mastery gaps for pull out support. They also need to identify any courseware curriculum gaps for larger group instructions. The ability to interact face-to-face with students in a flex academy is a powerful support system for students.

A La Carte Model

The **a la carte** model is when a student chooses to take one or more of their daily scheduled courses entirely online. It breaks from the traditional setting by allowing students to blend their learning experience, allowing them to take some courses online and others face-to-face. Students may take the online course(s) either on the brick-and-mortar campus (during a scheduled period of the school day) or off-site (from home). This differs from full-time online learning and the enriched-virtual model (see the next definition) because it is <u>not</u> a whole-school experience.

The online course(s) may be completed from a distance with a highly qualified teacher from afar, yet in some schools, students are provided a variety of in-person supports, like mentors or coaches in a computer labs or e-learning cafes. There is no doubt that this model disrupts the current traditional classroom model and the way we think about school, staffing, and student schedules.

The ability to *self-blend* or choose when and what online courses a student might like to pursue, rather than sitting in a face-to-face classroom each and every day is backbone of the a la carte model. Blending the student's schedule with face-to-face and online courses allows for student choice and changes the way we look at the typical school structure.

Online courses can expand school's course catalog, like it did for my daughter, Jolie. Her high school had a limited catalog of elective courses. Rather than take yearbook again or Spanish, the few choices available to her, we sought out alternative online courses. The virtual school in Clark County School District had a rich catalog of electives and was open to concurrent enrollment. Actually, concurrent enrollment numbers exceed their full-time enrollment. Many students across this very large county were opting to enroll in an online course with the district's digital learning school. Some schools assigned students to a learning lab, or study hall period, during the regular school day to work on their online courses.

Others allowed students the option to take a "free" period within their schedule so they could sleep in longer, or leave school early, promising to work on their online courses from a distance. Imagine an entire school that has teachers conducting face-to-face instruction as well as teach online courses and every student has an option to learning modalities.

Quakertown Community School District (QCSD) offers students in grades 6-12 the option of taking online courses **a la carte**; either at home or during the school day. They have created designated areas in a comfortable cafe style "cyber lounge" where students can work on their online courses during cyber periods at school. About half of all QCSD teachers teach at least one online course. Many of the cyber teachers host online and in-person office hours during their prep and cyber periods. These personalized, flexible learning options allow students to choose the best academic option for them and still participate in traditional face-to-face activities such as lunch, sports, and other extracurricular activities.[8]

- Video (3:57) - See QR code or the Internet Web address below:
  https://www.youtube.com/embed/adqwaFlEDQ4

The role of the teacher in the a la carte setting is truly 'from a distance' thus all teacher communication and support is also 'from a distance.' Motivating a student from a distance is difficult. Students do not get the benefit of seeing the teacher daily like their face-to-face class periods. Online teacher communications, via direct email, classroom announcements, or possible video recordings must entice students to *come to class* and *want to learn*. This is much different from a wink and a smile that teachers typically use to entice students in their face-to-face classrooms. Making a connection with students from a distance can be challenging. Teachers will need professional development in this new pedagogy. In many a la carte situations, onsite labs with adult coaches are established to help guide students' behavior and manage student attention to their online classrooms. This type of additional support is beneficial for both the teacher and students.

Knowing my daughter, Jolie needed to have another in the room to support and manage her time, we chose the required time in a learning lab during the school day. Though she would have loved to sleep in, rather than start her day with a two-hour block for online courses. With the assigned time to work on the courseware with an adult in the room, she had structured time each day to attend to her online psychology and French classes. Just like her face-to-face classes, she needed more time than the scheduled class periods to complete homework, but it was definitely a big boost in managing her time and being successful in a new and different learning environment.

As more colleges have online courses, as well as face-to-face classrooms, the a la carte model is a step toward college readiness. Career training is also moving to online modalities, making the a la carte model also a step towards career readiness. The self-discipline and self-motivation to work and complete online courseware from a distance is a skill that our schools need to instill in students for their future.

Enriched Virtual Model

The **Enriched virtual** model is commonly found in at the high school level in alternative settings. This is a whole-school experience in which students divide their time between attending a brick-and-mortar campus and learning remotely using online delivery of content and instruction. These alternative learning centers tend to focus on student populations that the traditional brick-and-mortar school have a tough time servicing.

In most enriched virtual models, students are typically only required to attend the physical location a set number of days in a shortened timeframe. For example, they may be required to attend twice a week (e.g. Monday & Wednesday) in a four-hour block (e.g. 8:00 a.m. to 12:00 p.m.). While at school, the time can be structured and scheduled, where teachers provide small-group instruction, study sessions, and lead students in project-based inquiry. Or the time can be unstructured, much more like a drop-in center where students are required to work on their online courses, with the guidance of their teachers nearby.

Many of the enriched virtual programs began as full-time online schools and then developed blended programs to provide students with additional support in a school building. Another growing arena is within alternative schools as they adopt online content and keep their limited attendance requirements.

Springs Studio for Academic Excellence is a K-12 school, serving over five hundred K-12 students in Falcon School District near Colorado Springs, Colorado. Using an **enriched virtual** model, students divide their time between attending on campus and learning remotely using online content and instruction, completing most of their course work remotely. Online courses provide a common instructional and content thread across all learning modalities—virtual learning, blended learning, and project-based learning.[9]
- Video (2:26) - See QR code or the Internet Web address below:
  https://www.youtube.com/embed/l3ZHHEV_ZoQ

When the virtual school in Clark County School District expanded to middle grades, offering full-time enrollment in grades 6-8 as well as high school, they adopted an enriched virtual model. It was difficult enough to get the mature high school students to complete online course completely from a distance, so the middle school program design required limited onsite attendance. Junior high students were assigned two days a week, either Monday and Wednesday for grades six and seven, or Tuesday and Thursday for eighth graders, to be onsite in class with their teachers.

While on site, teachers conducted face-to-face lessons, or students worked in courseware with their teachers facilitating the learning. Managing student schedules with assigned onsite requirements held student accountable for their own learning, while providing guided support. This model worked so well, that high school students that were falling behind were assigned "academic probation" and required to be onsite for additional support and ensuring that they too attended to their online courses.

Your Selection

As we look at the different models, it's important to consider what digital content is being used. Many software companies want to be your K-12 solution, but beware. Students want to *graduate* from digital content. The cute bug software in primary grades should be put aside when students reach intermediate grades. The funny animal-based software from grades 3-5, is no longer fun in middle school. I caution the use of the same courseware vendor in middle grades and high school, as students will become bored and tired of the same routines, practices, and user interface. As a district, purchasing a single K-12 product sounds like a great idea, but your students will not agree. I've seen too many quality software programs wane due to students' lack of interest and attitude of "*been there, done that before.*" Keep the digital learning environment fresh and unique. Allow students to graduate and progress out of digital software providers as they move in grade levels.

No matter the model, remember the change process that you must go through to adopt blended learning in your school or classroom. Some models, like rotation maintain teacher control of classroom pace and is easier to step into. Even the a la carte is not much change on the structures of a traditional school, but the methodology of being an online teacher from a distance is a large shift. Other disruptive models, such as flex, individual rotation, and enriched virtual models are extreme changes from today's traditional bell schedule and will take large leaps in design and pedagogy to embrace.

When adopting a blended learning approach, a teacher's role will change when digital curriculum relieves much of the burden of content delivery away from them. A blended learning teacher must adjust from being the one who drove students learning to a guided instruction model. Also, it will be important that teachers understand and know how to use the data from the digital systems to guide and support deeper levels of understanding. Finding the just right balance of digital instruction and teacher guidance will take time and practice, but it must begin with pedagogy of the digital learning environment and making a shift in one's mindset. More on how to help teachers step into the blended learning classroom in the next chapter.

NEXT STEPS

Questions to Consider

1. What blended learning model might be a suitable selection for your classroom, school or district?
2. Change is a process. How much change will you be asking staff and students to make - small steps into a hybrid model or large leaps into a disruptive model?
3. How will you ensure that your staff has a clear vision and understands the teacher role for the selected model?

Actions

1. Document a vision for your classroom, school, or district.
2. Identify any current digital software in use and note how the data it is being used. Is it driving instruction? Or supplemental to the learning process?
3. Leaf through Evergreen Education Group's *Planning for Quality Guide.* Found at: http://evergreenedgroup.com/wp-content/uploads/2013/11/EEG_P4QBooklet2013_v2-lr-1.pdf

Notes

1. Christensen, C., Horn, M., & Staker, H. (2013, May). *Is K–12 Blended Learning Disruptive? An Introduction of the Theory of Hybrids.* Publication.

Retrieved from Christensen Institute:
http://www.christenseninstitute.org/publications/hybrids/

2. Brame, C. (2013). *Flipping the classroom.* Vanderbilt University Center for Teaching. Web Article. Retrieved January 27, 2017 from https://cft.vanderbilt.edu/guides-sub-pages/flipping-the-classroom/

3. *How one school turned homework on it's head with 'flipped' instruction. (2013,* December 13). Web Article. Retrieved January 23, 2017 from: http://www.pbs.org/newshour/rundown/what-does-a-flipped-classroom-look-like-2/

4. Bernatek, B., Cohen, J., Hanlon, J., & Wilka, M. (2012). *Blended Learning in Practice: Case Studies from Leading Schools, Featuring KIPP: Empower Academy.* Publication. Retrieved from Michael & Susan Dell Foundation: http://5a03f68e230384a218e0-938ec019df699e606c950a5614b999bd.r33.cf2.rackcdn.com/Blended_Learning_Kipp_083012.pdf

5. Bernatek, B., Cohen, J., Hanlon, J., & Wilka, M. (2012). *Blended Learning in Practice: Case Studies from Leading Schools, Featuring Firstline Schools.* Publication. Retrieved from Michael & Susan Dell Foundation: http://5a03f68e230384a218e0-938ec019df699e606c950a5614b999bd.r33.cf2.rackcdn.com/msdf_firstline_06.pdf

6. Chang, C. (2016, August 16). *New Classrooms' Interactive Math Expands to 10 states.* Web Article. Retrieved January 23, 2017 from https://thejournal.com/articles/2016/08/16/new-classrooms-interactive-math-expands-to-10-states.aspx

7. Palmer, K. (2012, March 12). *At Flex Academy, High School Mimics the Workplace.* Web Article. Retrieved January 23, 2017 from https://ww2.kqed.org/mindshift/2012/03/12/at-flex-academy-high-school-mimics-the-workplace/

8. *Quakertown Community School District: A Systematic Approach to Blended Learning That Focuses on District Leadership, Staffing, and Cost-effectiveness.* (2016, April). Retrieved from Alliance for Excellent Education: http://all4ed.org/wp-content/uploads/2013/06/Quakertown.pdf

9. *Outcomes of Blended and Online Learning Programs in Schools Using Fuel Education Curriculum.* (2016). Publication. Retrieved from Fuel Education: https://www.fueleducation.com/content/dam/fueled/press-room/in-the-news/academic-outcomes-of-nine-blended-and-online-learning-programs-white-paper.pdf

CHAPTER 3
CIA OF BLENDED LEARNING

"Great blended learning builds upon a foundation of expert, in-person teaching."

Blended Learning Teacher Competency Framework (2014)[1]

Making the change to blended learning will not occur overnight. Change is a process, not an event. When faced with the need for change, we are asking staff and students to move from what is known and familiar, through a period of unknown as they make transitions. Having a clear vision of the future will help the adoption of your blended learning model.

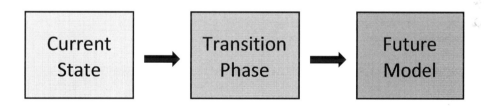

Know that the transition phase will be messy, possibly disorganized, and highly emotional. It will be easier to adopt a blended learning model with a strong plan and clear vision, supported with professional development that helps staff to shift their mindset. Later in the book, we will look at the seven steps of 'Planning for Success' which starts with a common vision. Blended learning pedagogy is an excellent starting place.

Curriculum, Instruction, and Assessment:
The CIA of Blended Learning

Let's start by looking at the foundations of any learning environment. When we think of the fundamentals of the face-to-face classroom three elements surface:

1) **C**urriculum: consists of the knowledge and skills in specific content areas that students need to learn.

2) **I**nstruction: the methods of teaching and learning activities used to help students master content.

3) **A**ssessment: the means used to measure student achievement with regard to identified subject matter competencies.

Every quality classroom is built upon these three elements - curriculum, instruction, and assessment, or CIA for short. The relationships among these three elements is what ties a classroom together to establish a quality learning environment. In the traditional face-to-face classroom, the relationship among these three elements is tied together with data driven decision making.

Imagine data generated every time a student interacts with the curriculum, in an easy to read and digestible format. That is the strength of blended learning - where digital curriculum delivers content, requiring less 'stand and deliver' instructional methods, providing teachers with time to analyze student achievement results and work individually with students, in large and small groups.

Just like a traditional classroom, blended learning models are driven by the same three CIA elements, yet with unique qualifiers:

1) *Digital* **C**urriculum

2) *Guided* **I**nstruction

3) *Authentic* **A**ssessment

Each of the three elements exemplifies the best of learning in the blended classroom. A balanced delivery provides a full Depth of Knowledge (DoK)[2], levels one through four.

Digital **C**urriculum, via **computer** access, creates an individualized standards-based learning environment with 24/7 access for each and every student and provides data feedback to instructors about student mastery or lack of understanding. Think of digital curriculum as a personal teaching aide for each and every student. Courseware can deliver basic skills and check for understanding, targeting depth of knowledge levels one and two (DoK 1-2).

Guided **I**nstruction from a highly qualified content area **teacher** who creates learning environments that challenge and support all students from skills gaps, basic understanding, and stretching students with higher order thinking skills. Guided instruction is a completely new mindset. It breaks from the traditional non-digital learning classroom pedagogy. The data from the digital curriculum helps teachers to identify and guide individuals and groups of students when intervention is needed. Years of practice also helps teachers draw on data from their own experiences where students tend to struggle or need scaffolding, as well as which topics could be considered power standards that students must master. Teachers no longer have to conduct large group instruction on depth of knowledge one and two, but can stretch the entire class to level three (DoK 1-3).

Authentic **A**ssessments use project learning requiring **students** to be critical and creative thinkers, working together in collaborative groups to communicate their understanding. Authentic assessments go beyond the simple skills-based assessments within most courseware by focusing on the skills that are needed to be successful in college, career, and citizenship. Through authentic assessment, students demonstrate their knowledge with real world applications, going beyond rote skill-based mastery into deep thinking analysis and communication, pushing students to depth of knowledge four (DoK 3-4).

Download and share the **CIA of Blended Learning Infographic** from the i3DigitalPD.com blog.
- See QR code or the Internet Web address below:
  http://i3digitalpd.com/the-cia-of-blended-learning/

CIA of Blended Learning

Digital **C**urriculum - COMPUTER ACCESS

Digital curriculum can be thought of as a teacher's aide with significant advantages.
- Baseline Instruction
  - Low level Depths of Knowledge (DoK)
- Aligned to Standards
- Engaging Digital Software
- Individual Data Points

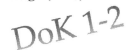

Guided **I**nstruction – TEACHER ENDEAVORS

With digital curriculum taking center stage in the learning environment, the teacher role changes.
- Extended Coaching on:
  - Power standards
  - Where students typically struggle
  - Scaffolding and extending content
- Small and Large Group, plus one-on-one Tutoring

DoK 1-3

Authentic **A**ssessments – STUDENT APPLICATIONS

In a classroom filled with digital tools students can stretch their thinking into analysis, synthesis, and creation while engaging in the Four Cs:
1. Critical Thinking
2. Communication
3. Collaboration
4. Creativity

DoK 3-4

The CIA of blended learning can be represented by a triple Venn diagram where each circle represents one element. In the diagram below, icons are used to provide a visual que for each CIA element: a computer for *digital* **c**urriculum, a teacher for *guided* **i**nstruction, and a student for *authentic* **a**ssessment. There are seven distinct regions in the diagram, some in a single circle, others in two circles. The sweet spot in the middle is where all three elements overlap. When designing a digital learning environment look for a harmonious approach and target the sweet spot in the middle where all the elements come together, creating a balanced and solid foundation in all three components of CIA of blended learning.

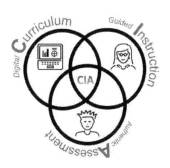

Blended learning is not a continuum, but a continuous movement among the three elements within the triple Venn diagram of *digital* **c**urriculum, *guided* **i**nstruction, and *authentic* **a**ssessment.

Helping staff understanding the relationship of the seven regions is important in creating a balanced approach to blended learning. Some digital content has project learning opportunities. This would lie in both the digital content as well as the authentic assessment circles. Then again, the teacher may introduce a collaborative team project that asks students to work together and think creatively to demonstrate knowledge and understanding of multiple concepts. Better yet, using the project from the digital curriculum, with teacher guidance to team and stretch students such that they are creating a project with peers - now that is "sweet."

The diagram could be used to evaluate your adoption of blended learning. The sweet spot in the middle is the ideal blend, but most days in a digital learning classroom will focus only on one element, or possibly where two elements overlap. Even groups of students may be in different regions of the diagram in a given classroom that is utilizing groupings and/or rotations. Once teachers fully understand the CIA of blended, have your staff self-evaluate their blended classrooms and daily activities using the circles.

Digital **Curriculum**

Think of digital curriculum as a teacher's aide with significant advantages:
- Engages student attention and delivers content
- Provides data with insight on students' strengths and weaknesses
- Has no limits as to when or where it can be accessed
- Is ideal for presenting and assessing student understanding and practicing skills

In most digital learning classrooms, digital curriculum typically comes in the form of vendor software or open education resources (OER). It is a rare situation when a teacher can create their own digital curriculum, that has all the components of an effective lesson; from an opening hook, review of previous knowledge, delivery of new content, check for understanding, real-world application, a summative close and tasks for students to demonstrate mastery (e.g. assignments and assessments). Developing online lessons is time consuming and very different from deploying pre-made content.

> **Develop vs. Deploy**
> Developing online lessons is time consuming and very different from deploying pre-made content.

Let me repeat this, because too often I see administrators who assume that Google® and mobile devices is enough for teachers to create a quality blended learning environment. Never before have we asked teachers to write curriculum, like that found in a textbook, supported with resources like ready-made practice sheets and assessments. Vendors have provided a full package of curriculum to educators for decades and teachers have done an excellent job of deploying these ready-made elements. So again, let me reiterate, *developing online lessons is time consuming and very different from deploying pre-made content.*

Typically, teachers gather pre-made resources from others such as publishers to deliver lessons. Rarely are they actually developing lessons from scratch. Teachers are good at curating OER materials, but this also takes time. Finding quality free internet resources is not enough. The question is how is the digital content being used to support and deliver instruction to individual students.

When an instructor puts resource links on the teacher website, it does not mean that they have incorporated digital learning into their classroom. You've seen it, links to Khan Academy™, CK-12™, and the online textbook on websites, along with subscription-based software like Study Island™, iReady™, or Dreambox™. These are just pretty window dressing if the teacher is not collecting individual student data to drive instruction. Just because the digital content is readily available does not mean students are using it.

Wonderful time for an example. If was the fall, Jocelyn, my freshman daughter had open house. Her math teacher was so happy to hear that I was a former high school math teacher and proceeded to share with me iXL™, where Jocelyn and her peers could access digital resources. "Twenty lessons free!" she said, followed with "Even more if she just uses a different login." The math teacher was so thrilled at the prospects. Her teacher website, which she proudly shared, had links to several open educational resources and the online textbook. Then she demonstrated how her Google® Classroom calendar has a link (yes- just one link) to the textbook. I could tell by the conversation that the teacher was not using the digital curriculum, nor any student data from the digital content to drive classroom instruction.

Later, when I asked Jocelyn about the digital assets, she said, "When she showed you iXL, I thought to myself, I'm not going there." And what 14-year-old would if not expected or required to do so.

I get it. Teachers are busy. Too often, just finding quality internet resources and adding links to their website is much of their extent into digital learning. These digital resources are not even supplement to classroom instruction. Just because teachers have access to digital assets (we all do, they are free on the internet), does not make them instrumental to student learning. Or that students are even accessing them, just ask my daughter and her classmates.

In the CIA model digital curriculum is crucial to delivering instruction. What teachers don't realize or understand is that digital curriculum can create time, when allowed to deliver content. As Steven Covey's seventh habit of highly effective people; Sharpen the Saw,[3] would say is that teachers are too busy attempting to saw down trees with a blunt instrument that they don't take the time to sharpen the saw and become more efficient. Teachers need to stop doing what they have always been doing - delivering low level acquisition instruction to the middle and allow technology to assist, so that they can become more effective. The use of digital curriculum in a personal learning environment preserves and enhances the greatest asset teachers can give to their students - themselves. Minutes with students is precious and must be used wisely.

> The use of digital curriculum in a personal learning environment preserves and enhances the greatest asset teachers can give to their students - **themselves**.

Even teachers that have 'flipped' their classroom by creating video lessons will tell you that digital content development is very time consuming. Developing digital curriculum, or locating and planning with quality resources on the internet, is difficult when most schools only provide a very small preparation period for planning. Thus, the need for high quality software or applications that can aid in the delivery of digital content is needed.

First, let me say I would highly suggest that central office work with vendor products to ensure alignments to standards and customize as needed. I have worked with numerous vendor products and there has not been a single courseware provider that was able to meet all expectations in Clark County. If you can't find what you need, or afford all the product you want, consider building digital content.

In Clark County, we realized the importance of providing teachers with high quality digital content. Vendor contracts were secured, but this becomes costly, especially as more and more classrooms adopt blended learning. Thus, resources were secured to write district-developed digital content. Believe me it was not a quick, nor an easy endeavor. We made mistakes along the way. And learned from our failures. One mistake was using part-time subject matter experts as course designers. It was too much to ask those who worked a full day, teaching face-to-face to reproduce the same quality digital lesson at night or on weekends. This created various voices and designs in the early courses. The best decision we made was to dedicate full-time team of designers who created consistency, high quality, low cognitive load digital content courseware in grades sixth through twelve.

I have a team of four designers (teachers on special assignment), one in each of the core content areas. Their full day is dedicated to creating a catalog of semester based courses aligned to district benchmarks and standards that could be used in all secondary classrooms across the one hundred plus middle and high schools. We established a consistent set of templates, icons, and lesson components to produce a product that could match any vendor courseware. Much like vendor products that teacher are accustomed to, we created teacher guides, students work documents, project learning opportunities, as well as formative and summative assessments components.

By using a cloud-based authoring tool, designers could make corrections to every digital classroom that was deploying the digital content. Since a third-party authoring tool was used, teachers with Google® Classrooms could use the district-developed content too. The links to the digital content could be easily distributed to students.

The full courseware with assignments and pre-made assessments were available inside the district enterprise learning management system (LMS). Within the LMS, teachers could determine what content they wanted to utilize, as well as customize the learning environment. No matter the deployment method, teachers could select what digital curriculum to use, by individual lesson, unit of instruction, or the full semester course. When the courseware was deployed in the LMS, teachers had full access to all elements and could customize assignments and/or assessment. Additionally, a professional learning community provided all who were implementing the digital curriculum to share ideas and practices. By designing our own courseware, district teachers were completely supported with digital curriculum aligned to district benchmarks and standards.

With district-developed digital curriculum, teachers were in a very familiar place: deploying content - not having to develop it. They had control of determining what and how they would deploy content built by another.

If your plan is to have teachers develop online content then ensure that teachers are provided with professional development in online design and given plenty of time to create quality content. A small detail like copyright is a huge issue in the digital design environment, especially when you are distributing content outside one's own classroom. The Fair Teacher Act does not extend beyond the walls, electronic or physical, of a single teacher. I cannot tell you how many times I've seen Disney® characters in the LMS or blatant out right distribution of copyrighted publisher teacher resources materials, scanned or even photographs of textbook pages that are freely distributed to others and breaking copyright laws.

Digital content development is not an easy road to travel. In Clark County, we have a team of secondary course designers working full-time to create digital content. Even with the help of additional subject matter experts (e.g. teachers in the classroom) and college interns, it takes six to twelve months to create a high-quality semester (sixty hours of instruction) course. The designers have no teaching assignments, no student work to grade, and have a full workday focused on digital content development with numerous supports.

No matter the source; vendor product, district-developed content, or even self-made playlists, digital content is usually delivered at low level Depth of Knowledge (DoK). At best, most digital content hits right at DoK levels one and two:

- **DoK 1:** *Knowledge acquisition* - recall and reproduce data, definitions, details, facts, information and procedures.
- **DoK 2:** *Knowledge application* - use of concepts and skills to answer questions, problems, accomplish tasks, and analyze texts and topics.

Digital curriculum is good at deploying instruction at a basic level and providing skill practice. It also creates an individualized learning environment for one, rather than the entire group like a direct instruction lesson to a full class held by the teacher. Digital curriculum is absolutely fabulous at capturing student data. It is this data, provided on each and every individual student, that teachers can use to guide instruction.

Guided Instruction

One thing digital curriculum cannot do is establish a relationship with students. That's why teachers will always remain the strength of the classroom. A teacher's human heart can reach out and touch another's heart. Teacher's smiles, kind words, and sympathetic actions demonstrate caring. They build a bond and friendship with their students, getting to know their likes and dislikes. Teachers can read body language and know when a student is sad or not feeling well. Technology cannot replace the human interaction that is so important to the learning and growing process.

> Technology cannot replace the human interaction that is so important to the learning and growing process.

Let teachers do what they are best at and use their passion to excite learners. With digital curriculum taking center stage in the learning environment, the teacher's role changes to one relying on relationships, human analysis, and intervention. Students respond to the human interaction, the caring heart, the smiling teacher in the classroom. Technology and digital courseware is good at data. Thus, teachers should use this data to create a learning environment that caters to the needs of the class.

In the blended classroom, the teacher will use their expertise in educational theory to analyze the digital data, identifying strengths and weaknesses with the digital curriculum, and coach students to success. When the digital curriculum treats every concept and skill as a single unit it becomes the teacher who needs to help students establish anchors. Teachers are needed to scaffold the learning and support students where they typically struggle. For their years of experience in the classroom, teachers know where students tend to have difficulty, and need additional support. They know what standards are essential, or "power" standards, for future growth in a particular content area. I like to say that teachers must focus on the five S's:

1) individual student support,
2) power standards,
3) where students routinely struggle,
4) scaffold the learning, and
5) stretch student thinking.

Let the digital curriculum do what it does best - deliver low level knowledge, DoK 1-2. Teachers need to extend students thinking to Depth of Knowledge level three:

- **DoK 3:** *Knowledge analysis* - think strategically and reasonably about *how* and *why* concepts, ideas operations, and procedures can be used to attain and explain answers, conclusion, decisions, outcomes, reasons, and results.

It's the responsibility of the blended teacher to create a learning environment that complements and extends the digital curriculum. Teachers should push student learning to higher levels of analysis and synthesis. Guided instruction may include small and large group settings, as well as one-on-one or small group tutoring or intervention. It most definitely should also have hands-on activities, investigations, and Socratic seminars. Teacher guided instruction is a great time to introduce higher order thinking and project learning, which leads right into different ways of assessing student knowledge via authentic assessment.

Remember, the human touch is important in every classroom, technology can never replace the human relationship between students and their teachers. Nor should student learning be left to the individual. Learning is a team sport, one that needs peers and adults to push each other to think beyond their own beliefs and knowledge. To **think outside the box**. Students need to develop both academics as well as social and emotional proficiencies to succeed in the ever-evolving digital economy.

To become successful beyond the traditional classroom students will need to learn how to apply core skills to everyday task. These real-world applications and problems are essential within guided instruction. Students will need to learn how to approach complex challenges with grit and perseverance. Teamwork will be a commodity that our students must adopt and master to become successful in college, career, and citizenship. These skills can be practiced while students engage in authentic assessments.

Authentic **A**ssessment

Authentic assessment is a must in a classroom filled with digital tools and curriculum, with access to the world-wide web, and teachers who push students to expand their learning. Digital curriculum relies heavily on recall and understanding. Guided instruction asks student to stretch to analysis and synthesis. Authentic assessment, or project learning, allows students to demonstrate understanding and mastery. Teachers will find they have more time, when digital curriculum aids instruction, allowing them to stretch student thinking.

Authentic assessments must push students to deeper depths of knowledge. They should challenge students within the Four Cs:[4]

> Authentic assessments require students to be active performers with the acquired knowledge.

1) Collaborate,
2) Communicate,
3) Critical thinking, and
4) Creativity.

With technology at student's fingertips collaboration and communication is easy, and creation should entail critical thinking in a fun and active way. In the blended classroom, students should be using technology not only to learn, but to create works that demonstrate learning too, stretching students beyond level three Depth of Knowledge into level four:

- **DoK 4:** *Knowledge augmentation* - think extensively about what more can be done with the learning and how the student can personally use what they have learned in different academic and real-world context.

Unlike the traditional tests found in the digital courseware which tend to reveal only whether the student can recognize, recall, or regurgitate what was learned, authentic assessments require students to be active performers with the acquired knowledge.

When digital courseware delivers content, teachers will find that they have more time in the traditional eighteen-week semester. This time could be used to add the extension problems in textbooks that were often skipped previously, due to lack of time. Add project-based learning to excite and challenge students.

The **Buck Institute for Education (BIE)** is a non-profit organization that creates, gathers, and shares high quality project based learning (PBL) instructional activities.[5] BIE has curated and gathered an online library of projects freely available to classrrom teacher.
- PBL explained video (3:49) - See QR code or the Internet Web address: https://www.youtube.com/embed/LMCZvGesRz8
- BIE Project Search: http://www.bie.org/project_search

Models and Lesson Planning

There are many ways to establish a blended learning classroom. The models will vary, but all should have a balanced approach to the three CIA components:

1) *Digital* Curriculum (computer access)
2) *Guided* Instruction (teacher endeavors)
3) *Authentic* Assessment (student applications)

Think of the CIA triple Venn diagram, seen above, with three overlapping circles and seven different regions, some in a single circle, others in two. The sweet spot in the middle is where the blended learning classroom has a balanced approach and a solid foundation in all three CIA components of blended learning.

Unit Lesson Planning

Lesson planning in the blended classroom is one place where teachers have a difficult time. If the teacher role, via guided instruction, is driven by data results, how does a teacher plan when data has yet to be determined? Now remember <u>not</u> all the teacher-led instruction in the blended classroom should be determined <u>after</u> students interact with the digital courseware. Teachers have prior knowledge in their content area that can help them determine the best way to complement the digital courseware – like prerequisite skills, misconceptions, and power standards. Beyond basic concepts (what is the knowledge and how it can be used) found in the online courseware (DoK1-2), teachers should be preplanning for higher order thinking skills (DoK 3-4); strategic thinking (why can the knowledge be used) and extensions (what else can be done with the knowledge).

Using the CIA components, teachers should look at the courseware units. By focusing on units of instruction, rather than individual lessons, the classroom teacher can set a minimum pace for unit completion, keeping students moving somewhat together. Making planning for class openers and closure on topics that most students are attending to in the same timeframe. **See the CIA unit lesson plan template and sample located on the following pages.**

Digital Curriculum

Planning lessons in the blended classroom begins with knowing what is in the digital content, so that the classroom teacher may complement it. Teachers need to preview the digital courseware and identify what students will be expected to know and be able to do. There are too many blended classrooms where the teacher had no idea what was in the digital courseware. This would be like planning without cracking the textbook and flying blind. If teachers do not know what is in the digital courseware, how can they predict where students will need support and guided instruction? They cannot wait until students interact with the courseware and the data sends up a red flag. Teachers need to plan ahead. Starting with identifying what is in the courseware and tasks students will be asked to complete.

Guided Instruction

Once teachers know what's in the courseware, they can plan for guided instruction. They will need to identify prerequisite knowledge and where students will need scaffolding. These topics could be used as class openers to set everyone up for success. Teachers also need to identify where students might have misconceptions, or areas that could be troublesome. These topics would be ideal as class closure activities to reinforce the learning. Courseware digital activities, like discussions and pre-test material, can be done offline in small and large group settings. Remember, it's a blended classroom. Blend the instruction too. Teachers will also need to identify resources that can be used to re-present material, especially for students who need to see it in multiple representation and require extra practice. Resources can be used in one-on-one or small group settings for struggling students.

Authentic Assessment

Teachers need to look for engaging activities that will stretch students by demonstrating mastery of concepts in creative, critical thinking, and collaborative ways. They should identify project learning opportunities to expand and extend the learning.

TEMPLATE: Unit Lesson Planning with the CIA of Blended Learning

 **C** = *Digital* **C**urriculum COMPUTER ACCESS <ul><li>Engaging software</li><li>Aligned to standards</li><li>Personalized learning space</li><li>Individual data points</li><li>**DoK 1-2**</li></ul>	Preview the digital curriculum and identify topics and activities presented. List what students will be asked to know and do.
 **I** = *Guided* **I**nstruction TEACHER ENDEAVORS <ul><li>Data driven</li><li>Small and whole group</li><li>Scaffold, support, stretch</li><li>Power standards</li><li>**DoK 1-3**</li></ul>	Determine what guided instruction is needed to support student mastery. Data will help diagnose groupings and individuals.
 **A** = *Authentic* **A**ssessment STUDENT APPLICATIONS <ul><li>Critical thinking</li><li>Communication</li><li>Collaboration</li><li>Creativity</li><li>**DoK 3-4**</li></ul>	Consider how to stretch student learning with authentic assessments: working with peers, real-world applications, projects, and productions.

EXAMPLE: Unit Lesson Planning with the CIA of Blended Learning

C = *Digital* **C**urriculum

COMPUTER ACCESS
- Engaging software
- Aligned to standards
- Personalized learning space
- Individual data points
- **DoK 1-2**

Preview the digital curriculum and identify topics and activities presented. List what students will be asked to know and do.
- Lssn 1 – What is a Polynomial + Quiz
- Lssn 2 – Adding and Subtracting Polynomials + Quiz
- Lssn 3 – Multiplying Binomials + Quiz
  - Practice: Area Model
- Lssn 4 – Multiplying Polynomials + Quiz
  - Journal: Area Model
- Lssn 5 – Polynomials Wrap-Up
  - Discussion: FOILed Again
  - Diagnostic Pre-Test
- Computer Scored Test
- Teacher Scored Test

I = *Guided* **I**nstruction

TEACHER ENDEAVORS
- Data driven
- Small and whole group
- Scaffold, support, stretch
- Power standards
- **DoK 1-3**

Determine what guided instruction is needed to support student mastery. Data will help diagnose groupings and individuals.
- Daily opener and closure
- Data-driven individual tutoring and small group
- SCAFFOLD: Combine like terms, Distributive property, Area of a rectangle
- *Misconceptions* +/-: Identifying like terms, paying close attention to negative terms, variables remain the same
- *Misconceptions* x & /: Forgetting the middle term, increased exponent of variables
- GROUPWORK: Area Model and FOIL
- OPTION: Jeopardy Pre-Test Prep
- RESOURCE: Khan Academy: Videos + Practice
  https://www.khanacademy.org/math/algebra/introduction-to-polynomial-expressions

A = *Authentic* **A**ssessment

STUDENT APPLICATIONS
- Critical thinking
- Communication
- Collaboration
- Creativity
- **DoK 3-4**

Consider how to stretch student learning with authentic assessments: working with peers, real-world applications, projects, and productions.

- Extension – Performance Task: *Polynomial Farm*
  http://www.radford.edu/rumath-smpdc/Performance/src/Emily%20O'rourke%20-%20Polynomial%20Farm.pdf

The selected blended learning model of deployment (e.g. Rotation, Flex) will help determine when students will engage with digital curriculum, interact with teacher guided instruction, and stretch into authentic assessment opportunities.

Rotation Models

Using a fixed time rotation, is an easy transition into blended learning. Rotation models maintain the class day and period schedule with little adjustments to traditional classroom instruction. Thus, the reason some call these models 'hybrids' of the traditional classroom. Using a calendar based, benchmarked curriculum, students move in a somewhat consistent path and the teacher can control face-to-face instructional topics, by allowing the digital content deliver *"when ready"* topics to individual students.

Station Rotation

Many elementary classrooms already use a station rotation model, the transition is rather easy to add a *digital* curriculum component. The key is to use the data from the software platform to drive *guided* instruction. At the secondary level a station rotation may happen over a three-day cycle, where one-third of the students engage on one of the three stations: a) independent digital learning, b) peer-to-peer collaborative work, and c) teacher small group instruction. This does not prohibit days of non-rotation for whole group instruction or full-class events. A typical station rotation week could look like the schedule below.

Station Rotation Weekly Lesson Model

Monday	Tuesday	Wednesday	Thursday	Friday
Teacher-led large group instruction	One-third rotations A - Indp. online B - Peer work C - Teacher group	One-third rotations A - Peer work B - Teacher group C - Indp. online	One-third rotations A - Teacher group B - Indp. online C - Peer work	Full class digital independent learning and 1-on-1 conferences

Lab Rotation

In today's classrooms with one-to-one devices a lab rotation doesn't mean students must leave the classroom to engage with digital curriculum. A lab rotation is much like the station rotation, just flipping between teacher guided instruction and digital learning. Full class guided instruction should focus on topics that include power standards, scaffolding and anchoring concepts, problem-solving, and real-world applications. Even on days that students are engaging with digital content, teachers should lead a full class introduction (possibly with a spiral review) and end the class with a closing activity (e.g. shoulder share one thing new you learned today). A typical lab rotation week could look like the schedule below.

Lab Rotation Weekly Lesson Model

Monday	Tuesday	Wednesday	Thursday	Friday
Teacher-led large group instruction	Full class digital independent learning and 1-on-1 conferences	Teacher-led large group instruction or peer pair work	Full class digital independent learning and 1-on-1 conferences	Authentic learning tasks and/or explorations

Flipped Classroom

There has been much buzz about flipping the classroom. This model reverses the typical classroom lecture and homework elements. Digital content can be used by students at home (or before/after school in an open lab) prior to the class session. This allows for the physical class time to be devoted to practice, projects, and discussions. This model works well when data from the digital curriculum is utilized to ensure student progress and understanding. Having students partake in the digital content outside the classroom provides more time within the classroom for Socratic seminars, peer-to-peer collaboration, and authentic assessment tasks. When students don't attend to outside digital instruction, in-class time should be set aside. One-on-one conferencing about digital curriculum progress should be scheduled each week to ensure pacing and digital courseware completion. A typical flipped week could look like the schedule below.

Flipped Classroom Weekly Lesson Model

	Monday	Tuesday	Wednesday	Thursday	Friday
Classroom Instruction	Teacher-led small or large group instruction	Peer-to-peer collaborative work and 1-on-1 conferences	Teacher-led small or large group instruction	Peer-to-peer collaborative work and 1-on-1 conferences	Authentic learning tasks and/or explorations
Outside Digital Instruction	Independent digital learning with data points to guide instructional needs				

Flexible Model

When time and calendar are taken out of the equation, student learning can be fluid. The flex blended learning model is often used at the secondary level when students become more mature and have the skills to manage their time and willing to seek assistance when needed. Digital content, or full courseware (designed in 60-hour semester courses), does much of the heavy lifting in terms of delivering instruction. This gives students and teachers more control over how they use their time. Teachers have time to work individually with students. While students can move through the lessons and materials at their own pace. Well, not exactly - there should be benchmark calendar points to ensure students are progressing through the courseware in a timely manner. Such an unit completion dates. However, for the most part students operate independently and receive help from teachers when needed. Students should be setting goals each week and conferencing with their teacher weekly to ensure they are progressing and understanding course material.

Speaking of data and meeting goals, teachers must use the data from the digital courseware to check for student understanding and determine best 'pull out points' for guided instruction in places where students commonly struggle. Guided instruction can be one-on-one tutoring, or in small or full class situations. Science labs and hands-on investigations should be incorporated into the learning environment. Ideally teachers can enhance the digital courseware with authentic assessments and peer-to-peer communication and collaboration with creative critical thinking projects in the course content area. A typical flex week could look like the schedule below.

Flex Weekly Lesson Model

	Monday	Tuesday	Wednesday	Thursday	Friday
Courseware	Independent digital learning in an online semester-based courseware with individual data points				
Classroom Instruction	1-on-1 conferences & tutoring	1-on-1 conferences & tutoring	Teacher small group instruction	1-on-1 conferences & tutoring	Authentic learning tasks

When using the CIA of blended learning consider how you can create a learning environment that has a good balance of all three elements. Consider the three elements carefully. Ask yourself, "What costs, or change processes, must take place to:

- allow *digital* <u>c</u>urriculum to carry much of the load?
- adopt a *guide* <u>i</u>nstruction role for teachers, driven by data analysis?
- embrace *authentic* <u>a</u>ssessments to extend learning and as evidence of mastery?

Keep in mind the three overlapping CIA circles when building a blended learning environment. Target the sweet spot in the middle where all three elements are balanced and come together. Blended learning is not a continuum, but moves among the three CIA overlapping elements at any given time.

NEXT STEPS

Questions to Consider

1. What are the best instructional practices of each element in the CIA of blended learning?
    - *Digital* <u>C</u>urriculum,
    - *Guided* <u>I</u>nstruction, and
    - *Authentic* <u>A</u>ssessment
2. How do you define the "sweet spot" or balance of all three elements of CIA in the blended classroom?
3. How will you use the CIA of blended learning to help teachers make the shift to blended?
4. What blended learning classroom model will work best in your setting?

Actions

1. Identify any *digital* curriculum available in your building or at your disposal (e.g. OER options).
2. Consider the change process that teachers and students, must go through when adopting *guided* instruction methodology.
3. Prepare for *authentic* assessments by scanning the National Education Association's Educator's Guide to the "Four Cs." See Note #4 below.

Notes

1. Powell, A., Rabbit, B., & Kennedy, K. (2014, October). *iNACOL Blended Learning Teacher Competency Framework*. Publication. Retrieved from International Association for K-12 Online Learning: https://www.inacol.org/wp-content/uploads/2015/02/iNACOL-Blended-Learning-Teacher-Competency-Framework.pdf

2. Webb, N. L. (2002, March 28) *Depth-of-Knowledge Levels for Four Content Areas*. Whitepaper. Retrieved March 9, 2017 from: http://facstaff.wcer.wisc.edu/normw/All%20content%20areas%20%20DOK%20levels%2032802.pdf

3. Covey, S. R. (2013, November). *The 7 Habits of Highly Effective People*. Simon & Schuster, 25th Anniversary edition.

4. *Preparing 21st Century students for a Global Society: An Educator's Guide to the Four Cs*. Publication. National Education Association. http://www.nea.org/assets/docs/A-Guide-to-Four-Cs.pdf

5. Buck Institute for Education. Website. http://www.bie.org/

CHAPTER 4
BLENDED TEACHER MINDSETS

"People in a growth mindset don't just seek challenges, they thrive on it."
Carol S. Dweck[1]

Making the transition from a face-to-face teacher to one that embraces digital content to support student learning sounds easy - right? You would think that teachers should embrace digital content as a way to make their job easier, but many may see digital content as a threat. The myth that computers can replace teachers - is just that, a myth. Technology cannot replace the caring heart of a human. Teachers will always remain some of the most influential figures in a student's life.

Software can deliver digital curriculum, but students need teachers who encourage them when they struggle and inspire them to set and reach their goal. Teachers provide guidance, lend a hand or an ear, and discern what's necessary for a student to succeed, stepping in with kindness and direction. The automation of computers will never replace the nurturing soul of the adult in the room. Our goal is to help teachers understand their new role in the blended classroom.

While working with Clark County, where there are more than 10,000 teachers, I've seen the full scope of educators when it comes to embracing technology and the use of digital courseware: from early adopters, to middle meddlers, and the slow to change. Moving to digital learning takes a mind shift in pedagogy and philosophy that embraces technology as a tool for instruction. Embrace the CIA of blended learning to help teacher relieve their nerves and feel less threatened when using digital content to help deliver instruction.

> When adopting a digital learning initiative, a growth mind set is a must.

Concerns that teachers typically bring when first adopting digital learning range from making the change from a comfortable known environment, to being replaced by technology, to a lack of control over pace and content, to fear of failure. These internal voices may scream doubt and worry loudly through teacher's heads. What we do to calm these concerns and reduce the internal chatter is key to helping teachers adopt a blended learning mindset.

Fixed and Growth Mindset

Based on the work of Carol Dweck, the idea of mindset is related to our understanding of where our ability comes from. A fixed mindset believes that their abilities, intelligence, and talents are fixed traits, unable to be developed any further. They tend to favor completing easy tasks, things that they know and are familiar with. People with a fixed mind set have an external locus of control, believing that things happen to them, which can lead to learned helplessness. Whereas those with a growth mindset have an internal locus of control and believe that they can influence events and their outcome. One with a growth mindset understands that talents and abilities can be cultivated through effort and continued perseverance. They tend to see setbacks as opportunities to learn and relish in taking on difficult tasks.

Fixed Mindset

Sticks with what they know

Avoids challenges

Fears failure

Feels threatened by the success of others

Growth Mindset

Desires continuous learning

Embraces challenges

Not afraid to fail

Inspired by others success

Everywhere you turn there is much discussion, articles, and push for preparing student for a growth mindset. Numerous articles are directed towards teachers on how to support the development of a growth mindset, however there is little information on changing a teacher mindset from fixed to growth. When adopting a digital learning initiative, a growth mind set is a must. Staff will be taking risks, finding themselves in challenging and possibly failing situations, and they will need to work collaboratively, learning from each other. The transition period will quickly identify those on the staff who have a fixed mindset.

Working together as a team, teachers need to adopt a growth mindset with reassuring belief statements such as:

- I belong in this digital learning professional community.
- My ability and competence will improve with my effort.
- This work matters to the future of our students and society.

Administrators and professional development providers need to ask teachers to reflect on their own mindset. Teachers should notice the areas where they have a fixed mindset and seek peer feedback wherever they can. They should reflect at the end of every day and ponder upon failures.

Blended Learning Teacher Competencies

As you take the journey down the road to adopting digital learning, look for guide posts along the way. Others have made the trip and have left maps to success. Research conducted by the Christensen Institute, Michael and Susan Dell Foundation, and the Evergreen Education Group have provided insight to how successful programs were designed and deployed. Even this book was designed to help with determining a best fit program. With ten plus different designs based in the practices of over fifty secondary schools, I'm positive that you will find at least one that will meet your needs. However, setting up a blended program is much easier than changing a teacher's mindset for blended learning.

The International Association for K-12 Online Learning (iNACOL) is a non-profit organization focused on research, policy, and quality standards for online and blended education. In a combined effort between iNACOL and researcher Beth Rabbit at The Learning Accelerator, a nonprofit with a mission to accelerate the implementation of high-quality blended learning in school districts across America, they published a whitepaper in 2014 titled: iNACOL Blended Learning Teacher Competency Framework[2] which identified twelve key competencies, organized into four large domains. Mindset was the largest domain. In the document, mindset is defined as *"the core values or beliefs that guide thinking, behaviors and actions that align with goals and mission of educational change."*

The Blended Teacher Competency Framework identifies four large essential domains that are needed when transitioning to a blended learning teacher:

- **Mindsets**: One's core values and beliefs. In blended learning, practitioners need to understand, adopt, and commit to a mindset that help them shift towards new forms of teaching and learning.
- **Qualities**: Personal characteristics and patterns that help staff make the transition to new ways of teaching and learning. Qualities include personal grit, flexibility, and transparency.

- **Adaptive Skills:** Generalized high order complexities that include skills which include reflection, collaboration, and problem-solving. The adaptive skills help practitioners tackle new tasks or develop solutions in situations that require organizational learning and innovation.
- **Technical Skills:** Basic mechanics and expertise helpful for execution and implementation of day-to-day classroom operations, such as data analysis, classroom management, and utilizing the software systems that deploys the digital content.

The iNACOL Blended Teacher Framework breaks the four categories further down into twelve specific competencies. The image below is a reproduction from the publication showing the four categories and twelve competencies in a circular target formation.[1]

iNACOL Framework for Blended Teaching Competencies

When you look at the circular representation, it is not a target, where one would seek the center bulls eye, but rather the competencies are three separate circles - unequal in size. The largest domain and first competency educators must embrace is mindsets, followed by the three identified qualities; grit, transparency and collaboration, plus a smaller set of specific adaptive and technical skills.

The largest and the first shift that has to happen is a teacher's mindset, to one that is orientated toward change and improvement. This includes embracing uncertainty and ambiguity as part of the practice to improve teaching and learning environments. Change is difficult. Along the way there will be bumps and need for corrections as you customize your blended learning deployment. Flexibility is key. Teachers will also need to model and encourage their students to be independent and self-directed learners. This will be a time for teachers to renew their love and passion for the classroom, for student learning, for their own personal growth.

Once you get into deployment, grit and flexibility, found in the second largest circle, or qualities category will become important. The ability to adapt and roll with the punches will carry staff far into an unknown and new learning environment. Peer communication and collaboration is essential to growing and reflecting on the transition to the CIA of blended learning. When the courseware delivers depth of knowledge one and two (DoK 1-2), it is crucial that the data from the courseware is used to inform teacher guided instruction.

Data analysis is the backbone of guided instruction. Digital systems have a vast amount of data. Teachers must understand how to pull courseware reports and use the data to review student progress in the digital software. Often, teachers start with periodic data use, but they need to move to a mindset of owning the data. Software systems can provide daily, up to the minute data, on individuals as well as the entire class of students. Teachers need to use this data to make instructional decisions, look for gaps in learning, and to determine how to meet large group and individual needs. This is an area that professional development will be needed. A professional learning community (PLC) with peers is an ideal setting for data analysis.

Professional Development

I'm a true believer in reducing teacher concerns about the digital learning classroom by having them become a digital learner themselves. Having them step into the role of an online/blended learner takes the unknown and turns it into the known. Learning via technology helps participants see that technology does not replace the classroom teacher, but rather changes their role. By being an online learner, participants discover the teacher's role and allows them to become familiar with the tools students will use and the instructional pedagogy. When stepping into the shoes of an online learner teachers have the opportunity to understand their student's control over pace and need for time management. Being an online learner builds student empathy and understanding of the role of a teacher in the digital learning classroom, modeled by their online instructor.

As you read in the introduction, at Clark County we built an extensive professional development program allowing teachers to opt into embracing digital classroom environments. The early adopters came running. These were teachers with a growth mindset, looking for new and exciting ideas. But when the professional development is optional, too many may not opt in.

Even few administrators sought workshops on blended learning, yet they were asking teachers to do "it." Even without knowing what "it" was. I remember a conversation with a building administrator who proudly proclaimed that she had read an article on blended learning and knew that it was the future, and told her staff to embrace it. When I inquired about a plan of action, she had none. Five years later the school had devices, software applications, even some digital curriculum. She had purchased all the easy visible products, yet little investment was spent on the intangibles, such as professional development, policies and procedures, or teacher expectations (see the Planning for Success chapter). Walking through the classrooms, little blending was actually happening. Much of the usage was just plain substitution of homework for software or digital work for skills practice. Rarely was individual student data being captured and used to drive instructional decisions. Teachers were still teaching to the middle and gaps in learning were still being left unfilled.

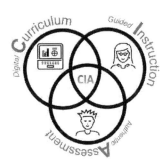

Understanding how the CIA of blended learning interacts, not only in the classroom, but also in deploying professional learning is essential. If all training is focused on the tool, then teachers don't change pedagogy. If there is no clear classroom design model, be it lab rotation or flexible learning environments, how do teachers know what type of guided instruction is needed. If teachers don't feel comfortable with designing (or curating) authentic assessments, students learning will rarely go beyond depth of knowledge three (DoK 3). Take one ring out of the CIA triple Venn diagram and there is little left, just three regions, rather than seven with a targeted sweet spot.

At i3DigitalPD we created a series of professional learning opportunities that target three distinct audiences: teachers, administrators, and content developers. We begin with knowing what is blended learning and determining the model that is "best fit" for your classroom or school. Then we look at the role of teachers. Helping them to adopt a mindset shift towards using digital content as an aide to classroom instruction and how to engage students in a personal digital learning environment. Lastly, we seek to understand how to differentiate instruction, based on the data encapsulated in the digital software. Sounds simple - right: 1) know what, 2) know how, and 3) know when.

Simple or not, if a plan for professional learning is not laid out, many staff will not seek it. A vast majority of teachers are like lambs. They enjoy the green grass of their current pasture, but if their leaders saw greener pastures beyond, they are willing to follow. Most are just waiting for someone else to lead and tell them what to do. It's important that a well laid plan is in place to help guide staff. At a recent international digital learning conference, a Canadian group shared their thoughts about supporting the transition to digital learning. I like how they put it: for every ten people who will take the digital transition training, two will take it and run (early adopters), six will need additional guidance and support, the others well... let's just say they have a fixed mindset and are too stubborn to change. I believe their words were, "They will suck the life out of you."

When thinking about what is needed as professional learning opportunities for teacher's transition to blended learning, consider the four domains of the iNACOL Blended Teacher Competency Framework and the CIA of blended learning. Use these two as guides to support the mind shift change. Share them both with staff. For without a shared vision and proper professional development, teachers and site administrators can fall into feelings of mistrust.

Era of Trust and Mistrust

Over the decades, administrators have gathered the visible makings of a classroom: teachers, students, and courses. The student information system meshed it all together and created a master schedule. Teachers were assigned courses. Students were assigned classrooms. Building administrators *trusted* staff to teach the expected curriculum. For nearly half a century we have *trusted* staff to teach face-to-face content aligned to standards and benchmarks. We gave teachers resources like textbooks and curriculum documents to draw upon. Administrators *trusted* that colleges prepared teachers and they knew staff would step up and handle their part of the bargain.

You see, colleges are great at instructing teachers on how to manage classrooms and deploy lessons, but few have ever exposed teachers to online classroom management or communicating and motivating students from a distance. Some of the poorest designed and least supported online classrooms are at the college level. Few offer an instructional design that you would ever want your K-12 teachers to model from. So, when we *trust* that teachers will prepare a high quality blended or online learning we are leaving our staff unsupported and unprepared.

Without proper professional development, teachers may feel a <u>mis</u>trust between them and the administration. Especially in situations where the administration has failed to cast a vision and developed a plan for rolling out blended learning, beyond giving teachers devices and buying software (which may include point and click training). Teachers need to feel supported in the instructional shifts required for blended. Software training is much different than the professional development needs of a mind shift. Use the CIA of blended learning for planning and pedagogical shifts to support the transition.

Pedagogy verses Tools

Kick off your blended learning adoption with a new vision for teaching and learning. Professional development begins with promoting the future of the blended classroom. Staff should be looking for new and diverse ways to improve student learning and achievement through the CIA of blended learning: *digital* <u>c</u>urriculum, *guided* <u>i</u>nstruction, and *authentic* <u>a</u>ssessments. Making the shift begins with these three core elements in the forefront of your preparation process. Professional development for teachers will be essential for continued growth towards best practices and innovation in learning.

Training on how to use devices and the nuances of the software is important for blended learning deployments. Teachers must have these technical skills the to know and understand the *digital* curriculum delivery system. It is crucial to know how to utilize the software system to assign digital curriculum and generate data on student learning. Since the digital curriculum will be aiding in the delivery of instruction, it is important that teachers understand how to track data on individual students and the class as a whole so they can target needs. The software and device 'point and click' training focuses on the technical category within tools and systems, not the teacher mindset. Though these types of trainings are necessary to building classroom management procedures and setting teacher expectations within the blended learning program. Refer back to the inner, smaller circles of the iNACOL Blended Teacher Competencies.

The blended teacher must be able to figure out how software works for each individual student, especially when it comes to adaptive technologies. This takes more insight and understanding, beyond just how software works, but when it works best and for whom. Teachers must be willing to take risks and chances, without fear of failing. Guiding instruction does not mean stepping aside, but stepping up to new challenges. Teachers will need opportunities to advance professionally in facilitation and balancing the elements of CIA in the blended classroom.

With technology in the hands of students, it's a wonderful time to push them to think critically and creatively. Authentic assessments should be a natural fit into any blended learning model. Ensure that teachers have professional development on project learning and the Four Cs: 1) Collaborate, 2) Communicate, 3) Critical Thinking and 4) Creativity. Students should drive innovation with higher order thinking skills to demonstrate their understanding and mastery of core concepts. Both in college and career, students will be asked to apply their thinking and so should our classrooms.

Matching Model Selection with Teacher Needs

Your model selection will determine the type of *guided* instruction setting teachers will be working from. For example, most blended learning models keep the teacher in the physical classroom, but the a la carte models have teachers working from a distance. Communication patterns alone will look very different in these settings. With daily access to students, teachers can immediately step in and support student learning. Yet, when working from a distance, communication and motivation is much more difficult. Consider how the teacher will be able to step in and support students from a distance. Leaders need to think through the expectations of both their students and teachers in the blended classroom. Document the practices that you want everyone to attend to. Be flexible and revisit your expectations often. Collaborate with staff on what is working and what should be refined.

Four Mindsets

Teaching is a craft, an art, and the core values stem from seeking instructional methods that better serve students' understanding and growth. The digital learning environment requires teachers to re-think their place, their role, and the needs of students when digital curriculum aides in the delivery of content.

As described in the earlier chapters, blended learning is not just one thing, but has many different models, ranging from a small shift in pedagogy to extreme disruptions to the classroom as we know it today. Thus, there are several different educator mindsets to consider when deploying digital curriculum. Over the past twenty years in this growing field, I have identified four distinct mindsets, as listed below. Each of these mindsets come at a different cost of change. Just like restaurant ratings, the mindset cost of change can be high (four-dollar signs) or low (one-dollar sign).

Online $$$$

Too often when digital content is first introduced, the initial thought is, "I'm now an online teacher." This is a huge mind shift change. Teachers feel out-of-control when the digital content takes the lead. The courseware determines the content, the delivery modality, and even the assessment elements. When students and teacher are physically distance communication is difficult. With no bell schedule, self-motivation is essential for both the teacher and student. Lack of control creeps in when teachers don't physically see their students daily. Teachers must work hard to maintain the human touch, the caring heart, in the online classroom.

Blended $$$$

When students and teachers see each other daily, it is much easier to control the learning elements, even when introducing digital content. Consistent social dynamics among peers and with the teacher in the daily face-to-face classroom allows teachers to take control of the learning environment. The role and expectations change in this environment, however there is comfort in the traditional bell schedule and the ability to pace student learning.

Innovative $$$$

Early adopters tend to be risk takers and enjoy the thrill of trying something new. They typically can deal with change and the need for iteration. The ability to take risks with others can support teachers. By creating a peer group that openly reflects upon the changing dynamics of the classroom when digital content plays a role can sooth the anxiety of possible failure. It's learning from failures that drive this mindset.

Designer $$$$

Open educational resources (OER) and learning management systems (LMS) have created an environment where many administrators believe teachers can create their own digital learning environment. It takes a rare person, with lots of time to curate OER content, craft a digital learning environment within a LMS into units of instruction based on the components of an effective lesson, with thought-provoking assignments and quality assessments – PLUS teach. That is asking a lot!

Throughout this book I will continue to reference these four mindsets in each of the program designs. When using vendor courseware, most programs will fall under a highly expensive online mindset to the relatively low cost blended mindset. Knowing what mindset is expected of staff is key to finding the right pedagogy for the specific digital learning environment. Student mindsets will need to be considered as well, they too have a high and low cost similar in the costs above.

Download and share the **Four Mindsets for Digital Learning Infographic** from the i3DigitalPD.com blog.
- See QR code or the Internet Web address below:
  http://i3digitalpd.com/four-mindsets-for-digital-learning/

It's important that professional development is a continuous process and targets the mindset needed specific to the deployment design.

Too often we see classrooms and entire schools that use technology only as a substitute. Schools no longer buy student agendas. Student no longer carry around backpacks full of books. And teachers no longer copy worksheets. However, the learning environment has not changed. Devices alone do not make a blended learning environment. New innovative learning environments restructure the classroom, with new roles and expectations for students and teachers. It starts with a balanced approach of *digital* curriculum, *guided* instruction and *authentic* assessment that teachers can buy into and grow with over time. Clearly delineate your staffing model, especially if you will be using adult mentors along with teachers and establish specific expectations.

NEXT STEPS

Questions to Consider

1. What personnel on your staff has a fixed mindset who may resist change?
2. Who on your staff has a growth mindset that can help lead change?
3. How will you use the iNACOL Blended Learning Competencies to help teachers make the shift to blended?
4. What is the cost of the mindset you are asking staff to adopt?
5. What is your plan for professional learning and building trust among staff and administration?

Actions

1. Prepare for the change process by reading Learning Forward's *Tools for Schools* Whitepaper, Winter 2011, Vol.14, No. 2, 4 Key Strategies: Help educators overcome resistance to change at https://learningforward.org/docs/tools-for-learning-schools/tools1-11.pdf
2. Read iNACOL Blended Learning Teacher Competency Framework. See Reference #1 below.

Notes

1. Dweck, C. S. (2006) *Mindset: The New Psychology of Success*. New York: Random House.
2. Powell, A., Rabbit, B., & Kennedy, K. (2014, October). *iNACOL Blended Learning Teacher Competency Framework*. Publication. Retrieved from International Association for K-12 Online Learning: https://www.inacol.org/wp-content/uploads/2015/02/iNACOL-Blended-Learning-Teacher-Competency-Framework.pdf

PART 2
TEN DEPLOYMENT DESIGNS

It's January, the start of the second semester of the school year. Winter break is over and students are coming back to a "fresh" start, a whole new schedule of second semester courses. The start is not so fresh for some. They had the unfortunate pleasure of enduring an eighteen-week classroom, sitting with their peers, listening to their teacher, working on assignments, taking exams, and yet in the end they failed to earn course credit.

My phone rings. It's a school administrator asking about digital learning options for students in need of credit recovery. Interesting enough, this usually is a middle school. High schools tend to start the year off in recovery mode and go year-round, even though summer attempting to recover credits through the full year using vendor courseware.

I typically start the conversation with, "Do you have access to courseware?" You won't believe how often the answer is no, followed with "Can you get me some? For free? We don't have any money." I guess that's the symbiotic relationship with central office and schools. We're magicians when schools are in need and the rotten bureaucratic police when schools don't want to hear it.

You see there is this mystical and magical delusion about digital courseware. It's online. *So, it should be free - right?* It's easy to access. *No setup or forefront planning required - right?* The courseware is all inclusive. *It does it all - right?* Therefore, it should be easy to deploy and easy for students to earn credits. *So easy you don't even need teachers - right?* Wrong. On all accounts.

The conversation typically is one of dispelling myths. One myth that I must fight over and over again is the need for a teacher. Students in recovery, those who failed to understand concepts and master skills when the teacher was in the room with them day in and day out, yes – still need a teacher to guide their way to success. How can we expect recovery students to earn a credit in a digital classroom, without the guidance and support of a teacher? Just because the digital courseware can deliver instruction, assign work, and provide exams to demonstrate mastery, does not excuse the need for a physical teacher. Keep the caring heart in the classroom.

Digital courseware is not magic. There is no white rabbit in my hat and no doves up my sleeve. The mirror and shadow game is one best left out of the classroom. But, I've got ten magic beans that just might make your courseware deployment an enormous success. That is, if you are willing to plant, water, and tend to the growth of your digital learning program.

There are many vendors in the digital content market selling online secondary semester-based courses. Many schools step into the market with a single focus, typically to increase the graduation rate with credit recovery programs. A single focus, for a product that has many options leaves much on the table. Why allow online learning opportunities only to a single population of students? Shouldn't all students have access to digital learning?

Vendor courseware contracts and deployment are usually an easy adoption for digital learning. In Nevada's Clark County School District, I manage several vendor contracts, document policies and procedures for usages, and guide schools with deployments. For many schools their first step into vendor courseware is with credit recovery in mind, thus the ringing phone in January.

I challenge schools to look beyond credit recovery. By working side-by-side with administrators at the nearly a hundred secondary school in Clark County, I've been able to identify ten designs for deploying courseware. These ten digital learning designs not only look beyond credit recovery, they challenge or disrupt traditional schooling, setting the foundations of innovative learning environments, that students and parents are crying for.

Digital Learning

Technology is a driving focus in today's world, from cell phones, inexpensive laptops, and smart devices. When was the last time you left your phone at home, did you feel out of sync? Rarely are phones even used to call another. More often they are used to access knowledge on the internet or via apps. They have even changed the way we drive, with music and maps. Reading and writing text messages are a faster way to communicate, than dialing a number, even if it is just a click of one button.

Students are already informally learning online, accessing "Do It Yourself" (DIY) videos and conducting searches on the internet. These self-selected, highly motivating environments are much different than digital courseware where learning is structured. Learning in a digital environment requires discipline, time management, and self-motivation. All skills needed in the adult workforce and college.

What I'm saying here is that providing students digital learning environments is preparing our students for the future. Digital learning environments should not be reserved for just the recovery students in dire need, nor the highly motivated who can 'learn on their own.' Every student should have the opportunity to use technology to learn, just as they will in college and in the workforce as many companies have turned to digital training programs.

This Part of the Book

Each chapter in this part of book will focus on a different deployment design for utilizing digital courseware. Like all good planning, we begin with a problem to be solved or an opportunity that has fallen upon us. Then we'll seek solutions using digital courseware. Finally, we'll think through design elements and considerations. For example, this section would have begun much like this:

Problem

You've purchased vendor courseware and are unsure how best to deploy to maximize utilization and increase student learning opportunities.

Solution

Look for creative ways to use online content to opens doors to digital learning to as many students and classrooms as possible.

Design

There is not <u>one</u> right way to deploy courseware. Actually, there are many different deployment design to consider. It starts with asking yourself, what problem are we trying to solve? Reflect on how courseware can be part of the solution. Then think through the program design process. Heed note on what to consider when planning for deployment.

<u>Considerations</u>
- Problem to be Solved
- Target Audience and Teacher(s)
- Digital Content Catalog
- Software Training on Vendor Courseware
- Professional Development: Online and Blended Learning Pedagogy
- Documented Practices and Procedures

As you read through this section of the book, you may find problems you are facing or opportunities you may have not considered before. I challenge you to have an open mind. Look beyond credit recovery. As you read, seek opportunities where all students have the option to learn digitally and for all staff to become actively engaged in a classroom filled with *digital* **c**urriculum, *guided* **i**nstruction and *authentic* **a**ssessment - the CIA of blended learning.

Download and share the **10 Models for Secondary Courseware Infographic** from the i3DigitalPD.com blog.
- See QR code or the Internet Web address below:
  http://i3digitalpd.com/10-models-for-courseware/

One Courseware Solution – Many Options

All too often schools are so busy seeking solutions to problems, like credit recovery, they don't see the forest among the trees. We get into the mode of problem - solution, fixed it, move on. So when the next problem arises we go seeking another solution. It becomes a one-to-one problem-solution narrow focus.

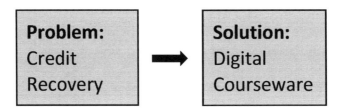

Rather than looking from a one-to-one relationship, consider the options that a digital learning solution can offer. Think beyond the single problem at hand, consider the many opportunities or hurdles that can be tackled with digital content.

Misfortunate predicaments happen suddenly. A student takes sick and will be out for a month. A male teacher has decided to take maternity leave (unknown to you that his wife was pregnant) leaving students with a substitute for eight weeks. These types of opportunities allow you to **think outside the box**. How to provide a quality learning environment for students, when instruction solely from an adult who cannot be with a student who is in the hospital, or an adult lacking content knowledge (e.g. substitute) would be difficult, yet with digital courseware the situation does not have to be so dire. Look for opportunities where digital courseware can be a solution. There are many:

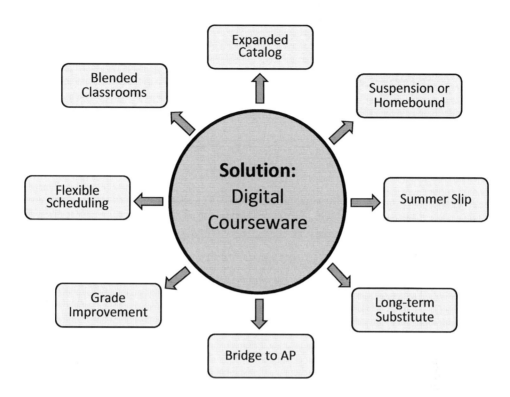

Digital courseware opens doors. Not just one, but many doors. A weak teacher whose poor students are left behind their peers, because the adult in the room cannot expose them to the full standards. This may be due to lack of knowledge or possibly the inability to manage a classroom full of rowdy teenagers. Yet, with digital content, already packaged in a semester-based Carnegie unit can help.

It was early August, I got a call from a school. The science teacher they hired over the summer from Ohio decided to stay in Ohio. They had found an alternative route to licensure (ARL) candidate with science background. The school administration was seeking digital help. The teacher was new to the classroom and would be attempting to manage thirty-five students each period and teach three different content areas in the day. Help!

Where should we begin; one brand new ARL teacher, over one-hundred eighty students, and three subject areas. Digital content could assist by ensuring students received semester courses based on district standards. By using the courseware for baseline instruction, the teacher was afforded the opportunity to develop skills in classroom management and understanding of the high school curriculum in a pace that did not feel like drinking water from a fire hose. Well, three fire hoses - geoscience, biology, and chemistry. The best part was that the new ARL teacher could use their love for science and demonstrate their passion by conducting small group hands-on labs and Socratic seminars. The balance between face-to-face guided instruction and digital curriculum, using the CIA of blended learning created an environment rich for both the students and the new ARL teacher.

The ten deployment designs will help you begin thinking outside the box. They could be thought of as a possible menu to digital content, when you are looking for a solution to a problem, or considering options to a new-found opportunity that fell into your lap. Digital content, just may be the thing you were hungry for, be it a small slice of apple pie, or a full blown four course meal. Speaking of meals, in Part III of the book we will look at design and master scheduling that really pushes well beyond the four walls of the typical classroom when digital content is utilized. I can't wait for you to see "growing up digital," truly a four-course meal from freshman year to senior college preparatory. Wait, I'm getting ahead of myself. Let's start with the menu of ten designs, to whet your appetite. As you read Part II of this book, begin to imagine the possibilities.

CHAPTER 5
TRADITIONAL SEMESTER-BASED ONLINE PROGRAMS

Problem / Opportunity

A long-term substitute is assigned to teach a full schedule, who has no content knowledge, and it looks like s/he will be there the full semester.

Only one or just a handful of students desire a course. It is not economical to set-up a full face-to-face class period with a limited enrollment.

Students are requesting courses that 'just don't fit' into their schedule. For example, an athlete wants to take a course in Psychology which is only offer the last period of the day, but that is the same period Weight Lifting is only offered.

The master schedule doesn't have room to meet all student requests. For example, only thirty seats are available in Honors English, but forty students have requested the class.

Solution

The solution would be to use digital content to provide students with the opportunity to take an online course rather than sitting in a face-to-face classroom with a highly qualified course instructor, when resources are limited. The online catalog could include core content or elective courses and only be limited by the vendor's courseware catalog and school staff licensing certification.

Design

A school can offer online courses as an option within the school day. This can be achieved by setting aside any period in the day as a virtual lab, allowing students to take an online course during any period of the day. Keeping the pace of the online course within an eighteen-week semester allows the student's schedule to be aligned with the school's master schedule. To instruct courses, you could use the same staff already teaching the face-to-face classes, other licensed staff, or check with your courseware vendor to see if they offer course instructors (at a cost).

Considerations
- Digital Content Catalog
- Available Teachers
- Professional Development: Online Mindset and Pedagogy
- Software Training
- Practices and Procedures (e.g. online student handbook)
- Student Orientation Program
- Scheduling within the Student Information System

Introduction

When you have a full catalog of online courseware why not use it to offer students the option to take online courses instead of sitting in a face-to-face classroom, especially if there are holes in your master schedule or student desire exceeds face-to-face offerings. There are times that online course selection is a better fit than a face-to-face, or in some cases having to deny a student the course of their wishes.

Using the eighteen-week semester calendar for both online and face-to-face courses maintains procedures already in place. Courseware is typically designed equivalent to the sixty hours per semester Carnegie unit. Students are familiar with semester long courses. No changes have to be made within the student information system when staying within traditional grading periods. Scheduling students into virtual periods throughout the day to work on their online courses will maintain everyone moving within the same bell schedule. Sounds easy, right?

Actually, it's a great first step into offering original credit online courses. It keeps the traditional bell schedule and semester grading terms. It also expands the school's catalog with both online and face-to-face options. You no longer have to deny student choices, when classes are full or canceled due to low requests.

Online Advanced Placement (AP) courses can expand your school's offerings. If your vendor product has AP content, why not open digital learning as an option for students looking to challenge themselves? Did you know that College Board certifies online content, rather than the individual teacher? The vendor had to submit and qualify content through the AP Course Audit to label their courses as "AP."[1]

Typically, AP students are highly motivated, self-disciplined, and very busy, so why not consider scheduling a period in the day to help them focus on their AP online course. You could support the AP student in a deployment model with a highly qualified teacher in the same room as the student when working on the AP courseware. For example, have the AP World History student scheduled into the same classroom in which a regular World History class is being conducted to work in the online AP course. This allows the teacher to interact and challenge the AP student when opportune time arise, like when the regular class is taking an exam or working in groups.

Online electives are another way to expand your school catalog. Many vendors offer a host of Career Technical Education (CTE) courses. Accessing courses found in the sixteen Career Clusters® and seventy-nine Career Pathways[2] is an opportune way for students to "try-out" a career that interest them, in a flexible online learning environment. With many employers turning to online training this is a fine way to prepare students for the workforce.

Blending the student's schedule with face-to-face and online courses allows for student choice and changes the way we look at the typical day for students. Teachers still teach courses, some face-to-face, others online. Students will need learning spaces for digital classes, such as a virtual lab or media center. Imagine an entire school that has teachers conducting face-to-face instruction as well as teach online courses, where every student has an option to learning modalities. This could be your building. Quakertown Community School District, in Pennsylvania did just that. See the Quakertown video link and QR code found in chapter two.

This model, often referred to as the a la carte or self-blend model, breaks from the traditional mold by allowing student choice to blend their own learning experiences, by taking some courses online and others face-to-face. Yet, at times the choice is made for them. The master schedule may not have room to meet all student requests, so online courses can fill the gap. Maybe the number of students who desire a course is too small and not economical to conduct face-to-face. Or rather than have student suffer through a long-term substitute "attempting" to instruct content they are not qualified to teach, use online courseware and have the substitute guide and coach students through the digital learning environment.

Digital courseware as a tool for substitute teachers is a win-win proposition. I wished my daughter's school would have done this in seventh grade science when they lost the teacher. Jocelyn complained the entire school year that the substitute didn't know anything about science and she was learning nothing. And it showed when she entered her eighth-grade science class. Digital content would have kept the students active in standards-based, semester-long courseware. The substitute could have monitored student engagement and ensured student progress through the digital courseware, relying on the software expertise to deliver quality science content. This would have kept the learning from fall upon the substitute to "teach" a subject with no background or knowledge within and students prepared for the next grade level.

Structures

Maintaining the bell schedule and the semester-based calendar makes adoption of this design an attractive option. You have courseware with a catalog of core content and electives. You have licensed teachers and students who desire online learning options. So, what more do you need? Well… don't think that it's as easy saying, "Okay, let's add online courses to the schedule."

Staff, students, and courseware are the 'stuff' that is required. Throw in devices and connectivity - but that is a "given" when using courseware. What about classrooms? Where will students go during online class periods? What are the online teacher's responsibility? How will students be orientated to online? What professional development and training does the staff need and when/how will it be scheduled? How will teachers communicate with students from a distance? Will you have proctored exams… question upon question that need answers. You really need to think through the 'how to' procedures and structures that need to be put in place. You can't just gather the goods and tell your staff, "Have at it."

It's like the time I purchased a wardrobe for my daughters at Ikea™. The box had all the 'stuff' I needed, from small nails, screws of six assorted sizes, and at least twenty of more boards of various lengths and thicknesses. You've been there, right? I grabbed a hammer and screwdriver (the 'given' elements) and laid all the 'stuff' out on the floor and thought, "Where do I start?"

I checked the box for the 'how to' instructions. You see, someone at the manufacturing company meticulously thought through all the details, processes, and step-by-step procedures needed to compile all that 'stuff' into a wardrobe. Without the "how to" guide by my side there was no way I was ever going to build a quality wardrobe for my daughters. Nor was I ever going to just gather all the goods and tell them, "Have at it." Okay, they were only eight and ten at the time, but you get what I'm saying here - right?

Don't leave your staff or students out to dry. Develop a vision and guide them through a planning process. Together, you can build a quality "how to" instructional manual. Don't feel that you have to get it right the very first penning. Iterations will lead you to a path of growth and triumph.

So let's start thinking through the structures needed for student success.

Classrooms

Go back to the problem you are trying to solve. Is there a handful of students who need online courses? Or is there a long-term substitute that needs a hand delivering high quality standards-based content? Having a target audience with a specific online course is much easier to deploy. For example, an online elective course that is not available face-to-face. When you start small you have time to work out the kinks before going full scale, or full catalog. Starting with one class, or one teacher is not a bad place to begin.

Long-Term Substitute

Clark County is a huge district. The fifth largest in the nation. Not only are the students transient, teachers come and go also. One high school had a Spanish teacher when they established the master schedule in the spring and offered five sections to students. Over 180 students were slated to take either Spanish I or Spanish II in the fall. Little did anyone know that the staff member would be moving out of state over the summer. The first day of school there was no Spanish teacher to be found and a long-term substitute was brought in to serve the students. This was an excellent opportunity to use online courseware to support students learning. Students received the full 60 hours of Spanish first semester content with mentoring and coaching from the substitute to ensure students stayed engaged and completed the courseware over the eighteen-week semester. The courseware had a calendar feature that established a pace and assignment due dates that helped the substitute manage student pace. Even course exams were all taken on the same date, in class. The school had not planned to offer an online Spanish course that fall, but circumstances led them to it and students were successful. Fortunately, this school was able to hire a licensed Spanish teacher at second semester.

When thrown into a situation with a long-term substitute, digital content is an ideal support system for students and the substitute. Mathematics and science are fields that are becoming more and more difficult to find quality teachers. All too many long-term substitutes are in our classrooms, with no content knowledge and poorly preparing students. Schools do their best to ensure that higher order thinking subjects are manned with highly qualified subject area teachers. Leaving courses like Algebra I and Biology, the freshman foundational and gatekeeper courses, with long-term substitutes. Deployment of digital courseware in such situations can ensure that students are being exposed to the expected curriculum benchmarked for the full semester.

Expanded Catalog

When more students need a course than the traditional bell schedule and staffing capabilities can support, digital courseware can expand a teacher's reach. You don't have to limit seats in courses, if you have a digital option available. In a small school, catalogs are limited especially in electives and available seats in honors courses. If your vendor courseware has options to expand offerings or seats why not take advantage of them? Create opportunities during the school day for students to attend to their online courses, either in a lab or open seating media center, where students can be monitored by adults, and teachers on your staff instruct from a distance.

Take a honors course as an example. Forty students have requested the course, not enough for two sections and too many for one. Remember, I come from a district that staffs at thirty-three to one. Using online courseware and the exact same teacher who is instructing the face-to-face classroom, additional online seats can be made available. This provides students a choice if they want a face-to-face learning experience or one that is completely online. No need to deny students the opportunity. Better yet, you could create a hybrid model that provides equal access to face-to-face instruction and online learning. More on this topic is included in Part III. Look at college hybrid in the Innovative Designs chapter.

Health is a high school graduation requirement in Nevada. Students are required to take Health 8 in grade eight and high school (HS) Health typically as a sophomore. Health is only a semester in length which makes it difficult to schedule. Many students will take the course in the summer before high school to "get it out of the way". This is a good time, since most students just finished Health 8 and much of the content is still fresh in mind. Many high school counselors suggest HS Health in summer before entering high school. One high school went so far as to inform parents that HS Health is only offered online in their school and if students wanted to take the course in a classroom setting they must attend a face-to-face summer school session offered by the school district.

At one high school, for ease of scheduling, the online HS Health was only offered as an early or late bird period without a daily attendance requirement. The entire Health course was taken from a distance, except for the proctored exams which student were required to attend during their scheduled early or late bird period for examinations. To stay within the eighteen-week semester, assignment deadlines were set to pace students. Students were required to attend class for exams a minimum of every two weeks. The Health teacher was assigned to monitor the early and late bird periods, proctoring exams and tutoring students.

The minimum attendance and required proctored exams helped the teacher make connections with students. During the school day the teacher attended to the online courseware classroom, motivating and guiding over three hundred students each semester to successfully complete the online course from a distance.

Both of high school programs above the structure was different. The online Spanish class was during the school day with continuous daily support from an adult who lacked content knowledge, but could guide and coach students through the digital courseware. The online Health model was outside the bell schedule, per se. Most interaction with the course instructor was from a distance, but students had the ability to get face-to-face instructional support any day of the week. Also, each school only had one online semester-based course and the students had no choice in the online classroom selection. The online courseware deployment model was chosen for them. These small programs helped lay the foundation for testing the waters, both for students and teachers.

Students

Preparing students to learn from a distance should not be left up to chance. Online learning takes a lot of self-discipline and time management. Skills that many students are just beginning to develop. The semester-based online courses help students by maintaining the same calendar as their face-to-face classes. Quarter grades and semester finals will run concurrent with all their classes, but just *going* to class is radically different. Having an assigned period during the day to work on online courseware will help students attend to their digital class. Scheduling a mentor, or teacher with the students to support the learning environment is ideal.

Student Orientation

I highly recommend that you also consider creating a student orientation for online learners. Please do not schedule a student orientation like one high school who gathered all their students in a lecture hall. The school counselor told the students they had been assigned an online course in a vendor product, then demonstrated how to login and locate the online class. Each student was handed a sheet of paper with the courseware Internet Web address. Students were instructed to use their Active Directory credentials to access their online course. Thank you and goodbye. As you can imagine, very few students successfully completed their courses, leaving the school frustrated with the software. But it was not the fault of the software. It was poor planning and lack of structures on the part of the school.

Orientation to online learning should be conducted in a hands-on setting. Students should be logging into the learning management system, accessing the courses, and being walked through the course layout and design. Have the online course instructor in the orientation to meet students face-to-face, look them in the eye, and share that they are all in the online learning environment together. Calendars with due dates for the entire semester should be set and previewed, reminding students that there are course deadlines and expectations.

Training on the software functionality should be part of the student orientation. Since communication will be primarily from a distance, the orientation should include a practice message to the teacher, which teachers should respond back to within 24 hours welcoming the student to the online learning environment. This demonstrates how two-way communication will be conducted in this unfamiliar learning environment when students and teachers are at a distance. Topics such as how to post to discussions and turn in assignments should be included in the orientation. Also, address how and where students will take exams and if they are proctored or not.

During the orientation talk about time management and student expectations. The more time spent in orientation, the less time teachers will have to spend down the line with technology questions and basic classroom rules and structures. Create reference documents for students and parents to refer to once orientation is over. Start with a contract that lays out the expectations and reminds students that online learning has the same attendance, grade, and honor code requirements as their face-to-face classrooms.

Just like the student handbook that outlines all the expectations for the traditional school day, students need guidelines for what is expected when taking an online course. It's too easy to assume students will attend to their online course daily, that they will complete all assignments, and take tests when required. Wait, students have a tough time doing this in the traditional setting, when the teacher is actively in the room daily to remind them. What do you think will happen in the online classroom when students are left to their own time-management skills?

It's important to document online student expectations. Consider these questions.
- Do students have to go to a physical location? Where?
- How will attendance be taken? In the lab and in the online class?
- Can students be truant from the online class? If so, what is the consequence? How is truancy defined?
- How does the student contact a teacher if they need help?
- How can parents view student progress and grades?
- Will there be required face-to-face tutoring should a student fall behind?
- Will exams be proctored? When and where?
- Can students withdraw from the online course if they do not like it? If so, how and when?

There are many things to consider when embracing online options. Programs can be structured such that students may take the online course(s) either in the brick-and-mortar campus (during a scheduled period of the school day) or off-site (from home). When teachers are from a distance, onsite labs with adult coaches are helpful to guide student behavior and focus student attention to their online classrooms. This type of additional support is beneficial for both the teacher and students. Finding a deployment design that works well for student success is important. Just because it works for staff, does not mean it's the best design for student success. Managed time, high expectations, and continued support are key to online course completions.

Teachers

Like the orientation for students, teachers also need structures in place to support their deployment of semester-based calendar online classrooms. They need to know what is expected from grading assignments, hosting tutoring sessions, proctoring exams, communicating with students and parents. It's a whole new world for them, just as it is for their students and parents. They too should have a handbook for teaching online.

It's important to document online teacher expectations. Consider these questions.
- How are students enrolled into the courseware system?
- How will attendance be taken in the online class?
- Can students be truant from the online class? If so, what is the consequence?
- Are teachers required to set assignment due dates?
- How often must they post class announcements? Set minimums.
- How does the teacher contact an individual student if the student is not responding to electronic messaging?
- How to inform parents about viewing student progress and grades?
- Will there be required face-to-face tutoring should students fall behind?
- Will exams be proctored? If so, who proctors them? When and where?
- Can students withdraw from the online course if they do not like it? Under what circumstances?
- Do the same school policies for quarter grades and late work apply?

Think through the expectations of teachers and students and then document your practices and procedures. The more details you provide, the better for everyone, from supervising administrators, classroom teachers, students, and parents. Don't wait until you need rules and procedures to make them. Start with high expectations, that you can scale back if needed.

Teachers will need training in the vendor courseware. They should be familiar with the content in the courseware just like they knew the chapters in a textbook. When given a text, teachers know when students should be quizzed or tested in the traditional classroom, this should also apply when teaching within online courseware. Teachers need to know what instructional part they have to carry, such as teacher scored assignments, exams, and course finals. It is essential that teachers have training in the learning management tools, like setting the calendar of due dates, communicating with students via class announcements, discussion boards, and feedback on assignments, and working within the gradebook.

A large part of training should focus on courseware data. Courseware collects day-to-day data on each student. It knows if the student logged in, where they went, how long they stayed on a page, and spent answering exam questions. Online courseware treats every student as an individual, gathering information about a student's understanding and misconceptions. It's the teacher's role to be able to interpret and analyze the data to know when and how to meet the needs of individual students and design a path to guide them to success.

The role of the teacher in this design is truly 'from a distance' thus all teacher communication and support is also 'from a distance.' Motivating a student from a distance is difficult. Students do not get the benefit of seeing the teacher daily like their face-to-face traditional class periods. Online teacher communications, via direct email, classroom announcements, or possible video recordings must entice students to come to class and want to learn. This is much different from a wink and a smile that teachers use to entice students in their face-to-face classrooms.

Creating opportunities for teachers and students to meet, such as office hours is ideal. This will help establish a closer relationship between students and their online teacher. When using on site teachers in your online courses create hours before or after school when they are available for face-to-face instructional support.

Don't expect or wait for students to come in for tutoring or help. As we all know, students are less than forth coming, especially before and after the bell. Ensure that teachers are monitoring student progress and requesting student attendance for one-on-one tutoring. Consider having procedures in place that allow the teacher to request a student attendance for tutoring and support, should they fall behind or have trouble understanding the material. Better yet, use time during the day for required pull out sessions. Also involve your counseling staff to ensure students complete courses and keep them on the path to graduation.

As more colleges have online courses, as well as face-to-face classrooms, this design is a step toward college readiness. Career training is also moving to online modalities, making the design a step towards career preparation as well. The self-discipline and self-motivation to work and complete online courseware from a distance is a skill that our schools need to instill in students for their future.

Mindsets

Being an online student, or teacher has a different mindset than that of sitting in a classroom conducting or receiving face-to-face instruction. Often in the traditional classroom setting the teacher is the provider of knowledge and students are passive recipients. In the online classroom everything changes.

Teacher Mindsets

The teacher no longer is the keeper of all knowledge. With the courseware delivering content, teachers now find themselves in an unknown predicament. Their role changes to one of data analysis and coach. And what does a good coach do, but analyze players strengths and weaknesses (data input) and pushes them to grow and excel (one-on-one guidance and support). For some teachers this is a hard swallow, as they love their content. They are passionate about sharing it with others. They want to *get up* and teach it to the group. Therein lies the problem - in the online classroom, students are seen as individuals, with individual strengths and weakness, that have to be handle individually.

Don't get me wrong, sometimes a small group or even large group settings are needed. Take motivation for example, classroom announcements should entice students to want to learn about the next unit of study. Teachers should praise students for thoughtful insights within the class discussion forum and celebrate top scores on exams. Whole group intervention may be needed, especially when the courseware misses standards, or does a poor delivery of concepts. This is where the teacher must have spent time going through the courseware to know it's weaknesses, so they can step in and ensure that standards are being addressed and mastered by students.

But for the most part, using courseware means dealing with students one-on-one. Motivating, guiding, and intervening one student at a time. This entails knowing each student's data, looking for student's weaknesses and stepping in to instruct as needed. It's not a creative art, like the "sage on the stage" was in the classroom, but a different kind of art. One that comes from the heart. One of caring. One that many of us went into teaching for long ago. To make a difference, one student at a time.

Student Mindsets

In the online classroom, the life of a student also changes. Students must *actively* pursue instruction. This is very different from the passive recipients, waiting to be instructed upon. They must take ownership of their own learning. Being absent for sickness, or travel, is no longer an excuse for not learning concepts. Attending class, doesn't mean 'just showing up.'

One of the most difficult transition for some students is attending their online class. Logging in is not enough. Attendance means actively engaging with the digital content. Clicking through pages, watching videos, and reading text is not enough to demonstrate engagement. Typically, engagement entails demonstrating understanding via a quiz, assignment, or exam. This is radically different than the traditional classroom where passive actions such as listening to lectures, watching videos or partaking in class discussions were acceptable attendance

Thus, the student's ability to manage time becomes important in the online classroom. Providing time during the school day is <u>always</u> a step in the right direction. You can lead a horse to water, but.... you know the rest. This is where the teacher, or an adult coach in the physical classroom is so important. Classroom management looks different, but the end result is the same - keeping students on task. Being on a computer has many distractions. The goal is to keep students actively attending to the courseware.

When students can work from home, the task is even more difficult. Think of all the distractions at home students encounter. This is where procrastination sets in. We've seen this in our own homes with our own children. I don't know about you, but shoes and socks are left throughout my home. My girls just don't seem to see the overflowing trash can or piled up dirty dishes. They are too busy watching TV or DV (digital videos on YouTube).

Calendaring due dates and sticking to a schedule is highly important in the digital learning environment. I've seen too many programs fall behind a pretense that allows students to complete courseware at their own pace and fail. In a calendar-based semester program, open due dates create a mad rush at the end. During the semester, students did not attend to the course. Teachers had no data to intervene. The last two weeks students rushed through numerous assignments, so many that the quality was well below par. Teachers were inundated with low level, high numbers of assignments that they too had to rush through to meet the semester grades deadline. Not a pretty site for anyone. Don't let this happen in your program. Create due dates. Have hard deadlines. Expect high quality assignments. Make students re-do work if it's not acceptable. Require teachers to communicate with students every week. Don't accept procrastination from students nor staff.

Changing mindsets is not easy. Matter of fact, this book asks you to change your mindset. It asks you to look beyond the typically credit recovery program for your digital courseware.

KEY POINTS

1. Start small and look to scale.
2. Keep semester calendar.
3. Set assignment due dates.
4. Manage student's time with an assigned period of the day.
5. Establish a student orientation.
6. Create a student handbook outlining expectation and procedures.
7. Document staff and program guidelines.

Notes

1. AP Course Audit: Online/Distance Learning AP Courses. Website. Retrieved February 10, 2017 from: http://www.collegeboard.com/html/apcourseaudit/online_learning.html
2. ACTE Career Clusters®. Website. Retrieved February 10, 2017 from: https://www.acteonline.org/general.aspx?id=8644

CHAPTER 6
SINGLE CONTENT SUPER CLASSROOMS

Problem / Opportunity

A single subject (e.g. math) teacher is needed to service more students than a traditional bell schedule allows or regular classroom can hold. Hosting several individual single subject classrooms (e.g. Pre-Algebra, Algebra, Geometry) may lead to some rooms with only a handful of students and others with too many students.

Solution

Using digital content creates an opportunity to offer a wide variety of courses in a single setting. Classes do not have to have a single focus, but rather a teacher certified in a single content area (e.g. social studies) area can service multiple subjects (e.g. World History, U.S. History, Government) in one virtual lab setting.

Design

Establish a "super" subject area class, where digital content drives the instruction and the highly qualified teacher is in the room to service and support students in the various subjects. Every student must have internet access, either in a lab setting or within a 1:1 mobile device environment. The course instructor pulls small groups of students in each subject area weekly to support and guide student learning and monitor progress.

Considerations
- Digital Content Catalog
- Teacher Selection
- Physical Location and Setting
- Professional Development: Blended Mindset and Pedagogy
- Software Training
- Practices and Procedures
- Scheduling within the Student Information System

Introduction

When looking to extend the reach of your staff, digital courseware provides an opportunity to go beyond the black box of the student information system and single subject periods in the school day. Classes can be created in the same content area (e.g. English), cutting across multiple subjects (e.g. English 6, 7 and 8). This type of "super" class, extends the reach of the highly qualified course instructor to many students in different subjects at one time.

You may have already been creating such learning environments within traditional settings. I've seen Spanish teachers host, both Spanish III and AP Spanish in the same class period, due to small numbers of students seeking advanced courses in the same subject area. With digital courses leading instruction, super classrooms can be created in most any content area, without over burdening the highly qualified instructor.

Super content classes can be used for original credit or recovery purposes. The goal is to ensure that every day students have access to their highly qualified teacher. The instructor's role is to support and guide students through the digital courseware towards success. Having a content area teacher in the room, students have immediate access to help when needed. Using daily data from the courseware, the teacher can identify when students need intervention and/or more in-depth instruction in the subject area.

It is important to establish regular times for teacher and students to interact either in one-on-one or within small group settings. This maintains the student-teacher relationship which is most important. Students must feel that they are not left to their own devices to complete the online courseware, but reminded that they are in it with others in the room, creating a sense of community. Regular teacher interaction holds students accountable to weekly progress and offers additional instructional assistance.

Structures

A single content super classroom begins by assigning one subject area (e.g. Social Studies, grades 9-12) hosted in the lab with a highly qualified teacher in the room. The digital content will carry most of the burden of delivering day-to-day instruction. The instructor will balance online learning with weekly guided instruction. Teachers may conduct whole class activities (great for hands-on investigations or projects to enhance the digital content), individualized small group instruction (by specific subject area or to fill learning gaps), and one-on-one mentoring. This design could be used for original credit or in a recovery setting.

Original Credit

When dealing with students seeking original credit and using a semester-based timeline, students in each subject area could be moving at the same pace. This allows the teacher to instruct individual subject areas with teacher-led small groups on topics within the week's scheduled agenda. This is an ideal opportunity when introducing new concepts or expanding on topics. In literature classes small-groups can be pulled aside on the required reading, taking students to deeper discourse, analysis, or synthesis. Small group instruction in super science classes may have the teacher conducting hands-on investigations and labs.

Teachers should use a rotation of subject area gatherings throughout the week, so that each subject is afforded time with the teacher. It is an opportune time to review concepts and introduce upcoming topics. The time together should include review of student progress and grades, holding students accountable to maintaining due dates calendared within the courseware.

Teachers should not leave all instruction to the digital courseware. They should consider a balance of *digital* c̲urriculum, *teacher* i̲nstruction, and *authentic* a̲ssessment, the CIA of blended. For example, a full-class opening or closing activity can pull students together to ponder real-world applications or thought-provoking extensions of learning within the core content area. The opportunity to be able to include explorations and investigations can bring out the best in each and every student.

Small group instruction should be scheduled and planned based on student data and the semester-based benchmarks. The schedule should not be so rigid that it prohibits access to the instructor the entire period. The weekly schedule below is for a super math lab, keeping Mondays and Fridays open for one-on-one private sessions focused on students who have fallen behind and need support, guidance, and motivation (e.g. coaching up). Mid-week, specific content areas are pulled aside for 20- to 30-minute teacher instruction, to introduce topics, scaffold learning, further analysis or expansion of concepts, or conduct hands-on investigations.

Weekly Schedule

Monday	Tuesday	Wednesday	Thursday	Friday
Private Coaching	Pre-Algebra Pull-out	Geometry Pull-out	Algebra Pull-out	Private Coaching

Using the semester-based benchmarked timeline and data to drive when and where students require intervention, the teacher can pull aside different subjects throughout the week. These small group instruction opportunities strengthen the relationship between the teacher and the students. It also reminds students that the online courseware is just part of mastering content. Scheduled time allows teachers to take student understanding gained with the digital content to level two or three in Depth of Knowledge (DoK 2-3) by adding in rich thought provoking discussion, student projects, or authentic assessments. Student-teacher weekly interactions also allows for monitoring that ensures students stay on track to successfully complete the online course on schedule.

Elective courses in Career Technical Education (CTE) are typically taught by a single instructor within a Career Pathway.[1] Such that one instructor teaches multiple levels (e.g. introductory, intermediate, and advanced) within the content area. Establishing a "super" content lab in CTE could be a natural fit. Many vendor courseware catalogs have grown in CTE areas, such as Business Management and Administration, Information Technology, and Health Science. Using a single teacher over several CTE courses, is one way to open more seats to career readiness. Rather than using a semester-based calendar, this may be a subject area where students could be allowed to roll into the next CTE digital course in the sequence upon completion.

Credit Recovery

Typically rolling enrollment courses are held in credit recovery situations. When students fall extremely behind in credits, often it is in core courses and usually in more than one subject. For example, students may lack credits in second semester Algebra and first semester Geometry. Setting up an environment that allows a student to roll into the next course upon completion of another is a fantastic way to establish a super content area class.

One high school established a super mathematics lab by pulling some of the most in need students, many of whom were attempting to recover credits, from every classroom each and every period of the day in mathematics. To accommodate all the students in need, a wall was knocked down between two classrooms. A highly qualified mathematics teacher along with a special education educator were in the super classroom working with the large group of heterogeneous learners who had access to laptops.

This high school was on an eighty-five-minute block schedule. In the super math class, a two-station rotation model was used to keep students engaged and not sitting at computers for extended periods. At any given time, half the students were engaged with digital content, while the other half of the class worked with course instructors either on: 1) courses content or 2) preparation for the Nevada high school mathematics proficiency exam.

Students taking Pre-algebra through Algebra II were placed in the super math class. Many of the students in the super math lab had several semesters of mathematics in need of recovery, as well as possible initial math credits. A goal was set to obtain one-half semester course credit every nine weeks. When a student completed one course, they immediately enrolled in the next math course in need.

Rather than have open seating, students were grouped according to their content area, allowing immediate access to others working on the same subject. If a student completed one course and moved into a second course their seating assignment was changed, so that they would be surrounded with fellow students who were able to support one another. This also helped the teachers with organizing coaching session within each subject area.

Super Mathematics Lab

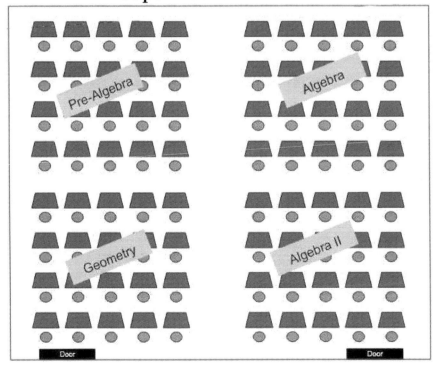

To ensure students stayed on pace, the teacher would meet with individual students each week to review their progress in the courseware. These coaching situations were designed to review student achievement data and conduct one-on-one tutoring as needed. It also maintained the human touch in the classroom, keeping students aware of the caring heart of their teacher. The student-teacher relationship is so important, and one that should not be lost, even in a fast and furious recovery program.

Super content area courses don't have to be so large, but can be small sections embedded into already existing settings. Jumping on recovery situations when they arise, rather than waiting for students' final years in high school, when they have an accumulated several lost credits. Ideally you want to put students into a recovery course, as close to the lost as possible, keeping content fresh in mind.

One middle school made every class a super content opportunity in math and English. These two subjects were offered every period of the day and successful completion was required to transition to high school in Nevada. When a student failed it was important to recover the credit as quickly as possible. The administration decided that come second semester students who had failed courses in the first semester were pulled from elective courses and placed into digital courseware for recovery. Rather than making radical changes to the student's schedule, they were slid into math or English courses that corresponded to the elective period.

Teachers who were teaching a class of seventh grade math might have a handful of students in their classroom also working on sixth grade math through Algebra content. In English, the same scenario was occurring. Students were in a supported environment, with a highly qualified content area teacher, who would oversee their progress and support their learning with private one-on-one coaching and instruction. When students completed the credit in need, they could return to the former elective course.

The ability to roll in and out of recovery mode is important when building a super content area course structure for credit deficient students. I cannot stress enough the goal is to ensure that students are supported with content area specialist, who can immediately rectify learning gaps and misunderstandings. Requiring the weekly teacher interaction with students to review progress and achievement data is crucial. See the chapter on credit recovery for additional best practices when dealing with students who have previously failed courses.

Mindsets

As with any time a school adopts digital learning environments, a "set it and forget it" mindset is easy to fall into. Do not let this happen in your classroom or school. In the super classroom, with several different subjects to attend to, a teacher can feel overwhelmed. It is too easy for teachers to fall under the belief that the courseware will do everything and that they are not needed. This cannot be further from the truth.

Content area teachers are important to the learning environment, for not only can they teach their content, but they also know where students traditionally have difficulty and remedies to help them over the hump. They know how to challenge students and add "fun" into their content area, well beyond just the curriculum standards. It is what we like to call the art of teaching and our student are the canvas we look to fill with bright colors and excitement.

A teacher's relationship with students can never be replaced by a computer. Yes, the courseware is well planned out and can delivery standards-based curriculum, but it cannot read a student's face and see frustration, lack of understanding, or hopelessness. Yet a teacher who is actively engaged in the digital learning environment can. They have the ability to step in and provide subject area help with a smile and a pat on the back.

The digital courseware can provide data about student progress and achievement, but it cannot motivate or excite students to want to know and achieve more. This takes the human touch, the caring heart, to look a student in the eye and push them to believe in themselves. To reassure students that they can do and be more. With content expertise, teachers can help students overcome struggles as they arise and lead them to the path of success.

Setting the stage and expectations for teacher interactions within the super content area lab is vital to its success. Teachers must be an active part of the learning process. They must be engaged with students on a weekly basis, to ensure quality student-teacher relationships. Their content area expertise being immediately on hand, does no good if they only sit back and watch students and monitor behavior. Helping teachers understand their role in the blended learning classroom is essential to creating a quality digital learning environment for students.

KEY POINTS

1. Consider what content areas warrant "super" classes.
2. With original credit, consider keeping the semester calendar.
3. For CTE and credit recovery, look at rolling enrollment or early exit.
4. Set assignment due dates to keep students on pace.
5. Require weekly teacher-student engagement.

Notes

1. ACTE Career Clusters®. Website. Retrieved February 10, 2017 from: https://www.acteonline.org/general.aspx?id=8644

CHAPTER 7
CREDIT RECOVERY PROGRAMS

Problem / Opportunity

Students are in need to recovery credits from previously failed courses.

Solution

Using digital content students are provided a standards-based curriculum with no limits on the time, place, path, or pace. Many vendor products provide credit recovery prescriptive or mastery-based options where students can test out of curriculum if they demonstrate understanding at a preset level determined by the school/district.

Design

Create digital learning opportunities for students to recover credits in a timely manner. Program design varies, but most important are the instructional support mechanisms provided to students, such as allotting time during the school day to work on courses, setting due dates, and having access to a highly qualified instructor for support and instructional guidance.

NOTE: Online courses are highly scrutinized by the National Collegiate Athletic Association (NCAA). NCAA nontraditional core-course legislation requires that even credit recovery programs must meet the same high standards and rigor as the traditional classroom setting and requires regular teacher-led instruction.

Considerations
- Digital Content Catalog
- Teacher Selection
- Professional Development: Mindset and Pedagogy
- Software Training
- Physical Location and Setting
- Student Expectation and Practices
- Policies and Procedures for Staff

Introduction

When students fall behind in credits, especially in core subject areas, they often have little options for recovery, Students do not want to sit through another entire semester of teacher-led instruction, when that method of instruction didn't work the first time around. Too often the need for credit recovery begins in the freshman year, but are left to be dealt with in the last two years of high school, when stakes are high and options are low. No senior wants to be sitting in a freshman math or English class for eighteen weeks.

Digital courseware opens the doors to learning opportunities with less complications than a calendar-based seat time classroom. Vendor products that are based on the Carnegie Unit, or 60 hours of instruction per semester course, are not tied to minutes per week, thus students can progress faster than the eighteen-week traditional semester schedule. But let's not fool ourselves into believing that the average credit recovery student is so motivated that they will fly through an online course without need for teacher intervention and support. It's not an autopilot system of recovery. The false impression of students quickly recovering credits in just a few weeks without teacher support runs rampant in our schools. Don't go thinking it's a "set it and forget it" program.

Program Design

Too often we have seen program designs where students were assigned courseware, given a login, and left to their own means. In such a poorly designed program, we hear loud cries from schools about the lack of success. Of course, they want to blame it on the courseware. That's definitely not the cause, any courseware would fail in those conditions. The poor students were set up for failure from the get go.

Program design matters! Let me tell you a story. It was the week after winter break. I got a call from a school administrator who was so adamant about changing the courseware because students were failing to recover credits. This was going to hurt the school's graduation rate. Only three students out of thirty in the assigned recovery lab had even finished a course in the last two months.

I always start these conversations with, "Help me understand your needs. Tell me about your program." This school had bought a teacher prep period to cover a computer lab filled with juniors and seniors who were credit deficient. The lab was the last period of the school day. The students were working on courses in various subject areas. This teacher was also assigned as the 'teacher of record' for science.

First, I must say that "teacher of record" is not my favorite term. Matter of fact I have removed it from my vocabulary. Either you instruct and support student learning, in other words 'teach' or you don't. Online courses like face-to-face classrooms, even credit recovery classrooms, must have a teacher.

The term "teacher of record" sounds like they are only there to record the final grade spat out by the autopilot courseware. Many administrators sell it to teachers as, "You don't have to do anything. We just have to put your name on the course in the student information system because you fit the highly qualified core content area requirement." I have seen department chairs, counselors, even administrators assigned as the "teacher of record" who have no idea how to log into the courseware, much less have any contact with their assigned online students. In many cases, any student work that would require a teacher to grade, provide feedback upon, or monitor student understanding of misconceptions were removed from the digital course to alleviate teacher workload. In most cases, the "teacher of record" didn't even record the final course grade. A school register posted the course grade in the student information system after the student completed the online course. Anyway... let me come down from my soap box and finish the story.

In this high school, six weeks ago the teacher went out on medical leave. A teacher from across the hall was going into the lab at the start of the period, took attendance, and checked if students needed an exam unlocked. Proctored exams within online courses are a Nevada state and Clark County requirement, yet you could not call this 'open and leave' action actually proctoring. Six weeks had passed with no adult in the room except for the daily check in from the staff across the hall. Students were not completing courses. The administrator called because "things had to change."

The administrator was frustrated. The kids were just not motivated. When I asked about student expectations, like unit deadlines or calendaring projected completion dates, there was none. The administrator was at his wits end. Graduation was only five months away. He wanted to focus only on the seniors and drop all juniors from the recovery program. To solve the lack of the teacher during sixth period, the computer lab would be dissolved. Students could work from home. Starting Monday another science teacher would be available to help students before school.

Here comes the real reason I was called upon to help. He asked, "Could you help they find a better courseware?"

What's wrong with this picture? Six weeks without a teacher. Removing the lab from the student's schedule. Unmotivated students were going to be sent home to work. But wait, when the students needed to take a unit exam or help with science, they must wake up early and come in before school. And I was being asked, "Can you get me a better, easier, less challenging courseware?" UGH! This is not a courseware problem, but a design problem that started bad and was getting worse.

Many misconceptions surround credit recovery programs where students are given control of the time, place, path, and/or pace. Let's begin with the fact that students in need of recovery failed when given all the structures of a traditional classroom setting, like an assigned class time during the school day, opportunities to work with peers, and immediate access to the teacher. Recovery students lacked the knowledge and skills to be successful in a highly structured setting, so giving them free reigns on control of the time, place, path, or pace is <u>not</u> advised.

Students need structure. It is a rare teenager that is motivated and organized enough to establish their own structures for success. Program design should start with the mindset that most recovery students failed in planning, preparing, and executing. As we all know, it's not enough to just show up to class. Students must engage and must be motivated. Few students have the desire to work in online courseware, "just because they need the credit." The fear of not graduating can pass if you just drop out. That is not the solution we are seeking here!

Time Management & Motivation

Successful recovery program designs are highly structured. It should begin with managing the student's time by assigning a period of the school day to work on recovery courses is a start. This provides a designated time for students to work on their online course. The environment, or setting of the designated period can make a difference. Consider how and where students will work online. We've seen too numerous computer labs with long rows of students working silently and too few open media centers with mobile devices where students can sit at round tables for peer collaboration. Worse yet was the school who threw together a credit recovery program in a small dark closet with no windows, poor lighting, white walls, three desktop computers crunched together on five-foot tables along the walls. Recovery students already feel bad enough about themselves, we don't have to exasperate the situation by treating them as less than worthy.

Even the title of the program name can make a difference. "Recovery" labs sound like an infectious setting. Using the name of the software product creates a school-wide stigma, should you want to use the product for other uses. Create a positive, motivating, vision casting name like "Graduation Lab" or a relaxing name like "Cyber Cafe" which can create a calming and de-stressful effect. The smallest of details like a name or a room can change a mindset.

What is hung on the walls can make a difference too. Blank white walls of a computer lab speak volumes. In many cases, no one cares enough to decorate. Motivational quotes, even if hand written, puts positive thoughts in students' head, reminding them to believe in themselves

Motivation comes in many formats and can be contagious. Successful programs celebrate course completions, with certificates on the wall, ringing bells, or just a simple act of having the room stop and clap for the student who just completed a course. Remember recovery students come from a failure mindset. We need to remind them that through hard work and determination they can succeed, one step at a time. This may mean celebrating small wins along the way, such as a single unit completion within a course.

In one credit recovery classroom, the teacher had created a huge baseball field where students got to move their player around the bases for each unit completion. Once a student completed the course they earned a baseball that they wrote their name and course title upon to display in the field beyond the home run fence, because they "knocked it out of the park." Now that's what I call motivation.

Staff Selection

If we see others succeed, we begin to believe that success is possible for us too. When someone else believes in us, coaching and cheering along the way, keeps us moving forward. We are motivated knowing that someone is counting on us, someone is invested in our success, is there to reach out to when in need, or better yet, knows when I need help even before I know it myself (which is possible given all the data available within digital courseware) and one who keeps a us on track to success. It is important to have the right setting <u>and</u> the right personnel in a recovery program.

In Clark County every high school has a credit recovery program. With over 40 high schools, I've seen a lot of good, bad, and downright ugly programs. It is always frustrating to walk into a credit recovery setting where the teacher is sitting behind a desk at the front of the room and can only see the backs of student's computers. The room might be quiet, but upon walking the room, it was apparent that few students were actually in the courseware working. Too often the teacher selected to monitor the lab had poor classroom management skills and unfavorable student results in the traditional setting. They just carried these unprofessional habits to the recovery lab. Our recovery students have unique needs and should have teachers who can 'step up' and 'step in' to help, support, and guide student learning.

Utilizing digital curriculum takes the need for direct instruction and lesson planning out of the picture, but that does not remove the need for a highly qualified subject area expert to guide student understanding. Especially in the core areas. Many recovery students failed mathematics, English, and science courses when they had immediate access to their content area teachers, yet they failed to take advantage of asking for help when help was in the same room. Don't expect recovery students to reach out and ask for help. That is highly unlikely. This is why teachers must monitor student understanding within the software and step in when they see data that clearly shows students' lack of understanding. If the program has a "teacher of record" design, who is ensuring the student is progressing, understanding, and will celebrate their successes?

Having a supportive caring adult can make all the difference. Clark County uses prescriptive courses, such that students can test out of units if they demonstrate mastery of the content on a unit pre-test. Please note that these types of programs do <u>not</u> meet NCAA non-traditional course standards. When speaking with some teachers who were concerned about students failing to meet the minimum level to test-out of the unit we talked about how to help students to prepare to take the pre-tests. Just like you might do in the traditional classroom, the day before a big test, why not review the major concepts, do a few practice problems, highlight key points. Remember some of the classes recovery students are trying to pass may be from years ago. Topics were long forgotten, but possibly still in there, but just need dusting of cobwebs. By creating these types of review opportunities students begin to realize their schools really care. That teachers want them to succeed. Students are impressed that teachers had taken the time to actually instruct them. It was a win-win for teacher relationships and student success in the courseware.

Some courseware programs have study guides for units of study. These documents can be used as a note taking opportunities or as a way to earn a re-test. At a large Clark County high school, the recovery lab teacher realized the potential of using the study guides <u>prior</u> to the unit pre-test. With coaching and support, along with the use of the study guides, student success rates climbed. When she left the school at the end of the year, this highly effective practice was lost.

The following year, the administration assigned another teacher to the lab. The inexperienced staff member was unaware of what the practices of the previous teacher. Pre-test preparation was lost. That year, student completions plummeted. The school chalked up the success of the previous year to the staff member, unknown that is was set practices and procedures that made the difference. Documenting expectations and practices would have helped the students and staff. Don't leave good practices to chance.

Structures and Protocols

Vendor courseware will often have decision points such as required levels of mastery that students must meet to continue in the program, otherwise adult intervention is needed, For example, if a student attempts a quiz and cannot demonstrate understanding (e.g. grade of 70%) then the program stops the student from continuing. Adult intervention is needed. This could be as simple as resetting the quiz. However, if instruction is not provided the likelihood of succeeding on a second attempt is highly unlikely.

The teacher should evaluate the student data:
- Did the students rush through the assessment?
- Were there concepts the student has mastered?
- Were there concepts the student misunderstood?

The teacher should identify weaknesses, conduct some one-on-one tutoring, and possibly ask the student to complete additional exercises (e.g. study sheet). The goal is to provide targeted intervention and prepare the student for the next successful attempt. This is difficult in a program designed on classroom management, such as jumping around to open and close proctored exam, rather than student success. Don't get me wrong here, proctoring of exams is important, but having practices and procedures in place reduce the need for management and increase opportunities for student support.

I suggest having a designated testing area for proctored exams. This supports classroom management and helps the teacher identify who is and is not progressing. If a student has not been in the testing area in a while, you know that s/he is not completing online course content. Having students move to a designated testing area demonstrates that testing is important and should be taken seriously. It also provides a quiet setting away from other classroom movement and distractions. The teacher can easily monitor a single testing area, more readily than having testing all around the room at any given time.

In settings with students taking various subject areas, cluster seating for specific content areas so students can work together and ask questions of one another. This is an excellent time for another story.

One high school had many students in need of English and math recovery. They had a recovery lab every period of the day, filled with at least thirty-five students in a four-by-four block schedule. Students were taking a variety of courses in any given period. The lab teacher was math certified and was stressed. She was spending most of her time jumping around the lab trying to open and close proctored exams and helping students with subject area questions, from English, math, science, and social studies at any given moment.

The administration was concerned that their students were just not recovering credits in a timely fashion. It had been nine weeks and only a small percent of students had completed a course. Upon review of the data, many students were attempting to recover English courses. This was not uncommon in a school with a large population of English Language Learners. Yet, the English credit recovery teacher was only available from a distance, mostly grading written papers and not interacting with students. Recovery teachers were not setting due dates, leaving students to flounder and self-select when they should be testing.

We worked through several design changes. All math and English students would be pulled from the small recovery labs, into a setting that would target their specific needs. The administration was open to turning a portion of the media center into a large area for student recovery. Two highly qualified teachers, one English and one math, were assigned to the large lab, which could hold over eighty students at any given time.

Math and English TLC – Teaching and Learning Center

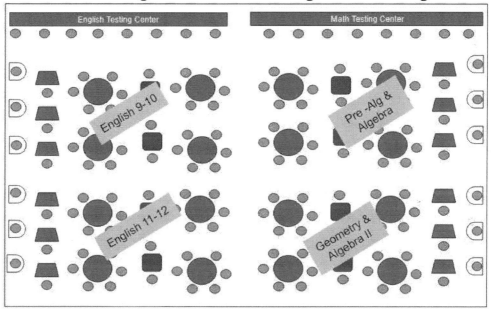

The large room had a designated testing areas and subject matter seating. See image above. This allowed the staff to concentrate on their subject and know when they were in designated parts of the room, they could anticipate the questions and foresee the instructional needs of the students. Teacher stress was reduced and student support systems improved. Rather than have isolated cubicle seating like that found in the smaller recovery lab, various seating arrangements were made available. This allowed students to work side-by-side with others who were attempting the same courses. Subject area testing centers were placed along the wall. This put student's backs to the main larger setting, so they could focus without distraction of peers and noticing classroom movement. It also helped teachers monitor testing students, for they could easily see their screens from most angles in the room. By setting student expectations, such as assignment and test due dates, students success began to rise.

Students will rise to teacher expectations, so set some in your recovery program. When the adults in the room don't care enough to set expectations, we are setting students up for failure, once again. It speaks volumes about how little we value these recovery students. Expectations such as completing one unit every one to two weeks, will keep students focused with a goal to aim for. This could be as simple as using the traditional school calendar to create a nine-week program schedule such that students are required to complete a semester course every nine weeks, allowing for the recovery of two courses in the same time it would take to recover just one course in a traditional semester-based calendar. Some courseware programs can create a calendar of due dates just by entering a start and end date, then cascade the unit assignments within the course. Take advantage of courseware built in calendar tools such as these, to keep students on track.

Documented Guidance

When training teachers for recovery programs it's important to not only provide the "point-and-click" how to run the courseware, but also equip them with guidance and expectations, just like you would for the students who are enrolled into the courses. As a school or district determines what is important and of value within the recovery program. For example:

- What is the master or proficiency level?
- Will exams be proctored? If so, what's the protocol?
- Can teachers remove content, if so what?
- How many times can a student retake a test?
- When and how should teacher intervention occur?
- Must students complete the entire course?
- Can they take zeros for work not attempted?
- Does your school/district have a minimum "F" or 50% policy? If so, does it apply to digital courses? How about credit recovery courses?
- Can student test-out of units? If so, what is the threshold?
- Are students required to take and pass course final exams?

Document your expectations. Create a reference guide that can be shared with all staff and substitutes when needed. Failing to document expectations will create an environment ripe for inequities. As one teacher put it, "If no one said I can't exempt all the teacher graded tests, discussions, and projects, then it must be okay." Don't just say it, put it in writing. Ensure that all staff, programs, and students have high expectations and document them, so programs can continue to be successful. Create handbooks for staff and students that outline the policies and expectations for taking non-traditional courses.

The limitations of systems, such as your student information system and/or the courseware will delegate protocols. Systems integration for enrollment is ideal. Manual input of student enrollments might be easy with a handful of students, but larger schools that have multiple periods of recovery labs can get overwhelmed very quickly.

Take the very simple idea of rolling enrollment. It sounds great conceptually. When a student completes one recovery course they can roll right into another needed course. Imagine all the manual enrollment, posting of grades, and new enrollments that must take place within the student information system for this to happen. The sheer man power, the communication protocols, and ensuring the right people have the proper assigned roles within the student information system to post grades off term are just a few of the pre-planning steps that must take place for the simple idea of rolling enrollment.

In Clark County, after a school year of pulling out their hair with a calendar-based student information system at the virtual school, even with multiple counselors and registers, the virtual school canned the rolling enrollment program. Tracking of grades, students coming and going, or never finishing courses was just too much, even for this non-traditional setting. They decided that nine-week sessions for their recovery program was best for everyone, adults and students alike. Using the nine-week quarter calendar already built into the student information system worked well. With a calendar and a set end date aligned with terms for posting of grades helped students succeed and staff with creating an environment ripe for success. So much so, that many traditional comprehensive schools moved to a nine-week sessions for their recovery programs. Clark County created new course codes for these nine-week courses that warrant full semester credits.

District policies or state legislation will require specific guidelines. For example, the Nevada legislation requires the designation of non-traditional courses to be identified within the student information system (SIS). The National Collegiate Athletic Association (NCAA)[1] also has the same requirement. Identification can be made within the course title or course code. Rather than have multiple course titles for an Algebra course, Clark County identified specific digits in the ten-digit course code to denote the type of non-traditional course from a full curriculum vendor course versus one that is mastery-based with prescriptive test-out of content courses (typically used in recovery programs and <u>not</u> NCAA approved). Another digit was used to identify the deployment manner which noted student-teacher instructional settings. Deployment designs ranged from independent study with no teacher-led instruction (non-NCAA) to a fully blended classroom meeting daily with the content area teacher for instructional purposes.

The ten-digit course code system was designed with NCAA regulation in mind, with full knowledge of what programs would and would not meet non-traditional requirements. Communicating various coding and courseware assignments with schools, staff, students, and parents required much documentation to ensure a full understanding of the importance of course codes and student enrollment procedures. You do not want to be the administrator telling a parent of the star basketball player that the student took a unapproved NCAA non-traditional online course and may lose their full ride scholarship.

Attendance protocols must be clearly delineated for funding purposes alone. Nevada distance education legislation requires that students must be enrolled in the student information system upon enrollment in the digital courseware. Attendance is taken for positive progress in the course and must be recorded in the student information system weekly. Imagine all the protocols needed to document these procedures to happen in the multiple programs across the fifth largest district in the nation.

Practices and procedures should not be left to a one-time announcement at a principals meeting, or a one-page flyer. Documentation should be available in multiple places such as the course identification directory. Establish training videos that can be access anytime. Create guides for specific roles; teachers, counselor and system administrators.

Also think about how you will evaluate the program. Set protocols for staff and students. Gather data to analyze effectiveness. Ask yourself:
- What expectations do we have of students?
- What expectations do we have of staff?
- How will we share protocols with the appropriate people?
- What data will be gathered and monitored?
- When and how often will data be reviewed?

There is so much data in the digital courseware systems. It's important to identify what data is of value and how it can be used to help meet program goals.

When setting up credit recovery programs work closely with the courseware vendor. They have seen many successful and unsuccessful programs. They know the best practices and the strengths of the tool. Speak with stakeholders about their role and expectations within the credit recovery program. Identify guidelines and create self-evaluation rubrics that will drive your program to success. In Clark County, I worked hard to ensure that policies, guidebooks, and reference materials were available to all schools. At the central office level, it is too easy to let schools find their own way. Better yet, create a roadmap for all. Below are samples of the self-evaluation rubrics created in tandem with the courseware vendor - as we both wanted the credit recovery programs to succeed.

Online Student Self-Evaluation Rubric

Exceeds	Meets	Approaches	Needs Improvement
Daily Progress			
Completed software orientation	Completed software orientation	Aware of software orientation, but has not accessed.	Not aware of student orientation within software
Uses calendar to identify what activities need to be completed	Makes daily progress	Jumps around within the course	Has login, but may not access course
Within the Course			
Keeps a course notebook	Takes notes	Reads course material	Does not read material
Always seeks built in scaffold activities, links and print resources	Accesses built in resources to help complete assignments	Skips over work deemed "too hard." Unaware of built in resources.	Clicks around, may be on non-course content websites.
Prepared for exams prior to taking them	Accesses notes prior to taking exams	Reads questions and all choices when taking exams	Quickly guesses on exam questions
Daily monitors progress in gradebook	Access gradebook to check grades	Periodically checks grades	Unaware or avoids gradebook
Interactions with Teachers			
Verifies with lab coach that they are on pace towards completion	Review progress with lab coach to help stay on pacing	Talks to lab coach about non-academic topics	Avoids lab coach
Maintains an open dialogue with course teacher (e.g. email or verbal)	Dialogues with course teacher (e.g. email or verbal)	Knows name of course teacher, but never "spoke" to them (e.g. email or verbal)	Unaware who is the course teacher

Online Highly Qualified Teacher Self-Evaluation Rubric

Exceeds	Meets	Approaches	Needs Improvement
Classroom Preparation			
Attended a software training and feels very comfortable with interface, and supports peers as needed	Attended a software training and knows where and can access how to guides and videos	May have been trained by another on site or self-taught using how to guides and videos	Has no software training and unaware of how to guides and videos
Has thoroughly gone through the course content and identified possible areas where student might need assistance	Has looked over the course content, syllabus, and gradebook	Has previewed the course gradebook	Is not aware of the course content
Monitoring Students Progress			
Sets individual students calendar start and end dates, holds students accountable to due dates, and adjust as needed	Sets individual students calendar start and end dates, reminds students of due dates	Sets individual students calendar start and end dates	Does not set calendar start and end dates
Knows each student's progress and where they should be to date and quickly turns around teacher scored activities	Monitors student progress daily – checking computer scored activities and teacher grading	Looks for teachers graded materials to be graded, but does not monitor computer scored grades	Does not check student progress daily. Waits to post grade upon course completion
Interactions with Students			
Uses the email and course announce features to keep students informed and motivated (e.g. "shout out" to students for good scores or discussion posts)	Uses the email (e.g. welcome to class) and course announce (e.g. spring break coming) features to keep students informed	Uses the email system to speak with individual students about grades only, does not use whole class announcements	Does not email individual student nor posts whole class announcements
Has established system for student access to teacher for support and tutoring (e.g. after school, at lunch) that can be accessed or required (e.g. failing grades)	Actively identifies students who need help, directs them to resources and best practices (e.g. study guides, note taking) with process to request tutoring	Directs students to others for tutoring (e.g. lab coach, peers) or directs students to resources within the courses (e.g. study guides)	No student support or tutoring system in place

Virtual Lab Coach Self-Evaluation Rubric

Exceeds	Meets	Approaches	Needs Improvement
Monitoring Student Progress			
Greets students as they arrive and takes attendance	Takes attendance	Takes attendance	Takes attendance
Knows individual student's progress and discusses daily with student	Knows individual student's progress and discusses weekly with student	Can locate individual student's progress if prompted	Unaware of individual student's progress
Interactions with Students			
Has established classroom behavioral expectations posted in several places in room and consistently holds students to them	Has established classroom behavioral expectations posted and holds students to them	Has established shared classroom expectations with students, yet not be posted in classroom	No established classroom behavioral expectations
Actively looks for and provides immediate assistance to students who may need help to make progress (e.g. watches for lack of screen changes/page turns, sees no new assessment attempts over several days, looks over handed-in work and quiz answers)	Actively seeks out students who may need help to make progress (e.g. watches for lack of screen changes/page turns, sees no new assessment attempts over several days, looks over handed-in work and quiz answers)	Responds to students who request assistance and occasionally looks for students who may need help	Responds to students who request assistance
Communication with HQ Teachers			
Daily communication with HQ teachers to share updates and concerns regarding student progress	Weekly communication with HQ teachers to share updates and concerns regarding student progress	Limited communications with HQ teachers	Few or no communications with HQ teachers

Academic Integrity			
Vigilant proctoring of students taking computer scored assessments. Has separate testing stations away from others, with screens visible and near teacher's station	May uses highly visible marker (e.g. flag, cone) to indicate which students are testing. Ensures academic integrity (e.g. no talking, no use of cell phones, no other websites)	Proctoring consists of opening computer scored exams at student workstation. No identification as to who is testing	Proctoring consists of opening computer scored exams and may student leaves alone in the room

Mindsets

Mindsets of staff and students will vary depending on how you set up the recovery program. Will highly qualified teachers be in the same room, or from a distance? Will the recovery program have scheduled time during the school day, or will students work from home? The more support structures there are the better for teachers and students.

Recovery students typically need someone who they can count on, to help them monitor their progress and celebrate their successes. When left alone, left to their own time management and their own self-directed learning, students can get buried in learned helplessness and self-pity. But with coaching and guidance, recovery students can find strength and reason to succeed. Look for ways to create recovery learning environments that encourage and embrace learning together - between teachers and students. It's best to set minimum expectations and hold students to them.

Having an adult coach, or mentor, with students daily is ideal. Even one that may have diverse courses throughout the day. The coach mentality uses tough love and praise to bring out the best in others. A good coach, is one that can learn alongside students. Don't let the coach say, "I cannot help you with math. I'm a history teacher." The better comment would be, "Let's learn this together. You teach me what you know. I'm sure between the two of us we can figure this out." The coach needs to have an open, caring, and flexible mindset when using a virtual lab approach. A coaching mindset would hold true even if the highly qualified teacher was in the classroom with students as well.

Often highly qualified teachers are from a far, leaving a large physical gap between students and content area teachers. Embracing the online mindset, which includes motivation through digital communication, via classroom announcements, comments on graded papers, and quick email 'check ins' will help both the student and the teacher be engaged in the learning. Setting due dates and holding students accountable to minimum pacing will be key to daily data review and ensuring students complete courses in a timely manner. Not seeing students every day is no excuse for not communicating and monitoring student understanding. It may be difficult to find time for tutoring and one-on-one support, but look for venues like prep, lunch, before and after school to provide face-to-face time with students and teachers.

Credit recovery programs are often the first reason schools/district buy digital courseware. This simple decision and quick purchase is just the beginning. Program design and documented guidance must be well thought out. Transcription of non-traditional recovery programs especially for NCAA must be top priority. Location, name, and even wall decorations should not be taken lightly when dealing with these fragile students. Know the local, state, and national policies and legislation for digital learning classrooms. Invest time in clear expectations for staff and students.

KEY POINTS

1. Design matters.
2. Staff personnel is key.
3. Manage student's time.
4. Set expectations and due dates
5. Celebrate successes.
6. Document staff/program guidelines.

Notes

1. NCAA Nontraditional Courses. Website. Retrieved July 10, 2017 from: http://www.ncaa.org/student-athletes/future/nontraditional-courses

CHAPTER 8
FRESHMAN ACADEMY

Problem / Opportunity

When students are transitioning to middle or high school, they need strategies for being successful in these new settings, such as calendaring multiple course expectations, note taking, meeting deadlines, and taking ownership of their learning experience.

Solution

Using digital content students can learn successful academic behaviors, including organization, time management, and goal setting. Provide students an advisory type course that incorporates teacher-led classroom instruction on "soft" and study skills with elective courseware that targets college and career readiness in a technologically driven global society.

Design

Create an elective advisory freshman or middle school academy course that incorporates a balance of teacher-led instruction and includes an online elective course where students learn to manage their time, meet deadlines, and set goals as they work through the digital courseware with teacher-led instructional support. Look for highly motivating digital electives with opportunities for project learning, such as college and career planning. Use a calendar of due dates that manages the classroom pace, where all students are moving through the digital content together, creating opportunities for peer tutoring and teacher support. Look for natural breaks in the digital courseware for teacher-led direct instruction in small and large group, plus opportunities for project learning. Weekly the teacher leads a class seminar where students communicate and collaborate with their peers in team building and problem-solving situations. The focus of the teacher-led instruction should support building strong study skills habits and soft skills which characterize relationships with others and how to be successful in life and work. Students will earn dual credits, one for advisory academy, as well as the digital courseware elective credits upon completion.

Considerations
- Elective Courseware Selection
- Teacher Professional Development: Blended Mindset and Pedagogy
- Software Training
- Classroom Expectations
- Schedule of Events: Balancing Courseware and Teacher-Led

Introduction

When students transition to a new setting, like middle or high school, they are often ill prepared for the changes in schedules and/or level of rigor. Students need advice on how to make good decisions, deal with peer pressure, and manage stress as they make these transitions. Advisory programs are an ideal situation to support students through soft and study skills as they progress through the challenges of school, develop study skills, and prepare for life long skills focused on success.

Typically, advisory is not held as a full length daily period, but rather as a shortened period or possibly one that meets periodically. This is due to the lack of quality curriculum and need for additional teacher preparation. Often teachers are given an outline of activities or topics with little guidance as to how to meet the lesson objectives. Teachers begin to feel it's "just one more prep" and time consuming. What if digital elective courseware became the curriculum where there was no prep, because the instructor does not teach the digital elective content, but rather instructs on the skills students need to be successful in them - like note taking, test preparation, time management, and meeting deadlines?

Another roadblock to daily advisory is issuing course credits, this is especially true when it's limited in minutes within the schedule. What if advisory could be conducted much like a study hall period that is scheduled daily with a teacher where students study and complete assignments from digital classes in which they will earn course credit. The advisory teacher guides students through courseware, while also providing coaching instruction on study and soft skills. Since the courseware is a full elective course, students can earn elective credits, as well as advisory academy credit, creating a dual credit opportunity and increasing a student's credit bearing options. The face-to-face course and online supplement should be set-up in a "no harm, no foul" situation. If students don't complete the full online elective courses, they still have earned the seat-time advisory academy credit.

During the face-to-face advisory academy class, the teacher leads instruction on the course objectives and engages students in powerful group conversations and Socratic seminars about school, life and career success. While in the digital classroom, students go deeper into topics that were just touched on in the face-to-face classroom. When students complete the online courses, they earn additional elective credits. If students do not complete the online courses, no harm, they still have the face-to-face advisory academy credit.

Think outside the box. Using digital courses in the early years, will help students to develop skills for independent, self-motivating behavior. It also allows students to become credit rich in their early years. Students have the opportunity to complete two semester courses, one face-to-face and one digital, in each semester. The diagram below demonstrates how in one period of a scheduled day, students can earn one full credit per semester, accruing two credits to a time slot normally held for earning only a single credit. Also, you are setting the foundations for digital learning habits that will carry student throughout schooling and into college and/or workforce.

Double Credit Earning Opportunity

Semester One	Semester Two
Advisory 0.5 credit	Advisory 0.5 credit
Digital Elective 0.5 credit	Digital Elective 0.5 credit

With proper support and planning students can complete one hundred twenty hours of seat time instruction in the face-to-face advisory academy, plus an additional sixty to one hundred twenty hours of elective credit within the digital courseware. In a traditional period, students can earn up to two full credits just by providing additional opportunities and guided instruction when including online elective courses into an advisory academy. That's starting off credit rich!

Course Content

The advisory academy blends online elective courseware with face-to-face instruction. Electives tend to grab student attention and lend themselves to project learning opportunities. There should be a natural blend in and out of digital learning and face-to-face instruction. When setting up the advisory academy, plan for a delicate balance between digital courseware and teacher instruction on soft and study skills, ensuring students meet the objectives for credit within the advisory portion of the academy, and providing enough support and encouragement to complete the elective credit from the digital courseware.

In the advisory academy the elective courseware becomes a supplement to the daily face-to-face instruction. The selected elective courses should expand upon a topic from the face-to-face classroom, such as career explorations. Adding the online learning opportunity allows for the development of skills to be a successful student, like time management, self-discipline, note taking, and test preparation. Classroom instruction can use these pathways to success in the advisory academy to lead classroom discussions, seminars, and/or team projects.

The focus of the teacher-led instruction should support building strong study skills habits and soft skills which characterize relationships with others and how to be successful in life and work.

The teacher should also provide mentoring and tutoring within the elective digital courses. The key is to create a balanced approach with class seminars and engaging project learning, where students communicate and collaborate with their peers in team building and problem-solving situations.

Digital Courseware

When first starting out as a digital learner, elective courses tend to be highly motivating and easier for students to complete in a blended setting. When given the proper support and guidance, with a teacher coaching the student through the courseware, helping them to manage their time with calendared due dates, and face-to-face instruction on study skills, students are prepared for success, not only in the online courses, but also, they will have the skills to transfer these habits to their other traditional classrooms.

One-semester digital elective courses are perfect for academy settings. Semester elective digital courses typically have plenty of room for teacher-led instruction. By using a calendar of due dates, all students move through the digital content together, creating opportunities for peer tutoring and teacher support, with the ability for additional guided instruction in small and large groups on required topics for advisory academy. Online elective courses that lend itself to project learning are ideal for advisory academy.

A middle school academy might use electives like these found in Edgenuity[1] courseware:

- *Online Learning and Digital Citizenship*
- *Strategies for Academic Success*

A high school freshman academy might like these topics found in Apex Learning[2] courseware:

- *College and Career Preparation*
- *Multicultural Studies*

Teacher-led Content

Students should engage in regular face-to-face instruction with their teacher and classmates. Teachers should monitor student progress in the digital courseware and determine opportune times to blend the online content with large and small group seminars. It's important that the teacher is fully aware of the content in the digital courseware, so that face-to-face instruction is not developed in isolation of the courseware, but seen as a natural growth out of the digital learning. For example, if a test is calendared in the week, the teacher might bring the class together to discuss test preparation skills. Maybe even ask students to work in groups to create digital vocabulary cards. Then students can discuss how this same activity could be used in other classes in their school schedule. Project learning built from content within the elective courseware extends the learning and builds student interest and skills for future grades, such as teamwork, research, and presentations.

The goal of teacher led instruction is to build habits that can be transferred to practices for school-wide success, lifelong learning, college, careers, and citizenship. College Board[3] provides advisory guides, grades 6-12, that can be used when looking for teacher-led activities.

One full credit will be earned in the one hundred twenty hours of seat time within the advisory academy over the course of one year, plus students should be able to complete two semester elective digital courses. Therefore, students will have earned one-full credit for the academy, with an opportunity for additional credits upon completion of the online electives. That's potentially two credits earned in a time that traditionally was slated for a single credit. Again, if the students don't complete the online electives, no harm. They still have the credit from the face-to-face advisory academy.

Structure

The advisory academy should be scheduled as a regular period in the day. Look for an elective course currently in your school district catalog that has advisory type of objectives and allows students to earn a Carnegie unit credit. Then identify digital courseware in your vendor catalog that closely aligns to these objectives.

In one high school they had eleven periods, with eleven different staff members teaching Freshman Academy. With little guidance, outside a course syllabus these eleven sections were having eleven different experiences. Utilizing digital courses would have at the very least provided similar experiences and provide guidance and opportunities for teacher guided instruction on skills for high school success.

Consider having all incoming underclassmen assigned to advisory academy. Having a single teacher to instruct the advisory academy is ideal. Depending on the size of your student population this may be the only course in his/her schedule, or just one of several. Students will need internet access, either in a one-to-one setting or in a lab.

Ensure that students understand the structure of the blended classroom and how the online courseware is just one part of the academy courses. Students will need to be orientated to the digital platform and courseware. Calendar assignments for the semester, so students can see that online courses are structures, not just "come and go" as you please. Set the tone for meeting expectations, within a guided setting.

Consider starting the course with a full week of face-to-face instruction prior to releasing student into the digital courseware. Use this time to build a foundation of trust among teacher and students, as well as among peers. This is a time that traditional advisory type of face-to-face instruction can be brought in, setting the tone for the entire course.

Let's look at a deployment design. At one high school all incoming freshman were assigned to Freshman Academy. The course was held in a computer lab, with a single teacher to instruct the course throughout the day. Some of the course objectives for Freshman Academy include:

- Learn the history and traditions of the high school community.
- Practice study skill techniques such as note taking, reading strategies, and test taking.
- Examine personal responsibility as it relates to school success.
- Analyze the decision-making processes.
- Research personal heritage and cultural background.
- Create an educational plan for high school and postsecondary education or training.

These objectives could be met with elective courses: *Career and College Preparation* and *Multicultural Studies*, with regularly held teacher-led seminars and project learning.

Overlay of Face-to-Face & Digital Courseware

Fall Semester	Spring Semester
Freshman Academy	
Global Studies Online	*Career and College Prep. Online*

Teacher-led instruction was interlaced with the online learning content. The Freshman Academy course began with a week of orientation and teacher-led seminars, prior to assigning digital courseware. Calendar due dates were assigned within the online course to help manage student successful completion. The teacher lesson plans included face-to-face seminar sessions, teamwork, and project learning. Below is an outline of the first month. The teacher started with face-to-face instruction for a full week, before introducing the digital courseware orientation. Notice how online work, including testing, is dispersed among teacher-led seminars and team projects.

Start of School Lesson Plan

Monday	Tuesday	Wednesday	Thursday	Friday
Orientation	Seminar	Small Groups	Seminar	Teamwork
Tech Orientation	Online	Seminar	Teamwork	Online
Seminar	Project	Project/Online	Project/Online	Project Share
Test Prep	Online Test	Seminar	Online	Teamwork

The balance of online and offline learning must be an integral part of the academy course. The classroom teacher not only guides and coaches students through the online elective courseware, but must also determine well-timed "teachable moments" to step in and lead instruction, assign teamwork, and project learning. This requires that the teacher has previewed the digital content and identified teacher-led opportunities that blend well with the digital content.

The premise of the academy is to build a skill sets for learning, both online and offline, creating a well-rounded learner prepared for future success in both soft skills, like interpersonal people skills, social skills, and communication skills, in addition to study skills that transfer to all learning settings, like time management, note taking, test preparation, overcoming procrastination, and taking ownership of their learning experience.

Mindsets

Underclassmen advisory academies set the tone for future success, in and out of online learning settings. It is important that both the staff and the students understand the relationship how online learning and face-to-face classroom instruction are designed to blend learning for a harmonious interplay and that the skills needed to be a successful learner apply no matter the setting.

It's too easy to think that students are 'wired' to be online learners because they are glued to their electronic devices. Don't be fooled. Students may love their technology, but this does not mean they will love learning on it, or that they have the skill set to be successful online learners. That's the purpose of the advisory academy; to help students build skills to become a self-motivated, self-disciplined learner.

The classroom teacher needs to adopt a blended learning mindset. One that sees the interplay between digital courseware and that of teacher-led instruction. Digital learning and face-to-face instruction should not be two separate disparate entities. It will be important to help teachers understand the interplay of the skill set of being successful within the digital content, to that of the study skills needed in all areas of success in and out of schools. It's their responsibility to help students not only to earn credits in the online courseware, but also to build transferable soft skills such as personal attributes that enable them to interact effectively and harmoniously with others.

Changing mindsets is not easy. The blended classroom, like the academy, is a wonderful place to start with digital learning. It keeps the teacher in the instruction and give students control over their learning. Once students learn to be successful in the online classroom, don't be surprised if they ask for and seek additional online learning opportunities. Look for other designs in this book to help build programs that meet student demands.

KEY POINTS

1. Build an academy for incoming underclassmen.
2. Select motivating elective course(s), aligned to advisory objectives.
3. Maintain a semester calendar for the online class.
4. Set assignment due dates in the digital course.
5. Expect the teacher to identify "teachable moments" within the digital content.
6. Teachers should incorporate soft and study skills regularly with seminars, teamwork, and project learning.
7. Students will earn a minimum one full credit for the face-to-face advisory academy.
8. Additional credit may be gained when/if students complete the digital course. *No harm, no foul.*

Notes

1. Edgenuity National Course List 2016. Website. Retrieved February 19, 2017 from: https://www.edgenuity.com/course-lists/edgenuity-course-list.pdf
2. Apex Learning Comprehensive Courses. Website. Retrieved February 19, 2017 from: https://www.apexlearning.com/digital-curriculum/courses/catalog
3. College Board Schools Advisory Session Guides. Website. Retrieved February 19, 2017 from: https://bigfuture.collegeboard.org/get-started/educator-resource-center/college-board-advisory-guides

CHAPTER 9
INDEPENDENT STUDY COURSES

Problem / Opportunity

Students are seeking flexibility in their schedule, such that they do not have to attend face-to-face class(es) each period.

Students are seeking a full-time alternative to daily attendance at a brick-and-mortar school.

Solution

Using digital content students can work from home, while teaching staff instruct from a distance. In the past, these types of programs may have been built within the alternative education setting with paper packets and textbooks. Today's digital courseware changes the format, but continues the independent learning opportunities for single classes or as a whole school experience.

Design

Create an independent study program designed for the self-motivated learner, seeking an alternative to daily face-to-face instruction. During a traditional bell schedule, independent study course(s) can be designed as early or late bird periods in the student's traditional schedule, such that they are required to attend proctored exams during these designated period, but not have to attend daily for attendance purpose, allowing students to work from home. To ensure student course completions a calendar with due dates pace students to finish courses either in a shortened timeframe (e.g. nine weeks) or maintain the eighteen-week traditional semester calendar. The independent study catalog can be limited in scope, based on staff availability.

A full-time independent study program allows students to work from home on digital courseware, with regular check-ins for scheduled proctored exams. Calendared due dates keep students on pace. Student schedules could be reduced with a course condensed timeframe for course completions and still maintain a full scheduled course load. For example, three course enrollments every nine weeks, such that six online courses are attempted in the eighteen-week semester, or six full credits per school year. Utilize individualized academic educational plans to outline student course load and time frames.

Considerations
- Digital Content Catalog
- Teacher Selection
- Professional Development: Online Mindset and Pedagogy
- Software Training
- Student Orientation Program
- Practices and Procedures for Students and Staff

Introduction

When you think about independent study what comes to mind? I'll bet you see a highly intelligent person, self-motivated learner, who is focused on a goal. You might picture an honors level student, or aspiring actor, musician, or athlete - those who know and understand the meaning and rewards of hard work. Independent study requires basic academic skills and a level of commitment, motivation, organizational skills, and self-direction much like the level required by young adults entering college.

Creating opportunities for students to take independent study digital courses reduces the requirements of face-to-face instruction led by a classroom teacher. Don't think that this means you don't need an instructor for your independent courses. The independent teacher should be present in the digital classroom, guiding student learning from a distance, coaching and tutoring students to successful completion. Just like the self-directed independent learner, the independent teacher must be committed, motivated, and have strong organizational skills.

What we don't want to create is students working in isolation and teachers who think they are just there to "record' the final grade. It is important that both independent students and independent teachers understand their roles and responsibilities before setting them loose.

Structures

Independent study programs can be as simple as allowing students to have a late start, early out, or 'free' period in the school day yet filled with a digital course. The catalog of courses can be limited and targeted or open. This will depend on the teacher licensure and staff assigned to instruct within the independent program. Ideally you will want to establish a pacing calendar for students, to prevent them from procrastinating. Regularly scheduled proctored exams will also ensure that students progress through the courseware in a timely fashion. Exams can be proctored by a staff member, or scheduled with the independent study courses teacher as this will keep an open line of face-to-face communication with student and instructor.

It's important that students are well orientated to the independent study program before setting them loose in the digital courseware. Handing them a piece of paper with a URL address and login information to "go home" and read is not enough.

Having the ability to work from home should be thought of as a special right, granted to those willing to make the commitment to complete and pass courses. Your school should have students sign contracts that outline pacing expectations, including proctored exam requirements, attendance policies, and consequences for falling behind, such as required tutoring sessions. Create a handbook and contract for your independent study program and use them to guide your student orientation.

High expectations should not only be established for students, but also your staff. Document expectations and procedures for your independent study teachers as well. They have a role in student success and let them know what it is and how they should interact with students within the digital course and at face-to-face proctored settings.

Determining a catalog of courses that can be taken within the independent study program is important. Some schools may only choose to have handful of courses available, others may open the entire courseware catalog. Much will depend on the teacher selection and support services your building can provide to students.

At one high school, they set up their independent study program with four teachers - math, English, social studies and electives. Science was not offered as independent study. Students enrolled were assigned independent study as the last period of the day. The four teachers were assigned independent study as their last period also. Each teacher was in the lab on a different day, rotating student access to teachers. This ensured each week students would have face-to-face contact with their independent study teacher. Students were expected to attend the physical class once per week to check in with course instructors, get help, and take proctored exams.

The table below shows the subject area assignments within the days of the week. With holidays often falling on Monday, the school assigned electives on Monday, keeping core content areas mid-week. Teachers nor students wanted to stay late on Friday so it was not scheduled.

Subject Area Rotation

Monday	Tuesday	Wednesday	Thursday
Electives	Math	English	Social Studies

Each teacher instructed multiple areas in their subject (e.g. US History, World History, and US Government) allowing for a rather sizable catalog. A large double lab room was used, opening sixty seats available in each subject area for independent study. Courseware calendars were set for the eighteen weeks of the term, but students could complete courses early. As not to overburden teachers, only first semester courses were offered in the fall term and only second semester courses in the spring term.

Full-time Programs

When you have a full catalog of courseware, you may consider having a full-time independent study program. Using a school-within-a-school design, a select population of students could work from home most every day. As one principal said, "Having students work from home is a huge cost saving on toilet paper alone."

Students would be required to attend the brick and mortar school once per week for proctored exams. This could be handled during the school day or at the end of the traditional school day. The time on site should also include the ability to get help and tutoring. Ideally keeping the workload to only a handful of classes at a time will ease the burden of a full day of testing.

As not to overburden students with a huge plate of digital courseware, student schedules could be reduced with a condensed timeframe and still maintain a full load by semester end. For example, by assigning three courses every nine weeks would consist of six online courses in the eighteen-week semester, or six full credits per school year. Unlike the traditional calendar-based schedule, when using a nine-week quarter plan, students do not have to wait for second semester to take a semester two course, such that a student could earn a full credit in one subject area in eighteen weeks.

To manage and document expectations, create an individualized academic educational plan (IAEP) that outlines student course load and time frames. It's important to consider academic load. Balance student classes with both core and electives. English and social studies tend to have a lot of reading. Math and science can be highly analytical. Create a schedule that balances not only electives and core, but also high reading and analytics. See the example below.

Individualized Academic Educational Plan

Student: Steven Brown   **Grade:** 10   **Test Date:** Tuesday

Semester 1: August - December

Course	Credit	Qrt	Start Date	End Date	Grade
English 10, sem. 1	0.5	1	Aug 14	Oct 13	
Earth Science, sem. 1	0.5	1	Aug 14	Oct 13	
Personal Wellness II, sem .1	0.5	1	Aug 14	Oct 13	
English 10, sem. 2	0.5	2	Oct 16	Dec 22	
Earth Science, sem. 2	0.5	2	Oct 16	Dec 22	
Personal Wellness II, sem .2	0.5	2	Oct 16	Dec 22	

Semester 2: January-May

Course	Credit	Qrt	Start Date	End Date	Grade
Geometry, sem. 1	0.5	3	Jan 8	Mar 14	
World History, sem. 1	0.5	3	Jan 8	Mar 14	
Health	0.5	3	Jan 8	Mar 14	
Geometry, sem. 2	0.5	4	Mar 15	May 24	
World History, sem. 2	0.5	4	Mar 15	May 24	
Driver Education	0.5	4	Mar 15	May 24	

The individualized academic educational plan document should be created as a student contract with attendance policies, and other student expectations such as required onsite tutoring if the student falls below a 'C' grade, and signed by both the student and the parent. Remember, independent study is a privilege. Not everyone is suited, nor self-disciplined enough to have the ability to work from home, therefore, high standards should be set to ensure that students understand their responsibilities. With such freedom and flexibility comes much accountability.

This same flexibility and accountability also falls upon the independent study teaching staff. Also you should document expectations for teachers, including expectations on how to support students who do not attend weekly proctoring, communication expectations (e.g. email, phone calls, text) outside the weekly face-to-face, and courseware gradebook management such as turnaround time on graded work and the ability (or lack of) to excuse digital work or exams. The teacher handbook should include what to do when students fail to meet minimum standards.

For example, in Clark County when a student does not meet the 70% mastery on a quiz, after the two attempts deployed automatically in the system, s/he must complete a study guide (a printable document provided within the vendor courseware) to demonstrate they are ready to re-attempt a lesson quiz for a third and final time. Upon review of the study guide, the teacher can check for understanding and possibly conduct one-on-one tutoring before resetting the exam. The Clark County policy on exam resets is 3-2-1:

- 3 attempts on quizzes (third only after lesson study guide),
- 2 attempts on tests (second only after unit study guide) and
- 1 attempt on course finals (no reset).

Students are pushed forward with the highest score after exhausting all attempts.

It's important to document all policies, so that there is consistency across deployment. Written policies can be shared with substitutes or other personnel stepping in to support digital courseware deployment.

In Nevada, we worked hard to change legislation such that if a highly qualified teacher was instructing the digital classroom from a distance then a non-licensed personnel could supervise the classroom where students worked on the courseware. This opened the ability to allow licensed teachers to focus on student learning and have support staff proctor exams. The independent study program in the Clark County virtual school took advantage of this legislation and housed non-licensed staff in labs to proctor exams throughout the district.

Full-time students in the virtual school's independent study program were scattered across the Las Vegas valley, so asking them to travel to the program office, though central in the city, was asking a lot. Yet by managing testing centers across the city was driving up cost. As more centers were needed, additional licensed staff were required. However, some centers only serviced a small number of students. The legislation opened the door to regional testing centers manned by non-licensed staff and reduced their costs.

Satellite testing centers allowed the full-time independent study students to stay within their local neighborhoods for educational purposes. The district's content area teacher had a set schedule rotating among centers so students were aware of when face-to-face tutoring support was in their area. Teachers had the ability to request student attendance when grades slipped.

The district program partnered with local high schools who provided them with a classroom. In exchange they allowed the school to use their staff to proctor exams for the school's independent study program. It was a win-win for the district's full-time and the school's smaller independent study programs.

Mindsets

As mentioned above, independent study programs require much self-discipline, both for students and teachers. A traditional bell schedule manages time for students and teachers, but when no bells are telling students when to attend, or teachers when to instruct, one must rely on organizational skills and follow through to complete needed tasks. It takes a highly motivated person to set their own schedule.

Even with the weekly face-to-face requirement for proctored exams and check-in with course instructors, some students will fail to meet the expected progress. Teachers must have a plan on how to encourage, nurture, and push student through the courseware. Policies should ensure that students have minimum weekly progression requirements and consequences if they are unmet.

Setting the stage and having documented expectations will establish checks and balances for independent study courses or a full-time school-within-a-school program. Selection of students and staff is crucial in assuring a quality independent study program with academic success.

Students

Independent study programs can be limited in scope to a specific grade, like upperclassmen only, or open to all students who have demonstrated the ability to be self-directed and motivated, or possibly a target population like teen parents. Guidelines for independent study should be the first place you start. Begin by identifying what characteristics students must possess to apply for independent study courses. Regular attendance and passing grades would be on the top on my list.

When given a choice to sleep in and take an independent study course, who wouldn't take that option? Students wouldn't mind leaving earlier in the day, or possibly having a free period. Know that everyone will come running for independent study, so have guidelines and expectations for enrollment that will help weed out those that can and cannot be successful in a learning environment that requires self-discipline and self-motivation.

As for full-time programs, you may find students who are seeking independent study just don't fit into the traditional school setting. They are uncomfortable in classrooms, have no need for the social crowds of schools, and may or may not be progressing. Again, it will be important to identify those who have a desire to be successful in a learning environment that requires self-discipline and self-motivation. Consider having trial periods, such as nine weeks, or one semester, where students can demonstrate their ability to succeed in a full-time independent study program.

Staff

Being an independent study instructor will mean little face-to-face time with students. Though this time is not formalized with instruction it should include coaching, mentoring, and checks for understanding prior to proctored exams. Instruction and most communication will be from a distance.

Independent study staff must have clear guidelines as to what their role is in the digital classroom. Though the courseware delivers instruction, the teacher is responsible for ensuring students are mastering the material. They have a responsibility to coach, tutor, and manage student progression in the courseware.

Too often teachers are sold by administration that independent study course instruction as, "Easy. Just record the grade from the digital courseware." Nothing can be further from the truth. If it was that easy, then why would we need teachers when they have a textbook that delivers instruction with quizzes and tests and we still ask teachers to instruct Because the role of the teacher is more than just delivering instruction, it's about knowing each individual student. Teachers connect with their students, demonstrate caring and concern. They guide and tutor students through material that is hard to grasp and enlighten students to real world applications. This too should be done in the digital classroom.

Independent study teachers are more than proctors and paper graders. They are the human touch to the educational arena. Like a coach, they encourage and challenge students to do more and be more than they ever thought possible. Just because the program is called independent study, don't leave the students flying solo through the courseware. Your staff should be leading the flight, mapping a route to success and student achievement.

KEY POINTS

1. Create program structures, including a student orientation.
2. Identify target populations and consider elements for the student contract/application.
3. Determine a catalog of courses.
4. Select and train teachers. Document expectations.
5. Maintain semester, or nine-week, calendar for online courses.
6. Set assignment calendar due dates and schedule proctored exams.
7. Remember, independent study is not a solo sport. It needs coaching.

CHAPTER 10
UNIT RECOVERY / GRADE IMPROVEMENT

Problem / Opportunity

Students fail an exam, unable to demonstrate mastery of standards-based instruction, yet instruction must continue to ensure meeting the benchmarks/standards and expectations for the course. This continued pattern leaves students with low scores in the gradebook, unprepared for the next unit (should it built upon concepts in the previous unit), and possible failure of the course at semester end.

Solution

Using digital content teachers can create and assign standards-based instructional units aligned to unit exams. These digital learning units can be assigned to students who failed to demonstrate mastery of content on the classroom exam. Upon completion of the digital instruction students can retest for grade improvement.

Design

Digital instruction can be broken down into chunks of learning units. When a student fails to understand the course material in a traditional classroom setting, digital content can be assigned to the student. This additional modality of instruction may help the student overcome misconceptions. When a student fails a unit exam the teacher can assign the same concepts in a digital format, for independent study and review, and allow the student to retake another unit exam for a grade improvement. Checks and balances must be put into place to ensure that the student completes the digital content and that this retaking of exams does not become a crutch to learning the first time around.

<u>Considerations</u>
- Digital Content - ideally an adaptive diagnostic program
- Professional Development: Competency-based Mindset (retaking exams)
- Software Training
- Practices and Procedures for Students and Staff

Introduction

Competency-based education requires students to demonstrate that they have learned the knowledge and skills they were expected to master. Yet in today's classrooms teachers are allowing students to fail to demonstrate competency, record a failing grade in the gradebook, and hope that the student does better in the next unit so s/he earn enough points to pass the class. Would it not be better if students were given additional resources and time to improve the grade and show they have learned the course material? Welcome to unit recovery.

In the traditional classroom there are a handful of students that fail a unit exam. They have not mastered the content and the low points in the gradebook have put them in danger of failing the course. Then why is it that we allow such behavior and continue forward with instruction as normal? Okay, I get it, because we have benchmarks to meet, so that all students are exposed to the guaranteed curriculum, yet such behavior has led our nation to a system of credit recovery, rather than remediating the problem upon exposure.

Matter of fact, some have even proposed a minimum "F" policy, which allows students to not meet the course standards and expectations. Yes, this policy may have reduced the classroom failure rate, it may even reduce the need for credit recovery, but does it help the student master core content? No. Now, isn't that what education is all about? Ensuring that we have an educated society, one with the basic fundamentals of subject areas that we as a nation have deemed necessary. We are failing our students. They are not failing our classes.

So how do we turn this around? Digital content provides teachers an opportunity to reteach material when students missed it the first time around without stopping the entire class or increasing teacher workload. By targeting exactly what the student needs, at the exact moment it has been exposed, when a student failed to demonstrate understanding on a unit exam.

Structure

Most teachers do not want to record a failing score in the gradebook. Most students don't want a failing grade either. Therefore, once the student's misconceptions and lack of understanding are revealed it's time to take action. Use digital content to reteach the standards that a student has shown they lacked understanding and mastery.

It's difficult for the teacher to stop instruction for an entire class when only a few students have failed to demonstrate mastery. However, having a teacher's aide to pull these students aside and reteach the content would be ideal. Well, that is exactly what digital content is - a teacher's aide. When you have courseware, you can put a teacher's aide in every classroom to support student learning.

Digital courseware and classroom instruction typically aligns to the same standards. Have your staff spend time upfront to identify units of study within the courseware aligned to classroom instruction. Generate a menu of digital content that can be used to reteach when students fail a unit of study. Recovery units could be identified at the district level in a large-scale courseware implementation.

Start small, possibly target 'gatekeeper' courses like Algebra, English 9, or Biology. The high failure rate in these courses could be reduced with additional instruction time for reteaching concepts digitally when a student fails a unit exam. Or look at senior year courses like U.S. Government, where unit failures put students at risk of graduation. Immediate unit recovery would be ideal in this situation. Think about structures you can put in place that keep students on track from the start. Be proactive and help students before they need credit recovery.

Independent Study

When students fail to grasp concepts, it may be due to lack of exposure caused by absences or inattention rather than lack of understanding. A failing score on a unit exam unmasks the student's blind spots and is a calling card for help. In most classrooms the failure of the unit exam is too late to remediate. At this point the instruction typically must move on to ensure the breath of the course material is covered. Thus students are left no choice but to accept the low score in the gradebook.

Providing students an option to earn the opportunity to increase a failing exam score is a win-win, both for the student and the teacher. Nobody wants to have failing grades hanging over them. Digital content is an excellent option for reteaching and relearning course material. Student motivation to replace a low score should be high, so providing an independent study option with digital content is attractive.

Once the deficiency is exposed by the low exam score, the teacher can assign digital content to reteach the section material. Teachers should set a timeframe for students to work through the content and also expect the students to maintain progress in the face-to-face classroom setting. One or two weeks would be appropriate. Some vendors have tutorial programs that pinpoint single concepts with adaptive diagnostic capabilities that allow students to target only the areas of misconceptions.

The ability to retest should be earned through the completion of the digital courseware, thus ensuring that students are prepared to obtain a passing score for grade improvement. Use data as evidence from the digital courseware to ensure students completed all learning tasks. I have seen schools that have students take the digital exam in the courseware for improvement. Other schools required students to take a teacher created test. No matter the type of retest, proctoring of the exam should take place.

In one high school, content area departments established common exams. When students failed an exam, the whole department worked together to identify and assign digital content to students in need of grade improvement. Since all teachers were moving at the same pace, testing occurred at the same time. They had set procedures for grade improvement, such that students had one week to retest on a designated day after school. Only students who completed the digital content earned the right to take a retest. Teachers rotated proctoring the retake pencil and paper exam. This school increased class passing rates and reduced the need for full course recovery drastically.

Policies and Procedures

Allowing students to retest is often a difficult sale to classroom teachers. Especially if additional work is being required for "those" students who did not prepare for the classroom exam. You must think through the policies and procedure you will put in place to ensure that students are preparing on initial testing, rather than using the unit recovery as a repeated instructional aid.

Think through what processes and procedure need to be in place. Here's some questions to consider:

- How will digital content units be identified?
- How will digital courseware be assigned to students?
- How long will students have to independently work through the assigned content?
- How will students earn the right to retest?
- Where and how will students retest?
- How will the improvement grade be generated and transcribed into the teacher gradebook?
- Will there be a limit to the number of units a student can recover?
- How will parents be notified of grade improvement options?

Having written policies and procedures in place for students, parents, and staff is highly recommended.

Across the nation more and more schools are looking to unit recovery as the key to reducing full course credit recovery. Highland High School in Antelope Valley School District, California saw a twenty-six percent increase in course passing rates in ninth grade Algebra and Biology after adopting a unit recovery program[1].

Some districts are using their virtual schools to support unit recovery. Within the Atlanta Public Schools at Atlanta Virtual Academy (AVA) middle and high school "students can recover unlimited units, in multiple courses, at the same time...while taking a face-to-face course at the student's home school."[2] Now that's putting the student in the driver seat.

Less than two hours down the road, in Ringgold, Georgia, teachers can register to use the Catoosa Online Academy's digital courseware to assign opportunities for students to relearn content electronically and the teacher determines how the student will retest[3]. Here the classroom teacher has some control on the assignment and retesting.

Unit recovery is an immediate remedy. We all wish we had enough time in the classroom to do this, but circumstances don't allow for after-the-fact recovery, so we have burdened our students with waiting until they fail an entire course before opening the door to recovery options. The time is ripe for a change in mindset.

Mindsets

Our education system is about ensuring that our students have the skills and necessary knowledge to become successful adults. Unit recovery, or grade improvement, is a way to help students understand actions have consequences, yet can overcome unfavorable circumstances. It requires students to demonstrate mastery of content and to take independent measures to successfully overcome hardship. Yet unit recovery will take a mind shift for both students and teachers.

Students

Unit recovery asks students to be held accountable for their learning and required them to master concepts. Too many years have passed with it being okay for students to fail exams and fail courses. Now we are saying that it's no longer acceptable. When faced with an epidemic of credit recovery programs, it's important that we look for remediation in the moment and recover units when students fail to demonstrate knowledge. Unit recovery requires holding students accountable for meeting course standards when gaps are exposed, rather than just moving forward.

For years teachers have led classroom instruction, so students may feel that it's the teacher's responsibility to reteach, not for them to have to relearn in an independent setting. They may feel that having them test after school, outside the traditional school hours may seem unfair. So be prepared for an uphill battle from both student and possibly parents.

Helping students and their parents see that unit recovery is an opportunity and not a burden will be important. Yes, learning does not stop in the traditional classroom, so the student is accountable for maintaining daily classroom attention, as well as independently relearning previous material. This is where adaptive software that can pinpoint student gaps and deliver instruction is helpful.

As more elementary schools use adaptive software, incoming secondary students will be prepared for self-directed digital learning, but until this happens students may challenge the shift to independent, self-regulated, mastery-based learning needed for a successful unit recovery program.

Remind students that they are responsible for their own success and unit recovery is an avenue to timely high school graduation.

Teachers

Teachers may find that unit recovery and grade improvement can be a large burden for just a handful of students. Yes, it is easier to just move forward and "hope" that students earn enough points to pass the course over the eighteen-week semester, however "hope" is not a strategy. Unit recovery is not only a strategy, but one that has proven to be successful.[1]

The initial setup and alignment of digital content to classroom instruction will be time consuming, but will pay off in dividends. When the alignment is worked on and shared across the school or district then all can benefit. Farming out the unit recovery program to a district virtual school is an option as well.

Helping teachers understand that they have <u>not</u> lost control of their classroom instruction and gradebook will be important. We do not want to feed into the myth that digital content can replace teachers. It is teacher's caring heart and burning desire for their students to do more and be more that make the unit recovery program such a success. Teachers don't want to record failing unit exam scores in their gradebooks. They want to give students an opportunity to master content. We just need to provide a venue to do so.

Ask teachers to help set policies and procedures in place for your school's unit recovery program. Build ownership. Keep data on recovery rates. Allow teachers to see the power and strength of changing their mindset.

KEY POINTS

1. Create opportunities for students to recover units, retake unit exams, in a timely fashion.
2. Use digital content as a teacher aide to reteach concepts digitally.
3. Set the tone with changing mindsets with teacher, student, and parents.
4. Select courses that have high need for unit recovery.
5. Put written policies and procedures in place.
6. Track the data on class passing rates.
7. Scale the program to other courses when ready.

Notes

1. *Case Study: Building the Path to Success with a Focus on Unit Recovery - Highland High School, Antelope Valley School District, CA.* Website. Retrieved March 7, 2017 from: https://www.apexlearning.com/resources/case-studies/building-path-success-focus-unit-recovery
2. Atlanta Virtual Academy Unit Recovery. Website. Retrieved March 7, 2017 from: http://www.atlanta.k12.ga.us/domain/10115
3. Catoosa County Public Schools, Unit Recovery for Traditional High School. Website. Retrieved March 7, 2017 from: http://catoosaonline.ga.cch.schoolinsites.com/?PageName=bc&n=212991

CHAPTER 11
BLENDED CLASSROOMS OR ACADEMY

Problem / Opportunity

Students enjoy using technology. Many students have already been exposed to digital software products in elementary school and may be looking to continue a digital learning experience at the secondary level.

Teachers desire to use digital content to blend the classroom learning experience.

Administration wants to ensure that students are receiving a full semester of curriculum aligned to district benchmarks and standards.

Schools seek to embrace blended learning in a small pilot, before rolling out full school.

Solution

Use digital content to blend the classroom with online curriculum and face-to-face instruction. Courseware aligned to content standards can be utilized to lay the foundational skills and knowledge, allowing the teacher the ability to enhance and expand upon digital content while focusing on "power standards." The data provided within the reporting systems of digital courseware informs teachers helping them to catch gaps in knowledge and intervene in large and small groups as needed. Data also can identify when students need to be challenged and pushed to deeper levels of knowledge and/or applications (e.g. project learning).

Design

Schools have an opportunity to utilize digital courseware to blend the student learning experience with online content and teacher-led instruction. Courseware can be used by individual teachers, select subject areas, or by administration to create a school-within-a-school blended learning experience.

Considerations
- Digital Content
- Software Training
- Professional Development: Blended Mindset and Pedagogy
- Balance in the CIA of Blended Learning

Introduction

Teachers have been blending the classroom experience with textbooks and teacher-led instruction for years. Textbooks come with numerous resources that allow teachers to establish lesson plans, create assignments, ask probing questions, and assess student mastery. Digital courseware not only does all this, it also delivers the lesson usually with video and engaging interactives as well. However, digital curriculum does not eliminate the need for a teacher. It just changes the teacher role. Digital courseware is like having a teacher's aide in the classroom, extending the teacher's ability to reach every student at their exact progress level. The classroom teacher no longer has to teach to the middle. Digital courseware can deliver instruction, providing time for the teacher to help individual students reach mastery, challenge others, or conduct whole group seminars. With courseware delivering baseline, level one and two depth of knowledge (DoK 1-2), the instructor can push students to deeper levels of thinking and understanding of the course material by taking students to DoK level three (DoK3).

Digital courseware provides an opportunity that no textbook can do. It can provide instruction in an engaging interactive environment. Most courseware incorporates text, video, and interactive elements that allow students to engage in the lesson and develop understanding of concepts without the need for the teacher to plan "stand and deliver" instruction. The role of the instructor changes to the complement of the digital content, seeking data to determine when and how to best help students reach their fullest potential.

Structure

Using the CIA of blended learning model of *digital* <u>c</u>urriculum, *guided* <u>i</u>nstruction, and *authentic* <u>a</u>ssessment, the classroom becomes one filled with multiple venues to learn and demonstrate understanding. The digital curriculum provided by the courseware becomes the baseline instruction for all students. The teacher provided guided instruction targets individual students needs for intervention and to extend learning. Assessment, beyond the structured assessments within the courseware, and the informal observations of teacher interaction should be pushed to an authentic level when requiring students to apply the knowledge in real world or project learning authentic applications.

Blended learning environments in the secondary classroom using digital courseware should be one that is balanced with teacher-led instruction and online learning components. Finding the "just right" balance between the two can be difficult to locate. The relationship between teacher and technology begins with a teacher that feels comfortable with "stepping off the stage." The mind shift required to changing the teacher's role, is moved from not being one who delivers content but to that of ancillary support. This is often difficult in secondary classrooms, with teachers who took years to master their specific content areas and did so because they thoroughly enjoy the subject matter. Turning over the stage and releasing student attention to technology can be a very troublesome shift for some. But if they can think of the digital courseware as an instructional aide, delivering basic skills and knowledge, and they - themselves as the expert that lead students to genuine authentic learning experiences, imagine the possibilities.

For example, when using a rotation model, a blended teacher can balance digital learning with teacher-led guided instruction. The digital courseware will expose students to the foundational skills and knowledge. Then the teacher can build upon these with hands-on demonstrations and student discussions or investigations. At the secondary level, the station rotation might be best served, by day rather than fixed minutes in a period.

In a simple station rotation, students are broken into two small learning groups. On any given day, half the students work on digital courseware, while the other half is engaged with their teacher. By allowing the courseware to conduct the direct instruction, the teacher can create investigative interactive lessons. And less of them, because half the students get the lesson one day and the next day another group of students get the very same lesson. In blended learning environments, teachers should still maintain the components of an effective lesson. See the sample station rotation model below.

Station Rotation

Introduction (whole group): may include a lesson hook, vocabulary introduction, review of previously taught material or brief introduction to new concepts.	
Odd / Even Days* One-half of the students flip between digital courseware and teacher-led instruction. *A third station could include peer work (e.g. authentic assessment)	
Group A - with teacher Group B - digitally learning	Group B - with teacher Group A - digitally learning
Homework Assignment: may include reminder of minimum completion of digital learning to maintain calendar pacing, activity assigned within teacher-led instruction, or authentic assessment extension. **Closure** (whole group): Reinforce concepts. Consider having students submit a ticket out the door with a brief summary of the day's work to hold them accountable for own learning goal.	

Not only can the courseware lead the delivery of knowledge it also conducts knowledge checks and administers unit exams, providing teachers with data that can drive lesson planning and freeing up time spent on grading. This will provide teachers with time to stretch students into true authentic assessments, such as project learning, that too often in the traditional 'sage of the stage' lecture setting, teachers had little time to do with their students.

Some staff may find that they want to conduct whole group instruction more often and a lab rotation is ideal for alternating days between large group settings. Having devices in the classroom, means students don't even have to leave the classroom in a lab rotation. Again, the teacher will still maintain the components of an effective lesson daily and utilize data from the digital courseware to drive the instruction. See the sample lab rotation model below.

Lab Rotation

Introduction (whole group): may include a lesson hook, vocabulary introduction, review of previously taught material or brief introduction to new concepts.	
Select Days All students are either on digital courseware or teacher is leading instruction.	
Teacher-led instruction	Digital Learning
Homework Assignment: may include reminder of minimum completion of digital learning to maintain calendar pacing, activity assigned within teacher-led instruction, or authentic assessment extension. **Closure** (whole group): Reinforce concepts. Consider having students submit a ticket out the door with a brief summary of the day's work to hold them accountable for own learning goal.	

Blended learning may look different in each teacher's classroom, depending on the balance established within the CIA model. Some teachers may pick and choose which courseware units they want to utilize with students and units of instruction they may want to lead. This is an easy, early step into blending the classroom. By picking and choosing units within the courseware, teachers can gradually release students into the digital curriculum and still maintain the ability to step away from digital content back into a more familiar traditional setting. This also helps students to slowly become familiar with the skills needed to be successful in the digital classroom in small steps, as the teacher becomes more comfortable with digital curriculum and their use of data within the system to guide instruction. Along the way students' exposure to digital content increases. This type of 'slow roll' into blending the classroom with digital content is often easier for both teachers and students as they gain confidence in their roles in the blended classroom CIA model.

One of my least favorite classroom model is the flipped classroom. I say this only because I've seen it used as a substitution for homework, rather than using the data from the courseware to drive instruction. Far too many schools have been in one-to-one environments for years and have never moved past substitution in the SAMR[1] model (substitution, augmentation, modification and redefinition). True blended learning with a good balance of the CIA redefines the classroom. So it becomes important that when creating a blended classroom, to find the symbiotic relationship of the *digital* curriculum, *guided* instruction, and *authentic* assessment.

Establishing a balance in the blended classroom is important. Knowing where and how digital content and guided instruction complement each other is key. Some teachers may elect to allow the courseware full reins to deliver the full course, where they use the data to pull small or large groups, and determine when to challenge and when to remediate. It's important in this situation that the teacher is more than a coach or mentor, but actually instructing content. Teachers should be conducting instruction, possibly filling gaps that the digital content was weak and providing instruction in areas that are difficult to understand and that students typically struggle with comprehending. A flexible learning environment, that allows for one-on-one, small group, and entire class instruction should be adopted in these environments. We would hate for students to feel isolated sitting behind a computer each and every day when a high qualified teacher is in the classroom. Their teaching talents should be utilized and guided by the data from the courseware.

No matter the classroom model, digital courseware is a time saver, and that time should be used to create engaging opportunities for students to demonstrate their knowledge and understanding of the course materials. Authentic assessments should be added to the blended classroom, allowing students to engage with the course content in ways that may not have been available in the traditional classroom, due to lack of time. Teachers should be looking for ways for students to actively engage in the four Cs: Critical thinking, Collaboration, Communication, and Creativity. With technology in the hands of students, they have the tools to stretch their thinking and demonstrate mastery of concepts in artistic ways. Teachers should look for the natural breaks in content to conduct group projects and other authentic assessment opportunities.

Blended Classrooms

Digital courseware can be used to extend the learning in any classroom. With a full catalog of courses, schools and teachers have an opportunity to look at ways to remove the traditional textbook for a digital delivery. Not that courseware is an equal replacement, but one that can be more engaging, more interactive, and more informative. The data alone that teachers have access to when utilizing digital curriculum is individualized for each student. The ability to have students move through and master content at a pace that is comfortable for each student rather than 'mass' movement of the entire class at the pace of the teacher alone is a win. Absent students in the digital world, have no excuse for not learning, or mastering content. Teachers can target instruction to individuals, small groups, or the entire class as needed.

As noted above, the classroom teacher may elect to move slowly into using courseware to blend the classroom, others may jump in full steam. For example, in Clark County sex education is required in the Health course at the high school level, yet some teachers are uncomfortable with the topic. With so many guidelines and regulations that govern the content it can be tricky to teach. Rather than risk tangent conversations and topics that can become uneasy or anxious in a large group setting, some teachers elect to use the digital courseware to deliver these units of instruction. Others have adopted to use the full Health courseware in their classrooms, opening opportunities to drive instruction from the teacher's point with seminars and group projects pushing student to demonstrate mastery with authentic assessments.

Sometimes a blended classroom falls upon a teacher and students, to ensure that students are exposed to the full and guaranteed curriculum. Building administration may find that one teacher is having difficulty keeping pace with their peers and that their students are not making the gains of others in their department when common assessment data is analyzed. The teacher in question could be a substitute or a regular staff member, but none the less is having difficulty meeting the standards and benchmarks of the semester course. This situation is a perfect time to add digital courseware to the equation. Using the courseware would ensure that students are exposed to the full semester curriculum.

At a middle school, the administration was concerned with a sixth-grade math teacher whose data was well below the department average. Students exiting the teachers course at the end of the year were also struggling in seventh grade math as they had gaps in their learning from lack of exposure to concepts that should have been covered in grade six. Digital courseware was a solution they turned to help both the teacher and the students. Using the calendar feature in the courseware, students were ensured to hit every concept within the semester course by the end of the eighteen weeks. Students were excited to have a new modality of learning. The teacher was a bit skeptic of their role in this type of classroom.

Teacher preparation was key to the success of the new sixth grade math class. It's important to ensure that the teacher was <u>not</u> being replaced by the courseware, but the courseware was brought in to support the learning environment for both the teacher and students. The new role of the teacher was more data driven, rather than lesson planning. It was geared toward student intervention and support. Calling for one-on-one tutoring, small group intervention, and whole class instruction on power standards in preparing students for success on common assessments. I must tell you it was not easy that first semester, but student achievement did increase. Student exposure to a full semester of content helped them as they progressed into grade seven. The teacher, with the help of guided blended learning professional growth opportunities and coaching, slowly began to see the value in digital courseware and understand their place in the blended classroom.

Digital courseware can ensure that students are being exposed to the expected curriculum. At an alternative school for exceptional students, the administration was concerned that the staff was spending too much time in remediation, leaving students little opportunity to access grade level content. By utilizing digital courseware students had access to grade level content, while the staff focused on support systems to help student understanding by scaffolding instruction in areas of needs as identified by students individualized educational plans (IEP) as well as from data in the courseware. As staff began using the CIA model they could maximize their one-on-one time with individual students.

Understanding the balance of the CIA of blended is very important when adopting a blended learning model. Being able to move among the seven regions of the three overlapping circles in any given day helped the teacher to see that blending the classroom is not about the digital courseware, but more about the foundations of all classrooms: <u>c</u>urriculum, <u>i</u>nstruction, and <u>a</u>ssessment. Go back to the CIA of

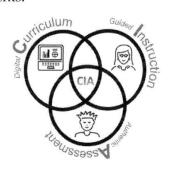

blended learning chapter to review models for the station rotation, lab rotation, flipped classroom, and flex designs for possible deployment options.

Blending a Subject Area

It may not be one teacher that is having trouble ensuring students are keeping pace in the eighteen-week semester, or mastering subject area content. It might be an entire subject area that would benefit from having a digital aide in the classroom, freeing up the teacher time to hone in on standards that are crucial to the subject area.

For example, Algebra as we all know can be a gatekeeper course in high school. Students come in at various levels of mathematical prowess that a traditional teacher led page turning textbook approach leaves many students behind and failing the course. However, with digital courseware all students can be exposed to the same content at a pace not left up to the teacher per se but allows the student to take additional time to comprehend concepts that are new and challenging, while other may have previously seen the material and can move along at a pace that does not bore them, nor impede others.

Using the CIA of blended learning, teachers can allow the digital courseware to present the semester-based curriculum and use the data from the system to support student needs for intervention, as well as engage students with higher order thinking. Small group or individual projects that allow for student voice and choice can bring together worthwhile, significant and meaningful application of the instructional concepts. Authentic assessments tasks should be open to all students and build upon the strengths of individual students, stretching their thinking in the subject matter and demonstrating understanding of its application in the real world.

Let's look at an authentic assessment in an algebra class. In this video from Edutopia and New York's School of the Future, a middle school algebra teacher demonstrates how he challenges his students to solve real-world authentic tasks.
- Video (3:57) - See QR code or Internet Web address:
  https://www.youtube.com/embed/HfwGqH9w-64

Teachers must allow the seven regions of CIA's three overlapping circles to guide, conduct, and create various learning opportunities for students. Ideally, teachers should always be striving for a balanced approach to learning while striving for the 'sweet spot' where all three CIA elements intersect.

After attending a blended personalized learning conference, an administrator went back to his school and sat down with all of his English 9 teachers. Far too many ninth-grade students were exiting English without earning credit and he knew that something had to be done to create a more student-centered approach to the subject. Using the English digital courseware as the foundation of the blended classroom and the expertise of his teaching staff to create relevance and rigor to a subject that is both difficult and tedious for many students the school turned freshman English into a grand new adventure.

Teacher buy-in was not easy at first. Like any change, becoming comfortable with digital courseware and seeing where and how student engagement could be pulled into the baseline curriculum with student voice and choice of reading selections and authentic assessment tasks took time. In the end more students were passing and enjoying the change to their traditional English classroom.

School-within-a-School

Blended learning as we have seen across the country is taking hold in many classrooms and schools. Sometimes it's difficult to figure out where to start. It all starts with having digital content. Providing teachers with high quality, standards aligned semester-based courseware is an easy first step. Having a full catalog of courseware opens the door to establishing blended classrooms and it can also lead to a full-blown digital learning program.

However, I caution you to think through this carefully and establish groundwork for blended learning success by starting small. Try using a school-within-a-school as a proving ground for others to watch, take in and consider, before asking your entire staff to adopt blended learning in every classroom.

Most schools have technology-driven early adopters who have taken off with curating open educational resources (OER) or possibly created videos of themselves to flip their classroom instruction. I will tell you that these staff member typically are <u>not</u> ready to give up their freedoms for digital courseware. Nor may they be peers, that others on your staff think they could replicate. It becomes important, when considering a proving ground for blended learning, you work with staff that are willing to make changes, willing to take risks, willing to learn from failure and re-iterate as needed. When teachers have this type of willingness, providing them with digital courseware is a step in helping them incorporate the CIA of blended learning.

A school-within-a-school approach allows various subject areas as proving grounds for the blended classroom, created by using digital courseware. Utilizing one math, science, English, and social studies teacher demonstrates that blended learning with digital courseware is not limited in scope. Having teacher's full schedule in the blended school-within-a-school allows the teachers to fine tune their practice and focus on one learning environment, rather than jumping from the traditional classroom to blended throughout their work day. It also helps students to focus as well, knowing that each class will have the same instructional practices - *digital* curriculum, *guided* instruction, and *authentic* assessment.

At one middle school the principal was interested in turning the school into a blended learning school, but knew that he would need a proving ground for this new way of classroom instruction to get buy in from his staff. Having access to digital courseware helped convince a handful of his staff that this was the right direction for student learning.

Over the course of one year we worked with his staff on what a blended learning classroom could look like, how the technology components work (both hardware and software), and visited several schools that had incorporated blended learning into their classrooms. The five staff members, one in each core areas, plus a special education teacher had no background in blended learning, yet they were open to students accessing digital curriculum with the instructional supports of their classroom teacher, and since they were a small school-within-a school the ability to create cross curricular authentic assessments peaked their interests. They had all the making of a high quality CIA model of blended learning.

The school advertised the new blended learning academy to incoming sixth grade students as an opportunity to become part of an innovative technology-driven learning experience. Parents were assured that students would not be sitting in cubbies stuck behind a computer screen all day, but would be engaging in a balanced and blended approach of digital and teacher-led instruction, with caring high quality teachers in each of the core subject areas in a new school-within-a-school design that allowed students to step outside the academy for electives, including highly sought-after band and choir. Over two-hundred students applied for the blended academy and became the proving ground for others.

Students and teachers alike, learned how to balance digital courseware and teacher-led instruction. Data gathered from the digital systems and from teacher-led instruction, from one-on-one tutoring, small group instruction, or whole class teaching, helped fine tune the design. Others from on the school staff watched carefully as they saw firsthand how blended learning was changing the look and feel on the classroom. Assessment data on school-wide interim and benchmark assessments showed that blended learning not only worked, but students were outpacing their peers in the traditional classrooms. This made rolling out blended learning into more classrooms the following year a much easier sell for the school administrator.

Mindsets

Creating a blended classroom and finding the fine balance between *digital* curriculum and *guided* instruction is not an easy task. When done well, teachers will find that the digital delivery of content allows them to challenge students with deeper thought and applications of the content. By allowing the digital content to carry much of the instructional burden (especial in lower level basic skill and knowledge), teachers will now have time to incorporate *authentic* assessments. However, the release of control to digital content is difficult for teachers and possibly some students.

Mindset also falls upon the administration. Blended learning is a challenging task. It may sound easy to just add a few digital assets to the classroom environment. There is a fine line between educational technology and blended learning. Blended learning builds from digital curriculum and using the data from its delivery to drive instruction. It allows students an individualized learning space, free from the pace of the entire class's speed set by teacher's daily lesson delivery. Don't get me wrong here. Blended learning should have benchmarks and pacing, but how quickly a student gets to the deadlines or if they need additional tutoring to get there is foundational to blended learning. Teachers have a vital role in the blended classroom and changing the role is a huge mindset shift. It's not as easy as telling your staff, "We are moving to blended learning." Administration must ask themselves, "What does my staff need to create a quality balanced CIA of blended learning environment?"

By providing high quality digital content to staff, they have a starting point, a base to build upon. Asking teachers to build or curate digital assets takes time away from the classroom design and much less time to grow a blended mindset through professional development workshops, webinars, and peer collaboration.

Let the technology do what it is best at – delivery of basic skills and acquisition curriculum. Allow the teacher to do what they are best at - guidance, coaching, and extending student learning. When there is a balance between these two elements, teachers have time to create true authentic assessment within the four Cs: collaboration, communication, creativity and critical thinking. Would you rather have teachers spend time looking and searching the Web for open educational resources, and apps, or building quality thought provoking students learning projects, seminars, and real-world applications?

Teachers need to understand the three elements of the CIA model for blended learning and how to design and deploy a learning environment that is balanced among all three. The digital content cannot lead instruction. The teacher must do this. Students cannot engage in authentic assessments without knowledge from both the digital curriculum and the teacher. The teacher still controls instruction, but finding the balance of all three CIA elements puts the students in the driver's seat of their own learning.

This is where you will find some students will need support. In a blended classroom, students must develop skills that may have never been asked of them before: self-discipline, self-motivation, peer collaboration and communication, thinking beyond skill and knowledge acquisition. Yet, these are the competencies that are needed in college, career, and citizenship.

Mindset changes will be needed for administration, teachers, and students when creating high quality blended learning environments that goes well beyond educational technology. Digital courseware is an excellent place to start.

KEY POINTS

1. Use digital content as a teacher aide to deliver instruction.
2. Provide digital content, rather than have teacher build or curate it.
3. Allow time for teacher to fine tune the CIA of blended learning.
4. Set the tone with changing mindsets.
5. Track the data on class passing rates.
6. Start small and scale up the program when ready.
7. Use the CIA of blended learning to create a balanced approach.
8. Design a classroom instructional model that blends digital and teacher-led instruction.

Notes

1. Puentedura, R.R., Blog. Retrieved on August 10, 2017 from: http://www.hippasus.com/rrpweblog/

CHAPTER 12
GRADUATION FLEX ACADEMY

Problem / Opportunity

Have numerous upperclassmen in need of a heavy dose of credit recovery.

Design

Using digital content, in a prescriptive or mastery mode, allows the ability for students to recover credits in an accelerated mode. By providing students a flexible setting, with a handful of core teachers supporting and guiding instruction credits can be earned more rapidly than the traditional semester-based calendar. The same setting can be used to earn original credits.

Design

Using a large open area create a flexible school-within-a-school design. Students can receive separate educational services within their home school location, separate from the day-to-day bell schedule. Assign a full day assignment of teachers in core (e.g. math, science, English, and social studies), which may include an additional staff member from special education or electives to the program. The Flex Academy provides students with uninterrupted and coordinated services to ensure credit recovery and maintain grade level original credit course load.

Considerations:
- Digital Content with a Large Catalog
- Target Population and Communication Plan
- Staff Selection
- Software Training
- Professional Development: Blended Mindset and Pedagogy
- Practices and Procedures for Students and Staff
- Student Information System (SIS) enrollment and Grading practices
- Schedule of Daily Events within the Program

Introduction

When students fall so far behind in credits and the traditional semester-base calendar and daily bell schedule can no longer support their ability to sustain and recover lost credits alternative schooling options are needed. However, these students do not want to leave their neighborhood school. They want to graduate with their friends. They have already established relationships with peers and adult staff at your building. Rather than ship them into alternative educational setting, where many will just drop out of due to travel or despair, why not create an alternative setting for them right there at your building.

Establishing the ability to retain under credit students and helping them along the path towards a possible graduation with their cohort group is both rewarding for students and the school. These potential dropout students can become actual on time graduates, or in some cases summer graduates or 5th year seniors, but none the less, graduates of your school. Instill pride in your students, your staff, and your school community with thinking outside the box.

Under credit students not only need to recover credits, but also must maintain the grade level course load to sustain their path towards graduation. The semester-base calendar and daily bell schedule cannot meet their needs. A new setting is needed to help them graduate.

School-within-a-School

Establishing a school-within-a school learning environment for this fragile student population, not only allows staff to focus on their particular needs, but also shows that they are an important part of your school and that their graduation matters. That's why I like the name "Graduation Academy" rather than less positive names such as "Last Chance" or "Credit Recovery" academies. One school used the name "TLC: Teaching and Learning Center." The name of the program matters!

With so many different student needs, in addition to senior required courses, a flex academy is an ideal selection. To pull this off, find a large location that is conducive to learning. We have seen libraries repurposed for graduation academies in Clark County. Books were moved to other locations in the school, allowing the graduation academy to inhabit the space, that also included small offices and workspaces off the large room, that were perfect for pull out and small group tutor sessions. See the example layout below.

Library Transition to School-with-a-School Graduation Academy

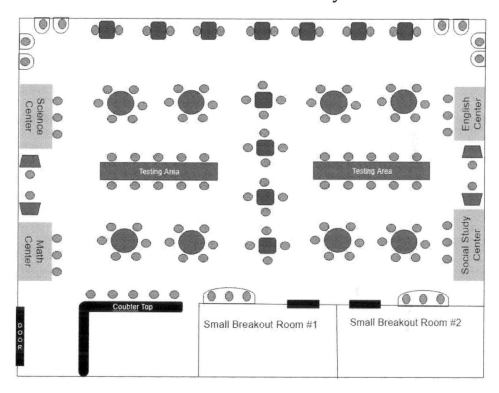

When dealing with students who are credit deficient, creating a learning environment for success will be begin with the selection of staff that have bought into their success. Students will need teachers in all four core areas (e.g. math, science, social studies, and English). Often special needs students will fall into this population, so consider adding a special education teacher to the academy staff as well. If your staffing allows, assigning a counselor and an administrator to the graduation academy will create a team designed for success.

The word "flex" should not be mistaken for unstructured. The layout of the flex academy should be considered carefully. The environment should be conducive to individual learning, group settings, and proctored exams. In addition, a quiet zone should be established. Each content area teacher should have an assigned space that they can call home base with a bulletin board to post successes and announcements.

The space should be more informal. No desks to sit behind. The expectation is teachers are moving about the room, working with students. They should be circulating among groups of students working at round tables or with individuals. Teachers must be tracking student progress within the courseware. Students also need some freedoms, but set work expectations that focuses the learning. Flexibility, within parameters, is essential.

Staff

Selection of staff for innovative programs is always instrumental. Graduation Academy teachers will be expected to take themselves off the stage and become guides and coaches of the digital learning environment. This is a complete mindset shift from the traditional classroom. Looking at students as individuals, rather than an entire class moving together at the same pace. Students will be at various places at any given time. Teachers will also have to manage multiple courses (e.g. English 9-12) in multiple terms (e.g. semester one and two).

Without proper professional development, most teachers are ill prepared to strike the fine balance needed for a digital learning environment where courseware delivers the vast majority of content instruction. Academy teachers must know how to use the digital platform to coach/guide the student, analyze data dashboards to determine when to step in for student support and intervention. I cannot express enough about professional development on the pedagogy of digital instructional practices. Also, teachers need training in the courseware to understand the technology and data behind the digital classroom, such as setting individual calendars of due dates for assignments to keep students on a path to success.

Teachers must have a good grasp the courseware design and how to use it. They will be responsible for students within their content area, which may cover many classes, and multiple semesters when dealing with recovery students. Teachers will need to be very familiar with the digital content, just as they would be if they were the one delivering it. The digital content should be reviewed to ensure there are no holes or gaps from district and/or state standards. It will be the teacher's burden to bear when it comes to required proficiency testing in their respective content areas, so they will have to fill any gaps or misunderstanding students may encounter. This can only be done by daily review of the data and knowing the digital content from start to finish.

If teachers are well versed in their digital courses, they can help prepare students for prescriptive, or pre-testing options. When students are attempting to recover credits, much time may have passed since they last engaged with the course material. To help support students, teachers can create topic review study guides for students to use prior to taking any pre-testing. This will help sweep away old cobwebs that may have formed on the student's long-term memory and support their best efforts in attempting unit pre-tests. This kind and caring gesture can also build student-teacher rapport, demonstrating that teachers truly care about student success.

Beyond their respective course assignments, consider having each teacher mentor a group of students as an advisory. This will give each student a personal coach vested in their success and path towards graduation. Advisory teachers should meet weekly with students on their team to set individual goals. Having advisory teams within the academy also generates an opportunity for friendly team competitions, such as credits earned or best attendance for the week. Celebrating successes within teams can be as simple as posting certificates for each completed course. Consider different colored certificates posted on the wall with student name and course title for each team. Not only does this create a friendly competition, but also allows students to identify other successful students that they can reach out to for help by noting who has completed the same course they may be struggling with.

Student selection will vary with their needs. May I suggest starting with student selection who are five (5) or more credits behind their graduation year cohort. Most students will be deficient in the core areas, but you find a few that may need a course that is not in the catalog of digital courseware. For example, physical education (PE) is typically a one-half credit course in most courseware, but students may need more several semester replacement credits.

This is where schools can get creative. Check with your curriculum division to see what alternatives there are to PE. In Clark County, Personal Wellness is a course that students can take as a PE credit. At one Graduation Academy, staff created a fun way to earn Personal Wellness credits, within the district's course goals and expectation in an offline setting, through direct instruction, food and fitness journals and hands-on explorations in advisory settings.

Scheduling

Having an individualized academic educational plan is important for student awareness and establishing course completion goals. Past experience, and lots of Clark County data, has shown that using a prescriptive or mastery-based mode student should be able to complete recovery and select elective courses in approximately six weeks. Original credit core subject area courses typically take nine weeks. A word of caution about sending students outside the graduation academy to general education face-to-face classrooms to earn the required original credit courses in a traditional eighteen-week calendar. This practice can lead to student failing courses *on purpose* so that they can re-taken them digitally in the academy within a shortened schedule. The academy should be all inclusive, meeting all needs of the full-time enrolled students.

Each student should have an individualized academic educational plan with projected start and end dates of courses. It is important to calendar expectations within the plan to ensure students meet graduation deadlines. With a condensed schedule, student's course load can be reduced to three online courses at any given time. Schedule electives and recovery courses for six weeks. Core original credit courses should be slated within two consecutive nine weeks. The sample schedule shown below includes the Advisory mentoring class which carries over the full term and provides students with an additional elective credit.

Flex Academy Student Schedule

Fall Term	Sem.	Type	Start	End	Weeks	Grade
Advisory	**1**	**Original**	**8/29**	**1/20**	**18**	
U.S. Government	1	Original	8/29	10/27	9	
English 12	1	Original	8/29	10/27	9	
Health	1	Recovery	8/29	10/07	6	
Algebra	2	Recovery	10/10	11/18	6	
U.S. Government	2	Original	10/31	1/20	9	
English 12	2	Original	10/31	1/20	9	
Biology	1	Recovery	11/22	1/20	6	

The daily events within the Graduation Academy should be flexible, running outside the traditional school day bell schedule. Lunch would be an exception. Yet, setting blocks of time for specific content may help students focus on their courses. Consider harder subjects like math, science, and English in the morning with afternoons slated for electives and social studies. Ideally, students should be looking at their data to set weekly goals and calendar their work week.

With their advisory teacher oversight and guidance students should be able to determine which courses they must attend to. Working with their advisor, students should create a weekly schedule with identified lessons and exams to be completed in each course by the end of the week. By setting and managing their own individual goals students learn success habits that can carry them into life beyond high school. With teachers by their side, cheering and supporting their achievements students can break the cycle of failure and begin to see graduation not only as an option but as an attainable target.

Graduation academies should start with credit deficient seniors. However, if space allows the same environment and staff could be used for underclassmen who need to recover credit, or others who want to take advantage of online courseware. For example, the first two hours of the day could be open for other students focused on graduation needs, be it for recovery or initial credit courses. Consider using this time for possible honors and advanced placement opportunities. Having other peers in the academy early hours focused on learning can set the day off within the academy with a tone for academic focus.

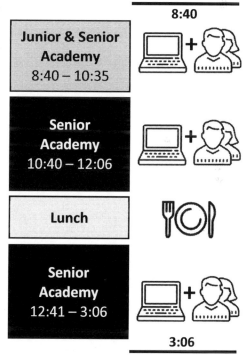

Try to maximize the space and staff to their fullest advantage. The schedule presented here is from a high school graduation academy that opened early hours to others with additional blocks of time just for senior academy students.

Mindsets

In the Graduation Academy the digital courseware drives instruction. The courseware controls most components of instruction from delivery to assessment. The teacher is more of a facilitator, guiding student success with one-on-one tutoring and support. Yet, that does not take their importance out of the equation. Matter of fact, their caring heart and ways are needed to motivate and lead students to success.

Teachers

The academy is much like independent study, with daily access to core teachers. Courseware data becomes vital to teachers. It will alert teachers when to step in and help students when they are not progressing and having difficulty in the content area. Unlike students who take online courses from a distance, academy teachers have immediate access to students. They have the ability to work face-to-face with students as soon as a problem occurs. Yet, they cannot sit back and wait for the students to reach out. They must have their eyes in the courseware data every day, tracking student progress or lack thereof.

Content teachers must be actively seeking students to help. They cannot sit behind a desk and allow the courseware to do all the teaching. Their role will be in a more one-on-one capacity helping students with the basic skills and knowledge presented in the digital classroom. It is a hard shift to step down from the instructional stage, when teachers love their content. It is this passion that should shine through when working with students individually.

Students

The advisory or mentoring group becomes vital to the success of the student-teacher relationships in the Graduation Academy. These coaching sessions are crucial to student and program success. Knowing that a caring adult is watching their every move, cheering them on, and providing tough love when needed, changes the student role. In the past, most of these students slide into their desks silently, unseen and they wanted it that way. In the academy this is no longer the case. Student success in center stage!

At first students may not like the added attention of their teachers and advisor. In the academy, students may have a tough time adjusting to the flexibility and freedom of choice. This is where the advisor must step in and shepherd his/her advisory team with a tool set of skills that will lead students to success, not only in the digital courses, but also into college, career, and citizenship. The goal is that over time, students will come to cherish their relationships with the academy staff.

KEY POINTS

1. Design matters.
2. Staff personnel is key.
3. Digital courseware drives instruction.
4. Teacher guidance and mentoring is vital.
5. Manage student's time.
6. Set expectations and due dates
7. Celebrate successes.
8. Document staff/program guidelines.

CHAPTER 13
SUSPENSION AND HOMEBOUND

Problem / Opportunity

Students removed from the general education environment on a comprehensive campus due to misbehavior need meaningful and equitable education opportunities.

Due to medical reasons, students are temporarily removed from the general education environment on a comprehensive campus and need continued equitable education experiences.

Solution

Using digital content allows high quality instruction to be provided to students who are removed from their general education peers while still being able to provide students with standards-based and benchmarked aligned academic support from a highly qualified teacher at a distance.

Design

Create a school-within-a-school design, where students are able to receive separate educational services without leaving their original school location while providing students with uninterrupted and coordinated educational services. A teacher guide, or coach, in the "time out" program works closely with the general population teachers to identify, deploy, and ensure student progress in digital content aligned with the concepts being taught in the traditional classroom. The highly qualified teacher can monitor and support student learning from a distance. When the student returns to the traditional classroom the s/he will be on pace with their peers.

Homebound students can use digital content to maintain course progress while on temporary leave from the physical school. Highly qualified teachers can monitor and support student learning from a distance, such that when the student returns to school s/he will be on pace with their peers.

<u>Considerations:</u>
- Digital Content Selection
- Staff Selection
- Professional Development: Online Mindset and Pedagogy
- Software Training
- Practices and Procedures for Students and Staff
- Student Information System (SIS) enrollment and Grading Practices
- Schedule of Daily Events within the Program

Introduction

When students must be removed from the general population of the school setting digital content can help provide a meaningful and equitable education opportunity. Courseware at the secondary level is already in a format that allows for lesson delivery and assessment of student knowledge. Using these design elements will benefit the student who must be removed from the traditional classroom for infractions that break school policies, such as weapons, drugs, or other poor judgements that would lead to removal from the traditional setting for weeks (e.g. 3-9 weeks).

In years past when a student was placed in situations like in-house suspension programs, teachers would send textbooks and packets of work for the student to complete while out of the general education classroom setting. This worked well when a student was out for just a day or two, even possibly a week. But when the time frame is lengthened to weeks, where students will miss units of instruction and does not have the ability to be readily assessed, these old practices breakdown.

Courseware is ideal for suspension or behavior programs and students out on temporary medical leave. Using the digital content's course outline, teachers can identify concepts that align to the general classroom instruction. They can assign specific digital content and assessments within the courseware to students while out of the classroom for weeks at a time. Digital courseware also allows the teacher to continue one-on-one instruction with the students from a distance, utilizing the communication platform within the content management system. Ideally, if the students are housed on the same campus, as is the case in many Clark County schools, the administration may request that the teacher take one day a week to visit the behavior program to provide one-on-one face-to-face instruction with the students. I would caution against having classroom visits on a daily basis, as this would lead to the instruction possibly reverting to a traditional direct instruction practice. Let the digital content platform do what it is best at: delivering content. Have the teacher focus in on what they are best at: identify gaps, targeting hard to understand concepts, and remediating where needed.

The key to a successful suspension program when using digital content boils down to the balance between digital content delivery and instructional supports. It is important to prepare teachers for such settings with proper professional development. Their role as a teacher "from a distance" can be difficult for teachers to understand. Too often teachers are under the assumption that the digital courseware will "take care of everything" and they neglect to instruct. Or at the other extreme, they want to do all the instruction and meet daily with students for direct learning experiences. Without proper professional development, most teachers are ill prepared to strike the fine balance needed for a digital learning environment where courseware delivers the vast majority of instruction.

Teachers must know how to use the digital platform to coach/guide students. They must analyze data dashboards to determine when to step in for student support and intervention. I cannot express enough about professional development on the pedagogy of distance instructional practices, but let us not forget the training needed within the courseware to understand the technology behind the digital classroom.

Staff

Teachers must have a good grasp of the courseware design and utilization. It will be upon them to identify and assign content that aligns to the instruction that is taking place in the general education classroom for the students assigned to suspension programs. Most courseware programs allow you to individualize student assignments within the same gradebook. This is ideal for suspension programs, where students are coming and going at various times and need a very personalized learning path for a short period of time. I caution against assigning the entire course to a student which could lead to frustration for both the student and teacher. Imagine if the student was to complete the entire digital course while in a six-week suspension and returned to the general education classroom. With the credit under the student's belt, s/he has no reason to partake in the remain weeks of the general education classroom. This will create a cycle of misbehavior and drive students to *want* to be suspended to earn credits without having to deal with the traditional classroom setting. Look at other ways to allow this to happen in your school. In such situations, upon return the student would be bored. The teacher would have no leverage. Thus, frustrations will lead to classroom disruptions, hurting the learning environment for all students in the classroom.

Having the right personnel is always key to the success of any program. Assigning a full-day digital coach/guide within the suspension classroom will keep consistency and establish a working relationship between students and an adult. Like any good coach, the staff member must relate well to students. This is <u>not</u> the place for a staff member with poor classroom managements skills. Hopefully the number of students assigned to the program at any given time is small, but these are students that can be difficult. A strong demeanor will be required, yet one with a caring heart. We want these students to be successful. They will need tough love. Praise and continued guidance, such as re-focusing the students will be needed daily, hourly, possibly several times in any given hour.

Like the content areas teachers, the suspension program coach will need training on the digital courseware. They'll need to monitoring student progress and success just as much as the digital classroom teacher. This will keep the lines of communication between the teachers and coach focused on student learning.

Setting Policies & Procedures

When everyone knows what is expected when a student is assigned to the suspension program, from the coach in the suspension classroom, the content teachers, and the students, the program can run effectively. Without clear guidelines and schedules the program can get messy rather quickly. It becomes important to document the expectations for each member of the program. It's seems easy to remove a student from the general population, but many questions remain:

- Do you have a location and a full-time staff member in the suspension room?
- What processes must take place within the student information system (SIS)?
- How will attendance be handled?
- What will students do for lunch?
- What procedures are needed for teachers to identify digital content?
- How long before digital content is assigned to the student in the courseware?
- Who will enroll the student and teacher into the courseware?
- What will you do with elective courses that has no replacement digital course?
- How often and/or when will the teacher and students see each other face-to-face?

- How will grades be transferred back into the general education classroom gradebook?
- What advisory behavior modification instruction will be provided to help students refrain from continued infractions?

Put expectations and procedures in place before they are needed. Otherwise you may have a suspension program that sits idle, which may lead to more behavior problems.

Daily Events

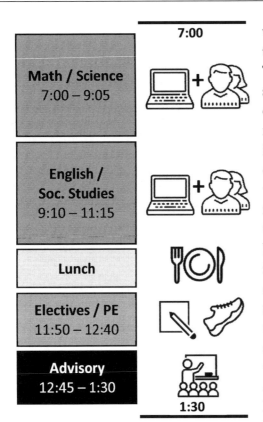

7:00

Math / Science
7:00 – 9:05

English /
Soc. Studies
9:10 – 11:15

Lunch

Electives / PE
11:50 – 12:40

Advisory
12:45 – 1:30

1:30

One big question to ask is, "What will the day look like for the students in the suspension or behavior program?" The traditional fifty-minute bell schedule is not conducive to working on digital content. It would be too much to ask a student to stop working in the courseware for each content area every fifty minutes, especially if lessons within courseware may be designed for multiple days over the week (e.g. a two-hour lesson with assessment). Use blocks of time to allow the student to immerse themselves into a single content area. Alternate days to get the most benefit of time and reduce transitions throughout the day. For example, block math and science together for a two-hour session and alternate days to balance cognitive load. The same can be done with English and social studies. Throw in an advisory program with behavior modification curriculum and lunch to break up the digital strain. Add in the electives or physical activity with hands-on tactile learning exposure in the day as well. Above is an example of what the daily schedule of events looked like at one high school.

At this school. there is a full-time coach/mentor assigned to the suspension program. During the morning students work on their assigned digital content, alternating days between subject areas. One day students focus on math and social studies, the next day science and English.

Each day a different content area teacher (e.g. Mon.=Math, Tues.=English, Wed.=Science, Thurs.= Social Studies) visited the suspension classroom to consult with individual students providing instructional support and tutoring. These same high-qualified core content teachers also instructed the online courses from a distance. The teachers created individualized calendars of lessons, assignment due dates, and graded student work within the digital courseware. It was essential that each student stayed on pace to ensure transition back into the general education program at the conclusion of the suspension term.

After lunch, students worked on elective projects, bookwork, or exercise. At the end of the day a counselor conducts an advisory period driven with behavior modification curriculum.

Having a solid framework for the student's day is essential to establishing a learning environment that is balanced and ripe for success. By providing an advisory program with emphasis on behavior modification one would hope that students develop tools for success once released back to the general population.

A well thought out program design is essential to success. A poorly designed program can lead to disastrous outcomes. No classroom structures can lead to behavior problems. Lack of teacher monitoring and coaching lead to incomplete assignments and students returning to the general population with gaps. Frustrations compound upon each other, leaving administration, staff, students, and parents exasperated.

A high school administrator called me completely defeated, as the digital courseware in their suspension program was ineffective. They were seeking an alternative software. However, during consultation the school shared their design and it became apparent the software was not the problem (it rarely is), but lack of an effective design model was the culprit. There was no single person assigned to the program. Each period a different subject area teacher wandered into the room. In between passing periods, when teachers exchanged places, a hall monitor would watch the students. This went on for six periods of the day, with six different staff members and a hall monitor who also walked students to the cafeteria to pick up their lunches.

Students were assigned content in the digital courseware, but they were not doing it or they were just *clicking through* and asking for assignment resets. Can you imagine, every period a different teacher enters the room, possibly asking the same question that the previous teacher did, "How are you doing?" or "Can I help you?". No progress monitoring was taking place. Students played the game, chatted up the various staff members, and did very little work. When it came time to leave, they were so far behind their classmates it just compounded the matter. I cannot say enough how program design and setting expectations for students and staff must be carefully planned, otherwise you end up with poor results.

Teacher-Student Interactions

A single staff member should be assigned to the suspension program to guide and support daily classroom interactions. This staff member must manage the room and students' behavior, but must also coach or mentor students when they have difficulty in content area courseware. Selecting the staff member best for mentoring student learning is crucial. Relationships between teachers and students can either help or hurt any classroom.

Too often a teacher with poor classroom management is assigned to the suspension program. What makes one believe that if the teacher could not handle a classroom full of students, that a small class of students that have already proven they have management issues will be a better fit for the instructor. In Nevada, given the high qualified staff is instructing the digital classroom from afar, the suspension personnel does not have to be a licensed teacher. Support staff can be tasked with the suspension room. With proper software training and solid job role expectations, even a long-term substitute could be assigned to the suspension program.

If available, having the highly qualified teachers interacting face-to-face with students can help motivate them and hold them accountable to courseware calendared assignments and assessments. If students knew that they had to interact with their instructor face-to-face each week it could help build a desire to complete assignments in a timely manner. It also helps the teachers to establish a schedule of when to review and analyze student data, check for understanding and weekly progress. Having only one day to engage face-to-face with the student, teachers can use the data from the courseware to identify individual gaps in student understanding and seek to address them.

In situations where students and teachers do not meet face-to-face, like in a homebound situation, the tools in the digital courseware become very important for communication purposes. Feedback, via announcements, within discussion posts, and on course assignments are vital to establish a feeling of mutual caring and respect between students and teachers. The timeliness of responses is key, so that the students know they are important. A twenty-four to forty-eight-hour turnaround time should be required of staff. Even if staff is not mandated to the suspension room, this should not stop them from taking the time to do so. Face-to-face interaction, or a phone to homebound students, says so much.

Transition back into the general population will also need procedures. For example, after the suspension term, or return from temporary medical absence, a student's grade from the digital courseware can be averaged and transferred into the teacher gradebook for assignments *"while away"* from the general education classroom. Since the student was working on digital content aligned and benchmarked to classroom instruction, the goal is for him/her to make a successful transition with transfer grades that reflect their understanding of these very same concepts.

Mindsets

In these short-term programs, the digital content will take center stage for instructional purposes. There will be little teacher-led instruction. Coaching and facilitation will be essential to the success of students returning to the general population with the skills and knowledge that they missed while away.

Students

Students who are isolated from friends, peers, and teachers can become frustrated with the whole school experience. Having to learn in a digital classroom will most likely be a new experience for students in these situations. Student orientation to the software will be important so that students know how to navigate the digital classroom, from turning in assignments to communicating with their teachers from a distance. Online learning doesn't have to be difficult, but students will need a mindset shift when it comes to self-discipline and self-motivation.

Maintaining an academic focus in the suspension classroom will help ensure that students understand that they must attend to their studies. Face-to-face visits from content teachers is helpful. If teachers only work with students from a distance, the amount of communication between students and teachers may determine student reaction to learning online. In the end, it is the staff member in the room that can make all the difference.

Staff

The staff member assigned to the suspension room has a big task in front of them, keeping students motivated to learn digitally and create a caring relationship to decrease student misbehavior. They too need to understand the digital courseware so that they can help students. They will also need an open line of communication with content area teachers. Like the students, at times they will need to be a learner, so they can tutor students.

Coaching is not always easy. You need to be both motivating and grounded in reality (sometimes called tough love). When working with students. the mentor in the room will need a positive demeanor and be able to help students see the good, the better, and the possible. It will be important to help students learn from their mistakes, be it in learning content as well as behavior that got them in suspension in the first place.

Depending on the design, a content teacher's mindset may vary. In most cases it will be one of teacher *"from afar."* This is not an easy road to travel. Content teachers must attend to students needs in a timely fashion and try to build quality relationships with students that might only be with them a brief time. They will need training not only in the software's communication tools, but also professional development to help understanding how to relate with students from a distance.

Digital courseware can help suspension and homebound programs create a learning environment that is held to high standards and expectations. One that keeps the students on track and prepared to return to the general population. It allows teachers to maintain ownership of the student grades and progress *"while away."* It is a fabulous way to get the most out of courseware in a non-traditional setting.

KEY POINTS

1. Have entry and exit procedures.
2. Determine program guidelines for:
   - selecting content,
   - instructional support, and
   - transition back.
3. Manage student's time.
4. Set expectations and due dates.
5. Document staff and student expectation, including communication.

CHAPTER 14
SUMMER PROGRAMS

Problem / Opportunity

Students have just finished the school year, but have failed courses.

Students want to create space in next year's schedule for their desired courses (e.g. band).

Students seeking to take Advanced Placement courses in the fall are hungry and want to use the summer months to start preparing for success.

Incoming students transitioning to your building lack the skills to be successful and need a bridge program to fill the gaps.

Solutions

Using digital content schools can build summer sessions for recovery, advancement, early preparation, or bridge programs. Since courseware provider contracts are typically year-round digital learning environments could be offered in the summer months.

Design

Create summer programs that takes advantage of digital courseware to help students; 1) immediately recover lost credits, 2) take rudimentary courses like Health or PE to open students schedules for the coming school year, 3) get a head start on Advance Placement courses or 4) build a summer bridge program for students transitioning to your building with identified weaknesses. Program design including timeframe, hours, and protocols will vary depending on the audience.

Considerations
- Student Audience
- Digital Content Catalog
- Teacher Selection
- Professional Development
- Software Training
- Practices and Procedures
- Schedule of Daily Events

Introduction

The lazy days of summer don't have to be so lazy when digital courseware is available. School with year-round digital content contracts don't have to throw away money on months that they typically do not service students. Better yet, why not consider a summer program that can both help students and utilize courseware that is already paid for during the hot days of summer.

Summer programs can vary in length, audience, and even months to serve students. Program design should begin with identifying the purpose for summer usage. Utilizing staff that may have already been using the courseware during the school year, can reduce the need for professional development and software training. This could also be a good time to bring new staff up to speed on blended learning techniques with digital content. To cover the expenses of staff, check into district policies about charging students for summer programs. In Clark County, per union contract, utilization of teachers in the summer is much cheaper than the regular contracted rate of pay. Most high schools in Clark County run at least one summer program utilizing digital content, typically focused on credit recovery programs and summer graduation.

Credit Recovery

It's the end of the school year and an immediate need just fell into your lap. Use digital courseware to service students who finished the school year with failing grades. A summer credit recovery program is ideal for getting students back on track. Students and their parents look forward to a timely graduation and would be willing to pay a small fee to support staying on pace to graduate with their peers.

A targeted approach that focuses on a few select subject areas will reduce efforts and cost. Typically, math and English tend to be the areas in greatest need of recovery. Offer a small catalog of math and English courses only. This will require only two highly qualified teachers, one in each subject. The catalog can spread the full spectrum in the content areas and over both terms, making the offerings very diverse.

Schedule

Summer months allow the freedom of more time to complete courses, but given a choice students would not schedule time for school. Take it upon yourself to schedule time for students by having them come to school to work on their courseware. Morning hours tend to work best. Forget about Friday. Both staff and students would rather have a three-day weekend. A possible schedule could might be Monday through Thursday from 8:30 a.m. to 11:30 a.m. each morning. With two staff members, you could even reduce their workload by having them alternate days in which they come to work. For example, the math teacher could come in Mondays and Wednesdays, while the English teacher is onsite Tuesdays and Thursdays. This allows teachers opportunities to work with students in their subject area and support student learning through the courseware. To maintain integrity of the program, ensure all exams are proctored.

Timeframe

Using prescriptive, or unit pre-testing options students should be able to finish recovery courses faster than a 60-hour Carnegie unit. With the courses so freshly failed, hopefully students can recall much of the content. Length of the program may vary from two to six weeks. Three weeks at three hours a day, over four days a week should be plenty of time to complete at least one if not more recovery half-credits. To maintain focus, have students take one course at a time. When students complete one course let them roll into a second course if needed. Otherwise let them go home for the summer.

Sample Summer School Recovery Program Schedule

8:30 a.m. to 11:30 a.m.	Monday	Tuesday	Wednesday	Thursday
	Math Teacher	English Teacher	Math Teacher	English Teacher

Catalog

It is too easy to bite off more than you can chew. Just because you have access to the full courseware catalog, doesn't mean you should offer it all. Ask yourself if you can support each course with a highly qualified instructor to guide students to successful recovery. A small focused recovery program is much better than one that is too wide and far reaching with not enough support.

Original Credit Elective Courses

Today's students are so busy and they want to do it all, from band, choir, student council, and sports. There is just not enough time in the day to fit it all in. Why not consider opening opportunities for students to create time in their schedule for the upcoming school year using digital courseware. There a few required courses that typically run one semester, that is backed with another one semester course that students are forced to take '*just because*' it fits into the student information system's little black box. An example of this can be found in Clark County's high school Health course requirement for graduation. Some schools will back it with Sophomore Studies or another frivolous semester elective.

Electives are often the reason students come to school. As a former mathematics teacher, I would love to say that core content areas are the backbone to a student's school day, but if you asked them core courses would fall far behind their chosen elective courses, especially in career and technical education pathways or the arts. Use the summer months for students to take some of the required half-credit elective courses, or possibly physical education and get them 'out of the way' so more choice electives are available in the fall. Students and their parents would gladly pay a small fee for a small catalog in the summer that will lead to a much broader and fuller catalog in the fall.

Catalog

The catalog should be targeted and small. Identify a few required courses that could be taken in your courseware that would benefit students, like Health, Physical Education, or Computer Literacy. This is not the time to offer a full catalog of courses. Have a specific audience and purpose in mind. Stick to the plan. Again, just because you have the full catalog, does not mean you have the means or resources to support a full catalog to success.

On-Site

Have students come into school. It is the best way to manage their time. With initial credit summer programs, you're not dealing with a recovery student who had a difficult time making the right choices. Yet, you are still working with teens who like to sleep in and enjoy a lazy summer. I cannot say enough, "Managing student's time is a key to success." Look at establishing an onsite schedule like Monday through Thursday from 8:30 a.m. to 11:30 a.m. each morning. Once the course (or two - if needed) is completed let the student go home for the summer.

From a Distance

Summer original credit electives might be an opportunity to pilot a fully online program, if you, your staff, and students are ready for it. If you are looking to implement a fully online program, consider onsite proctored exams to ensure the integrity of the program. Teacher preparation for a *"from a distance"* program will need more focus on digital communication skills and pedagogy. For instance, weekly electronic announcements that encourage and praise student progress are important. Without pedagogical professional development, too often announcements become nagging posts with deadlines and due dates. Electronic communication about student's assignments also should be more than numerical or alpha score. They should include guidance and redirection, possibly even allowing students to re-submit work with the support provided in the quality feedback loop. Teaching online or from a distance is much more difficult than showing up to a work location that requires meeting and communicating with students orally daily. If you go this route, prepare staff with proper professional development beyond the point and click of the software program. Too many teachers have failed to support students from a distance because they were sold on the idea of teaching online from home in their pajamas would be easy. Teaching is teaching. No matter the environment. It's demanding work to motivate and support student learning, especially from a distance.

Calendar

Online course or not, help students manage their time by calendaring assignments and due dates. Also, have defined start and end dates for the summer program. Three to five weeks should be plenty of time for an original non-core credit course during the summer. The Clark County online summer school program which offers both elective and core courses for original and recovery is calendared for five weeks with 24/7 access to digital content. Whereas the district traditional summer school program runs two sessions of a face-to-face, on site, four hours a day, five days a week, for three weeks. Do the math. It's a sixty-hour semester seat-time Carnegie half-unit per session. With the two face-to-face sessions, they only conduct first semester courses in session one and second semester courses in the second session. How convenient is that? Not. Therefore, more and more Clark County high schools are using digital courseware to offer summer sessions to students in a condensed timeframe in a varied and open catalog.

Summer Staff

Staff your program with teachers that understand the program design and expectations. Teaching is arduous work. Summer is no exception to the rule. Even with the courseware delivering the instruction teachers will need to guide student learning through data management, monitoring student progress, and stepping in with supportive guidance and instruction along the way. And yes, most quality courseware program that go beyond basic understanding and recall will even have papers to grade.

Advanced Placement Summer Prep Program

Speaking of students eager to get a head start on the upcoming school year, you may have students and teachers who want to get a jump on Advance Placement (AP) courses by utilizing summer months. Typically, this is done with required readings or research papers in a traditional setting. However, depending on the vendor's catalog, AP courses may be available to guide student preparation during summer via a digital format. Some vendors may also have an ACT or SAT preparation materials that can be used in the summer months.

Non-Credit Bearing

With the AP course summer program, since students are not looking to earn a summer credit the entire AP course does not have to be assigned or completed. Summer AP prep programs could pick and choose learning modules that target specific objectives. Ideally, the teacher that will be tasked with teaching the AP course in the fall would instruct the summer prep program. By selecting specific content, assigning specific discussion topics and due dates, students will be able to interact among their peers to collaborate and exchange ideas. The teacher may choose to assign courseware exams just as a pre-planning data collection to identify student needs for the coming semester.

Calendar

A word of caution, just like the other summer programs, the AP summer prep program should have start and end dates with calendared events and teacher interaction. Assigning courseware with no expectations has proven to fail. Just like the classroom, students will rise or fall to the expectation level. Even these highly motivated students will meet you at the 'no expectation' level and do nothing over the summer given the choice.

Creating an AP summer prep program can be the first step to getting your staff to use digital courseware as a supplement within their traditional classroom. Digital assignments, discussions, and instruction, via the courseware, can continue throughout the school year. Teachers can utilize the digital assessments to gather data on student understanding and gaps in learning along the way. Courseware does not always have to be use in a credit bearing setting, but bits and pieces of the courseware can be utilized to supplement the traditional classroom.

Summer Bridge

Summer bridge programs are designed to help students make the transition to the next level, or to a new school. Summer bridge could be used to orient students with skills for success or help fill gaps. Digital curriculum can be used with students who may lack the core content skills to be successful at the next level. Or use elective courseware to engage students in digital learning and prepare them for note taking, calendaring, and learning other self-directed skills.

Non-Credit Bearing

A short two-week program just prior to the start of the school is an ideal time to create a summer bridge program. Since the program is not designed to earn credits, the entire course does <u>not</u> have to be assigned or completed. Some courseware products have foundation course designed specifically for filling gaps in understanding. Teachers can identify and choose learning modules that target specific objectives. Students could be assigned different content and be in various places based on their specific needs.

Often schools like to use summer bridge as a time to bring students in early to orient them to the building and school expectations. This a fantastic opportunity to use courseware to teach skills such as note taking, calendaring assignments, and meeting deadlines. Even skills such as digital discussion and online assessments could be assigned to set a foundation for possible interest in taking more online courses in the future. Find a fun elective course that will peak student interest and they will find engaging. Assign specific lessons and guide students through skills that lead to success. Should the school so choose, the students might be given the option to complete the online course once school begins, to earn the digital course credit upon completion.

Credit Bearing

Summer bridge can be a kick off to credit-bearing opportunities when using digital courseware. One high school created a summer bridge program for incoming eighth graders. The two-week face-to-face program introduced students to the large school campus. Teaching included instruction focused on skills for success in high school, such as time management and calendaring events, as well as introducing clubs and sports. Digital courseware with a unit on preparing for college in high school was assigned to students. At the end of the two-week program students were given the option to finish the online course for a half-credit. During the first month of their Freshman Studies program students could take the proctored exams and complete the remaining units in the courseware, thus earning an elective half-credit for an online course they started in the summer bridge program. How is cool is that!

Mindsets

Summer term is quick. These short-term programs require the digital content to take center stage for instructional purposes, leaving any teacher-led instruction behind. Thus, teacher coaching and facilitation will be essential to the success of any summer program. Students must understand the importance of time management and self-motivation, with so many other things pulling at them, such as sleep, summer jobs, and friends. It will be important to cast a clear vision with written guidelines for students, parents, and staff.

No matter the program you select, start small. Prove success. Be sure to document guidelines for both students and staff. Topics to consider include:

- Start and end dates
- Onsite time, dates, and location
- Login expectations for students and staff
- Proctoring of exams
- Two-way communication between student and teachers
- Credit bearing versus non-credit bearing
- Credit extension into the school year

Consider using your summer success to scale into additional digital learning opportunities within the traditional school year.

The use of digital courseware does not have to end with the close of the school year. Contractually the product usage does not end at the close of the term. Summer is an ideal time to look for options to use courseware in alternative ways, such as recovering credits, earning original credits, or preparing students for the

upcoming school year. Look to maximize your vendor contract and students' opportunities in summer months.

KEY POINTS

1. Look for ways to extend courseware usage into summer.
2. Create a small pilot program.
3. Set teacher expectations.
4. Manage student time.
5. Calendar due dates.
6. Document program guidelines.
7. Look to scale successful practices into the traditional school year.

PART 3
PLANNING FOR SUCCESS

Having a menu of ten deployment designs, as seen in part two of this book is a great start. However, it is not like going to a restaurant, where you show up hungry, pick an entrée from the menu, and enjoy the meal. Designing a digital learning environment is more like being the restaurant owner, who had many different decisions they had to make so customers enjoy not only the food, but also the presentation, staff, and atmosphere.

Think about the last time you were at a restaurant. What drew you to that particular restaurant? How were you greeted and seated? What did the menu look like? Imagine all the ingredients that must be on hand to make your meal. How many people do you suspect it took to cook your meal? Did the presentation of the meal look appealing? How was the service? How many times did the waiter/waitress check in with you during the meal? What data did s/he use to know that you were done with your meal? Were you offered dessert? Were your drinks kept fresh? How was the check handled? Did the experience want you to come back, or stay away?

These are much the same questions that we must think about when establishing a digital learning environment - marketing, ensuring staff knows their job expectations, quality service, proper ingredients, presentation, monitoring data and knowing when to intercede, keeping the customer feeling like they want to come back again.

No one said it would be easy, but when you have a vendor that partners with you, who is just as interested in your success as you are, creating a path to success can be paved with previous knowledge (from other vendors clients) that can help you make some good decisions.

This Part of the Book

Each chapter in this part of book will help you chart out a roadmap to success in blended learning. The first chapter will share the ladder to success and the elements that you need to consider when planning a digital learning environment. It will help you with all the questions we asked above about serving the customer. Think of it as a checklist to verify and evaluate your progress when building innovative digital learning environments. Matter of fact, it has a rubric that your design team can use to monitor your headway. Check out the infographic that you can share with your staff.

The remaining three chapters will get you thinking about novel and pioneering designs over the course of years. I always caution schools to "**go slow, to go fast.**" Make sure you lay down a solid foundation, using the seven steps to success in chapter fifteen. Then find something small, that can be fine-tuned before pushing full steam ahead. There will be many stories of how others have carved a path, some with bumps. It is important to keep an open and growth mindset. We can learn from other's successes as well as their failures.

Knowing where and what you want to do, *before* turning onto a speeding highway is always best. Casting a vision and having a one, three, and five-year plan will keep you from biting off more than you can chew. Teacher mindset will be key to any program deployment. Helping staff embrace the CIA of blended learning will ensure that students are not left alone to learn in isolation, but are supported and stretched by their teachers, who monitor student data from the courseware to know when and where students need a caring adult to intercede - be it to remediate or extend the learning.

Think Outside the Box

As you read these chapters, you will find some ideas that go well beyond the traditional calendar and school year. You will be pushed to **think outside the box**. If you think of the ten deployment designs as possible ingredients, then the ideas presented here are the delicious meal made with mixing, stirring, and whisking the ten deployment designs.

"Growing up Digital" is one of my favorite chapters in this book, as it will get your juices flowing. Again, let me remind you, "**go slow, to go fast.**" This also means to make sure that you orientate your staff and students to the digital platforms, before expecting them to run fast and furious. Otherwise you just might crash and burn. Heartburn that is. It will break your heart to see frustrated students failing to progress in the digital courseware and disempowered teachers because they could not find their place in the digital learning environment.

No matter your design, it's important for your staff to create a fine balance among the three elements of the CIA of blended learning:

- computer *digital* <u>c</u>urriculum
- teacher *guided* <u>i</u>nstruction
- learner *authentic* <u>a</u>ssessment

I hope you are inspired as you read these chapters. I've had the pleasure to work with many administrators and schools that enjoyed pushing the envelope and think outside the box. Many of these designs started with questions: *"Can we…"*, *"How would we…"*, and *"What if …"*. Some started as a problem looking for a solution. Others were opportunities that were afforded when having digital courseware on hand. As you read, think about the questions that just might inspire you to **think outside the box**.

CHAPTER 15
LADDER TO SUCCESS

"The difference between blended learning and just adding computers to the way schools have always operated is that there is a regular and intentional change in delivery to boost learning and leverage teacher talent."

Blended Learning Implementation Guide 3.0 (2015)[1]

Planning for a digital learning program can be overwhelming. This book has been designed to help visualize the potential for digital learning environments. The question is where to begin. Think of it as climbing a ladder, you take one step after another step to climb higher and higher to success. Each step has things to consider, purchase, decide, plan out, and communicate to others. If we made a list, there are many items such as digital content, devices, staff, facilities, and so much more.

Go back and read the previous sentence. Notice that the items specified are visual and touchable; content purchased from a vendor, hardware devices, personnel, and classrooms. They are simple to gather, because they are easy to see and touch. Too often this is where the planning begins and stalls. These are the pretty shiny *"junk and stuff"* that so many programs are quick to seek out.

One school was so busy flipping through catalogs for colorful furniture, that when I asked about the classroom instructional practices they could not see the connection between the pedagogy with the classroom and the furniture layout. It was like kids in a candy store. They were filling classrooms with green, blue, and pink bean bags, gaming chairs, even picnic benches, with no consideration of how the teacher might engage students in learning.

I must tell you that when I went back to the school, the classroom teacher had brought in traditional desks, lined in rows, facing a whiteboard. Matter of fact she was sitting behind her desk, projecting a presentation at the time. The colorful furniture sat in the far corners of the room, collecting dust, while she lectured. Each student had a mobile device that they too could view the presentation, yet only at the click or speed of the teacher. Someone forgot to tell the teacher how the colorful fun furniture and modern technologies were supposed to change her instructional practices.

Too often, after acquiring the "colorful stuff" little investment goes into the necessary steps of building a quality digital learning program. The less visual items come at the cost of time and effort. Items such as professional development, planning milestones and benchmarks, or documentation of policies and practices, takes time.

Like spokes in a wheel, if a strut is weak or missing, the wheel begins wobbling and may topple over. So too can a digital learning program if attention is lacking in strategic areas. It is essential to have a roadmap or a checklist to guide leaders into investing time and resources judiciously. The program's design process, from initial planning through management and progress monitoring is essential to ensuring that your digital learning program enables students to be successful and excel academically.

Seven Steps to Program Design

The shift to digital learning is multifaceted. I like to think of it as a ladder to success. However, you do not have to move rung by rung of the ladder to climb to success, but you will need to tackle each step equally.

Don't get caught up in the bright colorful furniture or the sparkling new devices when you begin. Take your time in vendor courseware selection as well. Efforts should also be focused on operational procedures, preparing your staff for new classroom pedagogy and a mind shift to the CIA of blended learning, establishing expectations in the classroom for staff and students, and communicating a message home to parents and the community. There are many things to contemplate, examine, plan for, and execute.

Successfully implementing a digital learning program requires analysis and thoughtful planning. Knowing all the steps you need to take and having a progress monitoring system in place will keep your team focused. Below are seven steps to success when developing a digital learning program (link to infographic below):

1. **Goal Setting**
2. **Target Audience and Recruitment**
3. **Infrastructure and Devices**

4. **Model and Digital Content**
5. **Pedagogy and Professional Development**
6. **Facilities and Furniture**
7. **Structure and Policies**

Again, using the wheel analogy, if one of the seven steps is weak, or missing, the program becomes wobbly, loses traction, and may topple over. I have seen schools paint walls, establish a fancy logo or name, buy thousands of dollars in furniture, technology, and digital content, that didn't make if far before they begin to flounder, because they spent little time and resources in the non-visual essential items like teacher preparation, policies, and establishing performance benchmarks.

Download and share the **Seven Steps to Program Design Infographic** from the i3DigitalPD.com blog.
- See QR code or the Internet Web address below:
  http://i3digitalpd.com/7-steps-to-program-design/

Let's breakdown each step of the ladder to success.

Goal Setting

Adopting a digital learning program, even a small one (e.g. one classroom, or a pilot) begins with setting goals and understanding why the shift is necessary. Today's students are digital natives. They are less compliant to sit and listen. They are transient, with short- and long-term absences creating gaps in learning, when the only way to access learning is to be sitting in the seat when the teacher delivers it. Courseware is more forgiving. It can target individual gaps and personalize the learning space allowing for a student to pick up where they left off, day in and day out. It can assist the teacher with individual data points on every learner.

Establish clear measurable academic goals. Ask yourself, what data do you have today that can be used as a baseline? By utilizing the CIA of blended approach, teachers will have more time to take students to higher levels in Depths of Knowledge (DoK). The time saved by having the digital courseware deliver DoK levels one and two, provides time for highly engaging DoK level four authentic assessments. Using the data points, teacher led instruction can be targeted, specific to needs by scaffolding, supporting, and stretching student learning.

Progress monitoring of student data should be gathered often and not left until the end of the school year. This will allow you to adjust as needed. Especially in programs that are time-based like a nine-week online design. Ask your team, if students are given enough time to complete the digital courseware? Technology reports can be filled with so many numbers, it's hard to determine what is an important measurable data point to monitor. Find a few key factors to focus upon, like time on task, completion rates, and students' mastery-levels.

Adopting digital learning is not a solo sport. It takes a team. A strong leader will surround themselves with a committee of key stakeholders that can help champion the charge. This may include outside expertise and working with intra-district divisions like technology, curriculum, and professional development personnel. Use the expertise of others to create a cohesive group who can establish and a cast a vision for quality digital learning environments. As this book has shown in tales of the not so successful implementations, without a vision and proper procedures in place things can get off track very quickly.

The adoption of digital learning requires support-building before and communication during implementation. It will require discussions about reallocating funding sources and seeking new revenues to support a technology re-fresh. This is an area that I have seen many schools go astray. They purchase one-to-one devices with no plan for sustainability, lacking accountability for annual loss, damage, or age of equipment over time. Plan ahead.

Likewise, a digital courseware contract can be expensive. As digital learning takes off, and it will, usage will go up, increasing vendor courseware costs. This is why Clark County invested in developing their own digital courseware for secondary schools. Budgeting for growth in digital courseware usage is critical. You do not want to turn off the faucet when a steady stream of users have already bought into digital learning. Check out the section titled, *Structures and Policies* below to see how the limited number of seats in vendor contracts were stretched by setting simple expectations.

Target Audience and Recruitment (Marketing)

When building a digital learning program, communication is imperative. But what to communicate will be determined by who you plan to target. For example, will every student have online learning options? Or only credit recovery? Will your course catalog be expanded with digital learning options, including Advanced Placement and Career Technical Education courses? It's important to know the target audience.

Parents and students will need to know how they can elect into digital learning. Or are they just going to assigned to digital learning classrooms? Remember the poor schools that lost a teacher and digital learning came to the rescue. That was not a planned deployment, but an opportunity that landed upon the school and students.

Will you start with a small pilot, a few classes, or a specific grade level? Several Clark County schools have moved the Health requirement to online learning. Thus, every sophomore in these buildings are required to take Health digitally. Schools' deployments vary in design. Some have tried an independent study program (which failed miserably, due to lack of structures and policies, as well as the lack of maturity and time management skills of 15-year-olds). Others have embedded Health into the physical education traditional course as a nine or six week pull out (see the Innovative Programs chapter). A few schools use the digital content within the traditional semester long course in a blended classroom setting. No matter the program design, all schools had to communicate with parents and students about the new delivery of Health.

Once you have established who the target audience is, create a marketing plan. This could be as simple as a flyer or a paragraph in a parent newsletter. Either way you must communicate out the new digital learning endeavors in your building. Marketing should not stop when the doors open. Share photos of students working digitally, stories of success, and the data results that demonstrate promise. Create a short video of your program. Place it on the school website. Digital learning should be celebrated and embraced just like the other programs in your school such as sports, arts, events, and academic competitions. Share and market your digital learning endeavors throughout the school year. With marketing, you are drawing more staff and students' awareness, thus creating more interest and recruiting others to join in and think outside the box.

Infrastructure and Devices

Purchasing or leasing devices is the easy part. Deploying them can be difficult if you have not evaluated your infrastructure. Most schools today are investing in mobile devices, this will may require more wi-fi capabilities. Work with your district technology department to identify the capabilities and limitations of your infrastructure.

One high school was tired of waiting for infrastructure upgrades. The cinder blocks of the school building made it difficult to deploy the forty plus mobile carts in the building. The administrator contracted with a local wi-fi provider and placed digital hot spots throughout his building. An investment the administrator was willing to make, ensuring the building had adequate tools and structures in place so students could learn digitally.

It may sound like a small detail, but don't forget to plan for device management. From tracking devices, to deploying them in classrooms. Possibly even checking them out to students. What is your plan?

At some of the Nevada Ready 21 schools, a one-to-one mobile device initiative, they have huge deployment events at the start of the year. There are orientation videos, parent signatures to be gathered, and devices to cataloged before handing them over to students. Then at the end of the school the equipment must be returned. With populations upwards to 1,800 students it can be difficult. One school had no plan for the end of the school year. They let students take the devices home for the summer. Needless to say, they didn't all come back. Something else to plan and budget for, too.

I cannot say enough, have a device management plan. Keep a log of who, where, and age to track replacement needs. And budget accordingly.

Model and Digital Content

Access to devices and content will drive the deployment model. Throughout this book we have talked about various deployment models. Starting with the very general basic definition of blended learning, to the ten specific designs. But wait, I've saved the best for last. The next two chapters will really get you thinking outside the box. Anyway...

When planning for successful digital learning program, you will need to consider what model and designed you would like to adopt. Will teachers be using a rotation model that will require devices in every room? Or will the school be hosting virtual labs in the media center/library? You may have your digital learning committee conduct site visits either within your district, or outside. Often it is easier to grasp a concept by seeing it in action first. If you cannot get away, research other programs. The Christensen Institute's Blended Learning Universe (BLU)[2] is a repository of schools sharing their programs. Check it out. Clark County and a few of their schools can be found on BLU.

Selection of vendor courseware may sound easy, but beware. Not all courseware is created equal and sales representative tend to misrepresent their products. I love how every vendor will tell you their content is aligned to national standards. Someone back at the corporate headquarters pulled out a list of standards and checked to see how they match up to their product. Alignment done. Just because the alignment task was done, does not meet it met all the standards. What sales reps don't say is how much of the content is aligned, was it 50%? 70%? or 90%? Another grey area that vendors rarely address, unless you ask, is the length of the courses - or in other words, would it match up to a sixty-hour Carnegie unit. I've seen products who only build sixty hours content for honors levels courses, leaving other courses well below. Worse yet are the credit mill products that students fly through, with lots of click and little understanding. Beware.

Work with your district curriculum departments to ensure that the vendor courseware product you are purchasing meets your district standards. Some vendor courseware allows for customization. This may be needed, especially if the standards 'alignment' was low. Again, work with your curriculum department to ensure courses meet your district's expectation. For example, we have very specific requirements to Nevada (e.g. all students must take the U.S. naturalization test and report student scores to the state) that must be added in all U.S. Government courses, both face-to-face and digitally deployed. Since the curriculum expectation were Nevada specific, no vendor would have created digital content targeting this very specific requirement. Thank goodness, the vendor product in use was designed such that additional content could be easily added.

Even as you are shopping for courseware, consider systems integration options. How will student and teacher accounts be created? Will you need nightly batch uploads from the district student information system? If so, work with your technology department. If you can create accounts in the system, establish a standard format so that duplications are not created. This may sound simple, but if not thought through fully Robert Richard Smith could have accounts under Robert, Bob, Bobby, Richard, Rich, Dick, Smith or Smitty. UGH!

I cannot say enough about establishing a partnership with your courseware provider. I mean a true partnership, where the bottom line is student achievement. When both you and the vendor care about student success and not the dollar bottom line of the invoice, then you can establish a digital learning program that works best for you. Look beyond the sales representatives, to others in the corporation that will support your endeavors. Are they easily accessible? Do they deliver on promises? Can you count on them? Do they provide you with insight to where they are seeing concerns and possible opportunities? A true partnership brings much to the table. Don't you be the one to close the door after the sale. Seek a win-win environment for your staff and your students.

Speaking of students, ensure that you have not only selected a courseware product that supports diverse learners with such features as screen readers, translation apps, and chucked information, but you have also put in structures in your design model for special populations. Digital learning should be accessible to all students. Just like the traditional classroom, students with special needs should have the services they require to be successful in their digital classrooms as well.

Pedagogy and Professional Development

Don't let the software training provided by the vendor be the first and only place your staff gets professional development. The point and click training of the digital system is very important. Ensure that ongoing supports are available, as more teachers will buy into using digital courseware throughout the school year. Always use the vendor orientation module, it typically can be done anytime, anyplace.

Staff may also need training on the hardware. Some basics about the devices will help calm the nerves when students come to them with "I can't make this work." Digital devices are not as easy as "open your textbook to page __". Don't take for granted that teachers are digitally savvy. I still run into many who don't know what I mean by "Open a browser window."

Throughout this book, I have said much about the professional development needs of teachers when adopting digital learning - from the cost of change (model selection), to four different mindsets (Online $$$, Blended $, Innovator $$, and Designer $$$$) plus the shift to the CIA of blended learning. It starts with having with a growth mindset to being open to change. May I suggest re-reading the mindset chapter again.

How will you prepare your staff? Don't fall into a trust/mistrust situation. Teachers need guidance and support. Consider your options. Look for resources and opportunities within your district. Look outside as well. It's hard to create a learning environment that you, yourself have never been a student in. That's why I'm a huge fan of digital professional development for teachers. This helps with creating student empathy and viewing pedagogy. Hopefully your district has a learning management system where you can establish online/blended professional development opportunities to support the transition. Teachers will need to know what it is, why it is important, and how to do it. But first your teams must define "it." What is your plan?

Facilities and Furniture

Classrooms and furniture are easy to see, so many start here. They paint walls, design new learning environments with cool slick furniture, and set up labs. The one thing that tends to get overlooked is ensuring that classrooms have the power needs for digital devices. It's an easy thing to miss.

You'll need to figure out how you will set up an environment where thirty or more mobile devices are being charged each night. Some schools get creative with device storage, using restaurant grade shelving and magazine racks. Others choose to spend their money on charging carts. What's in your budget plan?

When it comes to facilities, I've seen a lot. Not all good, but we can learn from the bad.

- Knocking down walls
- Gutting libraries of books (or shared library space)
- Using the theatre for 'double' hybrid classrooms (see the Innovative Programs chapter)
- Using whiteboard paint on tables and walls
- Picnic tables in the halls and classrooms
- Shelving used to separate learning spaces

- Clustering blended teachers into a wing of the school
- Labs with mirrors on the back wall (would have been better served using monitoring software and a projector, allowing the teacher the ability to freely walk the room)
- Students stuck behind study carrels all day
- Dimly lit storage closet used for recovery program

Facilities and furniture are the fun part of designing a digital learning program. Enjoy it, but don't get so caught up that you let the other six steps to success suffer.

Structures and Policies

The entire book was designed to help you with building solid structures to your deployment models. The examples and stories should be a good guide to setting up structures and policies. Too often people tend to talk through policies and procedure and forget to write them down. I caution you that without a firm guideline of expectations that can be passed on to others in a written form, much will be lost in the translation over time.

Handbooks, letters, and other forms of documentation for students, families, and staff should be created to provide each with the tools and information they need to be successful in the digital learning environment. Much like a traditional handbook, it should include your mission, vision, and values - around your innovative learning environment. Handbooks and documents must establish a clear description of roles and responsibilities. Depending upon your model this may be for only the students and the classroom teacher. It may also include - online instructors who monitor student progress from a distance and lab monitor who guide/coach students through courseware. No matter the number of people involved, document a clear set of expectations.

Students

Student support is an integral part of a digital learning program, such as technical help, (access to courses, hardware, software, and communication tools), academic issues (teacher access, tutoring, counseling), and administrative support (enrollment processes, student/parent orientation). These items cannot be overlooked, or taken lightly.

An open letter to students and their family about the digital learning program should include:

- Brief overview of the program
- Online content access and policies
- Login and password information

- Technical assistance (vendor help desk, school technician, or classroom teacher)
- Student support services (e.g. school counselor, special education and ELL specialist, open lab access before/after school, FAQs)
- Academic Support (e.g. classroom teacher, online instructors, lab monitors/instructional coaches, tutors)

Check if the vendor courseware has documents that can be used or modified to meet your needs. This same information must be shared with teachers. Complete the communication circle with support staff and others that may take phone calls from families, so that concerns can be addressed immediately.

Blended learning, and other nontraditional forms of education, may find that the typical schools policies are may or may not be enough to ensure a quality program. When dealing with digital learning students consider policies and document expectations for:

- Academic integrity
- Academic dishonesty
- Acceptable use, including harassment and cyberbullying

It is important to lay a solid and strong groundwork. As it is always better to ease up, rather than hammer down later. Definitely check out the Online Student Rubric in the Appendices.

Consider this sample statement for academic dishonesty: "Regardless of whether the academic dishonesty is a first or second offense, if the incident is deemed severe, the student will be removed from the digital courseware."

Teachers

In most blended classroom when teachers see their students daily, there is less of a tendency to 'forget' about students in the digital learning environments. However, when using teachers from a distance, the online mindset is hard to grasp without expectations.

My stance is that either you instruct, or you don't. If a teacher has been assigned to a digital classroom, even from a distance, then it is their responsibility to instruct students. Remind teachers that they are the digital classroom teacher, and as such are the primary contact for students and parents/guardians about content-specific questions. They are to provide instructional interventional strategies as needed and to handle the instructional questions on content concepts, course materials, testing, and grading along with any modification for students with special needs.

Teachers should proactively monitor each student's progress using the courseware learning management system. Teachers should score assessments and provide feedback on the student's performance through formal means, such as assessment grades, comments, and progress reporting. Consider policies and document procedures for:

- Course completion and grading
- Interaction requirements
- Data analysis and intervention
- Professional development

These teacher expectations should also lay the groundwork for evaluation of staff. A good place to start would be the Online Teacher Rubric in the Appendices.

Lab Coaches

When using virtual lab personnel be sure to define expectations for them as well. This might include responsibilities such as:

- Maintaining regular contact with students
- Monitoring student's progress and needs through daily contact
- Monitoring classroom activities and progress of students
- Serving as liaison between the student and instructors regarding student performance and progress
- Proctoring tests and examinations on school grounds

More ideas can be found in the Virtual Lab Coach Rubric in the Appendices.

Structures

Setting expectations early in the program is important to the success further down the line. They set a consistent and equal path for all involved. Without policies and structures in place, people will do what is best for them, and not consider the ramifications to others. This is best illustrated with a story.

In Clark County, vendor courseware contracts and systems were set up with a per seat charge. This meant that every class a student was enrolled in was a cost. Alternative programs that placed students in six classes used six seats. Even if the student chooses to only attend to one course at a time. Other schools placed every student in need of recovery in the courseware, in a zero period with no monitoring or accountability. Many of these students did not even login, yet they were taking a seat that could be assigned to another.

To alleviate the burden such programs took on the limited number of seats shared among forty plus schools, a fourteen day of inactivity drop was scheduled within the system. This meant that if a student had not attended to a course in fourteen consecutive days the system would drop the student from the course. This matched the traditional classroom policy of ten days of absence the student lost the ability to earn credit.

The fourteen day policy was a hard pill to swallow for many schools, especially those that had not thought through their program design and progress monitoring. I recall one administrator who called me, begging for the removal of the fourteen-day policy. Their counselors were complaining that the fourteen-day inactivity was eating up their time. They were having to go back into the system and re-enroll students whose time had lapsed. The school had placed every senior who needed recovery into the courseware. No timeline or expectations were set. By the time the student finally felt like working in the courseware - days even weeks later, they had been removed. This was not a system issue, but the lack of planning and structures by the school. The school's counselors were exasperated by students who kept asking again and again to be re-enrolled into their online classes, because they had been kicked out. Students claimed no wrongdoing. It was a system issue. It just kept kicking them out.

My question back to the administrator was why would your counselors keep re-enrolling students who failed to attend to their digital course in the first place. Better yet, establish policies and expectations:

1) Limiting the number of students enrolled in the recovery independent study program at any given time, so that they can be monitored properly. No need for the full senior class to begin at the same time. And why provide them the entire school year to finish.

2) Divide the program into six- or nine-week intervals and set the calendar with assignment due date. Most classes were five units, plus a final exam.

3) Expect students to take a unit test every week. Recovery courses start each unit with a pre-test. This means if a student tests out that week, they have no work until next week. Otherwise they will be working through the learning material for the week. Use these face-to-face proctored settings as a time to monitor progress and take weekly attendance.

4) Determine if students can finish early. Spell this out for students and parents.

5) Have students sign a contract that clearly delineates the expectations, such as a maximum of six weeks to finish the course, weekly proctored examination until completed, attendance policy including the fourteen-day inactivity withdraw.

6) Don't allow for re-enrollment (unless the student has demonstrated responsibility and progress). Definitely not on an "as needed" basis. Consider re-enrollment to be seen as on the counselor's good gracious.

Putting these types of structures and policies in place reduced the counselors' headache and helped students to be more successful given the accountability measures.

As noted in the goal setting section, set-up a structure for progress monitoring. Determine how you will define success of your digital program. Set benchmarks. When will you gather data? What data? Review the data often. Make corrections to programs as needed to meet your desired outcomes.

Sometimes you just have to stop and push the reset button. If the current design is not working, then pause, re-evaluate, re-structure and move forward again. It's never too late to put policies and procedures in place. I know most buildings like to start the school year off and not make changes until quarter, semester, or the following year. But why put up with something that is not working. Get use to a cycle of iteration, iteration, and iteration. It's not about seeking perfection, but finding the perfect fit - which will continually change over time, and so will your structures and policies.

Evaluating 'Step' Progress

When designing a program, it's important to progress monitor and know where you are in each of the seven strategic areas. Now that you know the seven areas, it might be good to do a pre-evaluation. Ask yourself, "Where are we in program design?" and assess progress based on the following rubric:

- 0 points – Have not started in this strategic area yet
- 1 point – We're still generating ideas and brainstorming
- 2 points – Assigned a team and leader in this strategic area
- 3 points – The strategic area has a documented plan and timeline of events
- 4 points – Executing the plan and progress monitoring within this strategic area

Over the course of program design and through implementation come back to the evaluation rubric to re-assess your progress. Ideally you want to reach the four-point value in all areas. With each iteration, you may find needs for more professional development, innovative marketing materials, or refining policies and expectations. Again, refine - refine - refine, as many times as needed.

Summary

Don't get caught up in the "junk and stuff." Know where you are going and how to get there. Design a path to success. Use the seven steps here and the evaluation rubric to guide your planning process. Print out the infographic and share it with your team. Select leaders in each of the seven areas to share the responsibilities. Establish a communication plan. Celebrate successes!

Don't be afraid to ask for help when needed. When travelling an unfamiliar road, it's wise to have a guide who has been there before by your side. Use the program designs and stories in this book to help you determine possible action steps. When times get challenging, remember that failure is an opportunity to grow. Throughout the process, use the Stanford's design thinking model:[3]

- empathize with your staff and students,
- define the problem(s),
- ideate and brainstorm "how might we...",
- prototype, and
- test.

Cycle through this many times over. Always come back to the learner experience and your measurable outcomes. Adjust as needed. Remember iteration is a part of the growth mindset.

NEXT STEPS

Questions to Consider

1. Where do you stand today on the seven steps to success?
2. Of the seven steps, what steps do you feel good about and what areas need attention?
3. Who will lead each of the seven steps, to ensure a nicely paved path to success?
4. How will you use the seven steps to guide your planning?
5. Identify possible roadblocks and anticipate possible alternatives routes.

Actions

1. Conduct an initial survey on the seven steps to success.
2. Identify members for your site-based blended learning committee.
3. Tackle each of the seven steps and monitor your progress.
4. Browse the Digital Learning Now *Blended Learning Implementation Guide 3.0* publication, with its many resource links. See Note #1 below.

Notes

1. Bailey, J., Duty, L., Ellis, S., Martin, N., Mohammed, S. Owens, D.. . . Wolfe, J. (2015). *Blended Learning Implementation Guide 3.0.* Publication. Retrieved from Digital Learning: http://digitallearningnow.com/site/uploads/2013/09/BLIG-3.0-FINAL.pdf
2. Blended Learning Universe. Website. https://www.blendedlearning.org/
3. Platner, H. *An Introduction to Design Thinking: A Process Guide.* Publication. Retrieved from Institute of Design Stanford: https://dschool-old.stanford.edu/sandbox/groups/designresources/wiki/36873/attachments/74b3d/ModeGuideBOOTCAMP2010L.pdf?sessionID=573efa71aea50503 341224491c862e32f5edc0a9

CHAPTER 16
INNOVATIVE DESIGNS

"As we advance further into the information revolution, we need to prepare our students to participate and fulfill their full potential to be successful in a future society that is more entrepreneurial, creative, innovative."

What's Possible with Personalized Learning? (2017)[1]

Digital content may change the way classrooms look and feel for today's students especially when compared to the schools their parents attended, but then again so does our society. Still many things about the classroom learning environment remain the same - students learning individually and together, a mix of small and whole group instruction, hands-on investigations, critical thinking, and creative demonstrations of student understanding and mastery of standards.

Blending digital content with face-to-face instruction and allowing student choice in path, place, and/or pace may change age-band grade levels determined by semester calendars. An individualized learning environment that is based on mastery of content, not time in a seat will be better served in a society that is more entrepreneurial, creative, and innovation. It's time to re-think the factory model of schools. To **think outside the box**.

Digital learning does not have to be limited by periods in the day or weeks in a semester. Consider using digital content with classroom instructional support to increase teacher reach and shorten the length of time to earn credits. With years of implementation and numerous data points from Clark County, we have found that given proper support and direction, semester-based digital courses can be completed within nine weeks. Even shorter in recovery mode. Better yet, when adding a virtual lab to the instructional time the student-to-teacher caseload can be distributed throughout the week.

Hybrid Designs

Colleges are noted for holding class every other day, while students are expected to continue the learning when not in front of the instructor. We've all experienced it - right? Go to class on Monday, Wednesday, Friday, or Tuesday, Thursday, and expected to read one to two chapters in the book between classes. With a lab rotation. students don't have to wait for college to learn how to manage their time and become self-directed learners.

Using a lab rotation model, students can access digital content a few days a week and have access to teacher-led instruction the other days. When using two separate learning spaces, one with a highly qualified teacher, the other possibly in a virtual lab, assigned to a media center/library, or slated as a 'free period' for study, a teacher's reach is extended.

College Hybrid Design

In a traditional classroom, a teacher can only reach the number of students they have enough desks for. In Clark County, rooms are packed with thirty-five to forty desks. Yet using digital courseware alongside teacher instruction the room no longer has four walls. **Think outside the box**.

This is best illustrated with a story. One high school was struggling to meet the Health requirement for every sophomore (approximately 700 students) given only one certified health teacher on staff and no budget to hire others. Together we designed a model that doubled the one teacher's reach using digital courseware and the CIA of blended learning.

Let's start by doing the math. Health is a semester-based course, so we needed to design a model that could service half the students, or three-hundred and fifty students each semester. One teacher, three hundred and fifty students in five periods of the day, meant class sizes of seventy students. Wow, that's a lot of kids to service every period of the day, five days a week. What if we could cut the work in half? Half the students. Half the lesson plans. Half the grading. Again, **thinking outside the box**.

The high school had a classroom within their library area, digital courseware, and a laptop cart available. Rather than put all seventy students that the teacher had to service each period in the classroom, half the students would work on the digital courseware in the library, while half the students met in the classroom for teacher-led instruction. The next day, the student population would switch places. The instructor would teach the same lesson to the other half of the students. Thus every two days, only one lesson plan was needed. The courseware delivered much of the instruction and testing, with data points to drive the planning for classroom discussion, extensions, and authentic assessment experiences. This cut the teacher grading in half and student engagement doubled with project learning. It was a win-win.

In this design the teacher reach doubled from thirty-five to seventy students, over five periods a day, totaling 350 students each semester. Double that as she got an additional 350 students in the next semester, for a grand total of all 700 sophomore students in the school serviced by a single teacher. Not only did the teacher extend her reach, she had a teacher's assistant in content delivery with digital courseware with less grading, fewer lesson plans, and deeper authentic learning experiences for students by using the CIA of blended learning.

College Hybrid Classroom

1 teacher	Monday, Wednesday, and Friday	Tuesday and Thursday
5 periods	Group A in classroom with teacher Group B in library digitally learning	Group B in classroom with teacher Group A in library digitally learning
Seventy students each period, half in the classroom with the teacher, the other half in the library engaging with digital courseware. Each week students flipped days to balance access.		

The college hybrid design could be used in a full semester course as well. Doubling the number of students, a teacher services in the course over the year. The design works because it is supported by digital courseware, pre-made to a standards-based Carnegie unit, with frequent checks for understanding and computer graded unit exams. The teachers are provided time to create quality teacher-led instruction that pinpoints power standards, scaffolds the learning, and stretches students to authentic assessments. That is the beauty of the CIA of blended learning.

The college hybrid design maintains a traditional master schedule. Attendance can be tricky, but just needs a clear line of communication, or possibly co-teachers within the course section inside the student information system. Students stay in the semester-based timeframe as their peers. Teachers can set grading benchmarks within the courseware to keep students moving through the digital courseware together. It also makes the student information system happy.

Mass Hybrid Design in a Lecture Hall

Colleges are also noted for holding classes in lecture halls to a large number of students. And I'll bet that most secondary school have a theatre that could be used for instructional purposes, beyond serving the performing arts students. What a better way to prepare students for college, than replicating a college experience.

I got a call from a friend, who was griping that her husband, a local social studies teacher, was being asked to teach in a lecture hall. Due to budget cuts, the school had lost staffing and was trying to **think outside the box**. They had a small theatre with two hundred seats (and expandable by a moveable wall to another hundred seats). The teacher was going to be assigned to the theatre for his U.S. Government classes. He knew he would have no problem lecturing to this large of a group, but was worried with the grading of papers and ensuring that all students succeeded. By goodness, it was senior year and a failure in U.S. Government would mean no graduation. Now that was pressure.

With five days of lecture each week, there was bound to be students who would tune out and fail. The setting was doomed from the beginning for both the students and the teacher. Basically, the school was not thinking far enough outside the box.

The school had access to digital courseware, but only thought of it as a credit recovery solution. Yet, in the blended classroom, digital content could be thought of as a teacher's assistant. It can deliver content, grade papers, and provide instructors with data points on individual student progress. This poor U.S. Government teacher needed an aide and these seniors need an opportunity to prepare for college. It was a perfect storm.

Mix together one highly qualified teacher, digital courseware, and innovative thinking. All the ingredients for a mass college hybrid design. Add a laptop cart to the theatre. Open the movable wall to create a second learning environment. Students would alternate the days in the week that they accessed the digital content and meeting with the classroom teacher. Students could have been assigned a separate learning space for attending to their digital courseware, like the media center/library or a virtual lab. By using a hybrid design, the student's daily schedule would be split between virtual learning and classroom instruction.

Students attended to the digital courseware that targeted acquisition knowledge or depth of knowledge (DoK) level one and two instruction. The teacher had a long history as a U.S. Government instructor, so he knew where students typically struggled, needed scaffolding, and how to stretch students into authentic learning. Though he may love to lecture, students needed his social studies expertise in other pedagogical instruction. The key was to let the technology do what it was best at and allow the teacher to demonstrate his animated spirit and love for U.S. Government in other ways. Too boot, students got a college-type experience. That's what I call college readiness.

Mass Hybrid Classroom

1 teacher	Monday, Wednesday, and Friday	Tuesday and Thursday
5 periods	**Group A** in theatre with teacher **Group B** in lab digitally learning	**Group B** in theatre with teacher **Group A** in lab digitally learning
One hundred students each period, half in the front of the theatre with the teacher, the other half in the back half of the theatre (e.g. virtual lab) engaging with digital courseware. Each week students flipped days to balance access.		

Again, using the CIA of blended learning to balance *digital* curriculum, *guided* instruction, and *authentic* assessment in a traditional semester-based calendar, keeps students, teacher, and the student information system all in a familiar setting and context. Extending a teacher's reach with digital courseware, such that one teacher can reach five hundred seniors with half the lesson plans and half the grading. Now that is innovative thinking.

Mix and Match Online with Traditional

When thinking outside the box, schools should consider how they can create learning environments that mix face-to-face learning with online learning courseware. When you allow the digital courseware to take the lead, online courses can be finished in nine weeks (or shorter) with proper supports. In quarter, or nine-week sessions students are fully focused on the courseware, day-in and day-out, in a virtual lab setting with individual one-on-one tutoring and coaching. Allowing the digital content to drive, means the teacher mindset is from the standpoint of an online teacher, even though they may be in the same room as the students, their mindset should be one of guiding the instruction of which the digital curriculum leads. There may be a limited amount of time for teacher-led instruction (e.g. whole group discussion) and possible authentic assessment activities in the nine weeks as well, but the focus would be on the completion of the digital courseware and less blending.

In Clark County, the virtual school breaks their independent study program into nine-week blocks, allowing the first three week for late arrivals. Thus, in nine weeks (even as little as six weeks) using digital courseware students typically have sufficient amount of time to earn a half credit in most vendor products. Using this data, we can create a good mix and match of online and traditional courses to extend credit bearing opportunities.

Nine Week Flip

Image physical education (PE) in one-hundred plus degree weather in the desert. Ouch - right? When using digital courseware, we could reduce the amount of time students were enrolled in a traditional PE classroom, by in mixing digital courseware such that a student earns a full credit in PE and an additional one-half credit in Health. As noted earlier, Health tends to be difficult for most Clark County schools to schedule into a traditional setting. Finding another one-half credit course to match it within a traditional schedule can be tricky. This is where the online courseware for PE was ideal in a nine-week rotation.

Much like the hybrid design with different days in the online courseware, matched with days face-to-face with the classroom teacher, nine-week quarters can be mixed. Students could be assigned online Health for nine weeks and online Personal Fitness (an equivalent for PE) for nine weeks, plus a face-to-face traditional PE for an eighteen-week semester. In doing so, students earned one full credit in PE and one-half credit in Health, during a single period in the day.

Nine-week PE/Health Mix and Match

Semester A		Semester B
9 weeks = Lab	9-weeks = Lab	18 weeks = Classroom
Health Online Content	*Personal Fitness* Online Content	*Physical Education* Face-to-Face
One-half of the students are pulled from PE class each semester to attend to online courses. Using an online PE course (or an equivalent), students earn one full credit in PE, along with one-half credit in Health for a total of 1.5 credits by the end of the term in a single class period.		

The size of PE classes were reduced and the reach of the Health teacher doubled by using online courseware and thinking outside the box. Students were excited that they only had to dress out one-half of the school year, and were able to document their 'out of school' exercise in Personal Wellness to earn a full PE credit. The best part was that the design stayed within the black box of the student information system, keeping everyone satisfied.

When mixing and matching, if you have a full year of digital courseware in Personal Wellness (PE), use it and add in a nine-week face-to-face Driver Education course into the design. Driver Education is an elective all teens should take – keeping the roads safe for everyone!

Nine-week PE/Health/Driver Ed Mix and Match

Semester A		Semester B	
Personal Fitness, s1 Online Content	*Personal Fitness, s2* Online Content	*Health* Online Content	*Driver Education* Face-to-Face
Students spend three nine-week sessions in digital PE and Health courseware, plus a nine-week face-to-face Driver Education session to earn two full credits in a single class period of a traditional schedule.			

Pull-out Design

Speaking of Driver Education, another design for Health and PE came from the days of pull-out for Driver Education. In a traditional six period bell schedule, the ability to pull students out of PE for thirty hours of instruction for Driver Education maintained the full seat time Carnegie unit in PE. Many students complete the online Health course in a five-week summer session of the virtual school and the data showed that it was possible to complete the online Health course in less than thirty hours. Using the Driver Education pull-out design for online Health, students are being pulled out every six weeks from PE. They still earn one full credit in PE, plus one-half credit in Health, during a single period in the day.

Six-week PE Pull Out

Semester A			Semester B		
6 weeks	6 weeks	6 weeks	6 weeks	6 weeks	6 weeks
PE or Online Health (1st group)	PE or Online Health (2nd group)	PE or Online Health (3rd group)	PE or Online Health (4th group)	PE or Online Health (5th group)	PE or Online Health (6th group)
One-sixth of the students are pulled from PE class every six weeks to attend to an online Health course. At the conclusion of the term students have earned 1.5 credits.					

Students are pulled from several different PE teachers when being assigned to online Health. Again, class sizes in PE were reduced and the Health teacher extended their reach to more students over time. However, the six-week pull out design is less friendly to the student information system and requires a good deal of planning and communication among teachers and staff for attendance. And it leaves little time for much more than the consumption of the digital courses.

Mixing Cores

The examples above use an elective with already overburdened staff PE course, but the use of courseware to drive instruction in a shortened period of time also works for core classes. In a more independent study courseware-driven instructional environment, students can complete core one-half credit courses in nine weeks, and elective courses in even less time. Knowing this, we have an opportunity to offer more courses in a traditional semester term. Students can earn credits faster when the digital courseware drives and the teacher guides instruction provided in the digital curriculum.

A fast track to graduation can be created with courseware that allows students to complete digital courses, at school, assigned to a lab (for time management), in a shortened timeframe. It's quite simple to manage the mixing of core courses when the same group of students take similar grade level classes, such as World History, U.S. History, and U.S. Government exchanging with English 10-12. In a nine-week design for each semester course, a student can complete two full credits in a single class period of a traditional schedule.

Flipping Grade Level Core

Semester A		Semester B	
English 10 semester 1	English 10 semester 2	World History Semester 1	World History Semester 1
Students spend a traditional eighteen-week term immersed in digital courseware to complete two full courses (semester courses are taken consecutively each nine weeks) in an expedited fashion. An English teacher and social studies teacher exchange students at term. Students earn two full credits in a single class period of a traditional schedule.			

With this design, the teacher reach is doubled. By allowing the digital curriculum to drive instruction the teacher's role changes to one of coaching and mentoring. Even though the teacher may see the students daily, this online mindset is <u>much</u> different from the blended mindset who has more time with students in a traditional term. Remember the cost for an online mindset is much higher than that of a blended teacher. Success and failure will reside with the teacher support systems in the fast track design. The teacher's mindset can make or break a program. If the teacher sits back and does not engage, students may feel unsupported and fail to complete courses in a timely manner. If the teacher over instructs, stopping the class too often for large group interaction, students may not have enough 'on-task' time in the digital curriculum to complete the course in nine weeks. Finding the right balance between coaching and guiding students is the true art and craft of teaching digitally.

Rolling Enrollment

A nine-week, digital courseware instructional environments are ideal for alternative education or targeted population groups. Especially when students tend to roll into and out of the environment, like that of adjudicated youth, or teen parents. When a student's life takes a hit, the traditional eighteen-week, butt in the seat, semester calendar does not make sense.

Digital courseware is an excellent choice for alternative secondary schools targeting special populations in need of an educational setting that is flexible. With courseware, the learning environment can be geared to meet both emotional and educational needs. For example, in a high school for students coming out of addiction recovery programs, students need a more flexible calendar to earning credit towards graduation, not one so rigid and locked into an eighteen-week seat time calendar. A schedule that could support possible relapse, with the ability to pick back up where a student left off. Not one tied to teacher lectures or the semester posting of grades. They need a system that allows for credits to be earned in a rolling fashion, possibly even one that did not mean taking six classes at a time, but focused on only a few at any given moment.

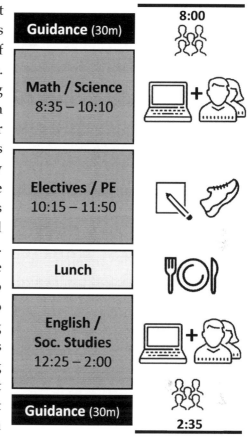

In rolling enrollment settings, it is important to create a structured setting, yet flexible. For example, the day could be set in a series of three 90-minute blocks of time for students to attend to their online classes and engage with staff. Two blocks for core and one for electives, which could include physical education outdoors for a brain break and building a sense of community among students and staff. Mixing one high reading course, such as English and social studies, with one analytical course, like mathematics or science, along with an engaging elective creates a well-balanced approach to a student's daily schedule.

Teachers can support digital instruction with large and small group activities, plus individualized mentoring. Wrap around services at the start and end of each day can focus on life and coping skills. In the morning session, students set goals for the day. In the afternoon session, they reflect on time management and obtainment of daily goals. This type of highly structured day is one I recommend not only to alternative schools, but also to programs such as on-site suspension programs. See the previous chapter on behavior programs.

When using a rolling enrollment environment, it is important to ensure that students are progressing and obtaining credits in a timely fashion. To keep students and staff focused, use an Individualized Academic Educational Plan (IAEP) to guide student enrollments. Set up a schedule for students within a rolling enrollment that outlines a semester at a time to ensure students don't fall further behind. With digital courseware taking the lead, nine weeks is sufficient for core classes, six weeks for electives, and recovery classes tend to vary. A good starting point for recovery courses is six weeks. Most students will finish much earlier, but in a rolling enrollment environment that will not matter. The key is to keep a minimum pacing guide to help students manage their time wisely and earning credits.

Ideally, attempt to reduce the student workload, such that they are engaging in a small number of classes at a given time, rather than a full load of six courses. Three courses at a time is a good number, allowing for variability over the day for students. Thus, my preference for the three-block schedule example above. Most alternative programs provide more latitude in student schedules. In Nevada, the IAEP must demonstrate a minimum of six courses over a traditional semester timeframe. Check with your district policies and state legislation.

A sample IAEP below, shows how students can tackle multiple classes in a term using the nine and six-week scheduling of courses, over the course of a school year. Semester based original credit courses are taken consecutively. A balance of elective and recovery courses compliment original credit courses, such that a student is only assigned three digital courses at any given time. Notice that additional courses are already listed and available for students to roll into should they complete others early.

As noted in the flex academy chapter, alternative learning environments for targeted populations can be created in comprehensive schools in a small school-within-a-school program. When we create these types of alternative programs in a comprehensive building, students don't have to leave their neighborhood schools when needing someone who can think outside the box, beyond the bell schedule, and the eighteen-week semester-based calendar. Digital courseware gives every school the option to create rolling enrollment opportunities.

Rolling enrollment is an easy concept to grasp, but difficult to put into action. Most student information systems are designed for calendar-based, semester long courses. As are most school policies and state legislation. It's important to check all laws and regulations that might govern non-traditional learning environments. This includes NCAA nontraditional requirements.

Individualized Academic Educational Plan (IAEP)

Course	Sem.	Type	Start	End	Weeks	Grade
CORE COURSES						
Geometry	1	Original	08/14	10/13	9	
Geometry	2	Original	10/16	12/22	9	
World History	1	Original	08/14	10/13	9	
World History	2	Original	10/16	12/22	9	
English 10	1	Original	01/8	03/14	9	
English 10	2	Original	03/15	05/24	9	
Biology	1	Original	01/08	03/14	9	
Biology	2	Original	03/15	05/24	9	
ELECTIVES						
Career Planning I	1	Original	08/14	09/22	6	
Computers	1	Original	04/09	05/24	6	
Health	1	Original				
Spanish II	1	Original				
Spanish II	2	Original				
RECOVERY COURSES						
Algebra I	2	Recovery	02/20	04/06	6	
Geoscience	2	Recovery	01/08	02/16	6	
English 9	1	Recovery	09/25	11/09	6	
English 9	2	Recovery	11/13	12/22	6	
Spanish I	2	Recovery				
PE	2	Recovery				

Electives and Advanced Placement

Too often schools get so caught up in being inventive for credit recovery students, or those troublesome areas like Health, that they stop looking for other ways to create opportunities to use courseware for extending the catalog and enriching student digital learning experiences. Electives and catalogs with Advanced Placement courses are a wonderful place to be innovative.

Semester Electives, Plus Project Learning

Electives vary with each vendor catalog. Some have only a single semester course in electives that are a typically yearlong at your site. This may look like a detriment, but when thinking outside the box it becomes an opportunity for extended project learning. Or just think of it as a full semester of highly engaging authentic assessment. Using the CIA model, a semester elective from a vendor catalog can be turned into a full year course in a blended learning classroom.

Use the digital content to set the foundation in the first semester with instructor guidance. With a blended classroom mindset and approach, the first semester is filled with the foundational knowledge and skills. Then in the second semester, the teacher can extend the learning within the content using project learning and research-driven collaborative group work to extend and personalize instruction. Art History, Sociology, and Psychology may only be a semester digitally, but can be extended into a yearlong course by adopting the CIA of blended learning.

One Semester Elective Extended

Semester A	Semester B
Blended Classroom with Digital Courseware	Extended Project Learning and Personalization
One semester courseware can be stretched to a full year with extended learning opportunities into the second semester, using the CIA of blended learning.	

When using a hybrid design where students work select days in the lab and other days with their teacher, a highly sought after elective teacher can extend their reach to even more students.

Advanced Placement by the Handful

Most advanced placement (AP) courses are deeper extensions of high school general education courses. A student may choose to take U.S. History or AP U.S. History, Biology or AP Biology, English 11 or AP Literature and Composition. Even elective courses like Psychology and AP Psychology, or Calculus and AP Calculus. Every school offers general education courses, but may find it difficult to offer AP courses in the same content area. Vendor courseware with a catalog of AP courses just might be a way to open this door.

In an AP course all the lesson planning and presentation has been already put into an highly rigorous learning environment. Matter of fact, to even use the term "Advanced Placement" on a course, vendors had to submit their course to the College Board for approval. Thus, there is no additional prep for the general education teacher to extend their services to advanced placement students.

When creating a catalog, why not allow students to choose to take AP courses using digital courseware. But don't send them to a virtual learning lab. AP students could work on digital courseware in the back of the classroom of a highly qualified instructor who is teaching a general education course of the same or similar content. Layer the two, general education and AP courses into the same class period. The instructor can focus their time with the full class of traditional general education students, with an additional handful of students using digital courseware taking AP level content. Extend the reach of the instructor to both sets of students. They should use the data from the courseware to attend to the needs of the AP students as well.

Since the content is similar in nature, though not to the same depth, the AP students may benefit from hearing the general education classroom instruction. The key is having immediate access to the teacher. The instructor can use time that the general education students are actively engaged in peer work or taking exams to meet with the AP students. As with many AP courses, additional study sessions after or before school can also be arranged for more in-depth analysis and preparation for College Board AP examinations.

Layer Advanced Placement (AP) with General Ed

Semester A	Semester B
General Ed Traditional Face-to-Face	General Ed Traditional Face-to-Face
Advanced Placement Digital Courseware	Advanced Placement Digital Courseware
Layer general education classrooms with Advanced Placement students using digital courseware in the back of the room, with immediate access to the course instructor.	

In Clark County, most every high school offers Psychology, yet very few have enough students to schedule an AP Psychology course for students who want to continue their pursuit of learning more. By layering an AP course within the general education course, students no longer had to be denied this opportunity and it allowed schools options previously not available.

Let me caution you about using AP courses without structures. One high school enrolled a very ambitious student into an AP Statistics digital courseware. The student was even provided a period in the day to attend to his online class. It was not an optimal location, as he was assigned to the virtual lab with numerous other digital learners, mostly credit recovery students. The credit recovery highly qualified math teacher was his assigned instructor, but as often happens with independent study courses, the teacher was less attentive, lacking to provide student coaching or even progress monitoring. After nearly eighteen weeks in the virtual lab, the student had not finished even one unit of study. The school was left in a quandary. Staff had failed the student. The student had failed the course. And the student *was* on track for graduation with honors as salutatorian. I cannot say enough that proper structures and expectation must be put in place for staff and students, even the highly motivated, so that students achieve and succeed in digital learning environments.

Summary

Digital courseware provides opportunities to be creative and innovative in design. Look outside the box for ways to create blended classrooms that extend the reach of excellent teachers. The college hybrid design is ideal for opening doors to more students who can engage with a highly effective and successful master teacher. And to boot, it prepares students for managing time in a college model. Definitely a win-win. The hybrid design allows for a balanced approach to the CIA of blended learning, extending students into rich authentic assessments with teacher guided instruction.

When letting the digital courseware drive, students can complete courses in an expedited fashion. Though little time is left for a balanced CIA. Teachers become more of a coach and mentor to the digital content. Yet it opens doors for gaining additional credits in creative mixing and matching of face-to-face classes with digital courseware. Also rolling enrollment becomes an option for students who want to accelerate their program, or may have fallen behind and need several recovery courses to graduate on time. These types of programs are ideal for alternative settings and in a school-within-a-school program.

Think outside the box. Outside the typical class periods. Beyond the student information system. Be creative. Ask yourself, "How can we use digital courseware for innovative program design?"

NEXT STEPS

Questions to Consider

1. Does our vendor courseware catalog have electives, including Advanced Placement options that we could use creatively?
2. Who are the master teachers in my school/district and how can I plan a college hybrid program to extend their talents and skills to more students?
3. What will it take to use the nine-week quarter and rolling enrollment options for earning semester credits?
4. What district policies and state laws address student enrollment options for alternative learning settings, such as reduced course load?

Actions

1. Review data on digital courseware completion times.
2. Check vendor courseware catalog for electives opportunities.
3. Identify master teachers for possible college hybrid programs.
4. Use the nine-week quarter for earn semester credits.
5. Consider options for rolling enrollment, beyond credit recovery.
6. Review policies and legislation pertaining to alternative settings, including distance and competency-based education.

Notes

1. Friend, B., Schneider, C., Patrick, S., & Vander Ark, T. (2017, February). *What's Possible with Personalized Learning? An Overview of Personalized Learning for Schools, Families, & Communities.* Publication. Retrieved from International Association for K-12 Online Learning: https://www.inacol.org/wp-content/uploads/2017/01/iNACOL_Whats-Possible-with-Personalized-Learning.pdf

CHAPTER 17
GROWING UP DIGITAL

"Technology has allowed us to rethink the design of physical learning
spaces to accommodate new and expanding relationships among learners,
teachers, peers, and mentors."
Reimagining the Role of Technology in the Classroom (2017)[1]

Today's kids are digital, but that does not mean they are digital learners. Technology may drive the way we live. Most students in secondary schools have a cell phone in their backpack. Believe me they are not using it to learn on, especially not in a formal learning environment. Oh yes, they may be looking up things they are interested in, or watching a video on "how to do it yourself," but these are areas of interest. It's more informal learning. No need for mastery there.

Asking students to learn math, English, science and social studies online, in a digital format can be difficult. It will be important to set the groundwork, lay a solid foundation of the digital classroom. Students may be resist, especially those who have learned how to play the game of traditional education so well. Now you are changing the rules on them.

Go Slow, To Go Fast

When designing digital learning environments teacher preparation is just as important as student readiness. Personally, I'm a huge fan of **"go slow, to go fast**." This means start with something small, something easy for both students and teachers. Use a tiny pilot. Watch it closely, refine as needed. Set everyone - the students, the teachers, the digital courseware - up for success.

Since the courseware is new to both students and teachers, think of ways to create a learning environment that allows for familiarity with digital learning as little pressure as necessary. For example, core classes are high risk. In Nevada, some are even tied to high stakes tests like end-of-course exams. If a student fails a core class, or is unable to grasp concepts in the class, it could possibly hurt their graduation. Yet elective classes can be fun and engaging, typically requiring less homework. Given a choice, start with electives.

Courseware Orientation

I've seen too many schools fail to prepare students and teachers for the digital learning environment because they were so quick to enroll students and staff into the digital software classrooms. Remember the early days of any classroom. Time was taken to orient students to the rules and teacher expectations. Simple directions, such as where the turn in basket is and where they can find posted grades was shared. Teachers pointed out how to locate the calendared assignments and what to do if absent. The need to orientate students to the digital classroom is just as essential, if not more so to setting the foundation for success. Classroom teacher's orientation in the face-to-face environment had years of experience to scaffold and build upon. Yet the digital world may be a first for students. Turning in electronic assignments, raising a digital hand, and communicating in a virtual discussion can be new for students. New for teachers as well.

Always start with the orientation in the courseware. Most vendor products have a student and a teacher "getting started" online learning module. All too often schools are so quick to start that they place students immediately into the system and say, "Go to class." What they fail to do is set the students (and staff) up for success, via the orientation module. In most systems the orientation is not part of the class, but a system-wide feature found outside of

> All too often schools are so quick to start that they place students immediately into the system and say, "Go to class."

the digital classrooms. Typically, it is short, approximately thirty to sixty minutes, which entails watching a few videos. Some vendor products may even have a printable certificate of completion. Use it to validate student preparedness. I've seen many programs struggle with their deployments, because they skipped the orientation and everyone floundered.

After the orientation learning module, try letting students become familiar with the digital system in a fun and engaging elective. This will allow students time to understand how the online classroom is designed, from where to find assignments, how to turn in work, use the discussion board, and email their teacher. This will also help the staff gain knowledge in how to work with the system's gradebook and data reports. Most importantly, where to find course syllabus, identify teacher graded work, and assignment answer keys.

While working with some alternative education sites, who were new to digital learning, we devised a plan that would use a study skills career planning elective course as the initial experience for students and staff. The content addressed how to manage time, take notes, test-taking skills, and preparing for college and careers. Minimal risk content, yet very important to setting the stage for high school success. The data had shown student completion times were low and grades were high. This type of course creates an early easy win for students, as they learn the digital system. Teachers also have a low risk opportunity to gain understanding in the course structure and features such as teacher graded work, locating and reading data reports, and managing the gradebook. A win-win.

Everyone in the school worked on a single course for a brief period of time. This created a community of learners - both students and teachers, surrounded by others who were engaging in the exact same digital learning environment. Students had friends they could talk to about the course content and functionality. Teachers had co-worker that they could collaborate with about assignments and student data.

No matter the subject area, every class allotted time to digital learning for one week. Every teacher was assigned a group of students to monitor. The entire student body was enrolled into the same study skills career planning digital course. On the first day of the deployment, the first hour of the day was dedicated to students going through the courseware orientation, starting off the deployment with a solid foundation in the system. Throughout the day, teachers set aside half the class time for digital learning. As they would wander the room, look over students' shoulders, pose questions, and coach students through digital lessons. There was no sitting behind the teacher desk. The expectation was for staff to be an active and physical presence in the digital learning environment. Students were encouraged to work together and not to sit behind a computer screen in isolation.

The digital courseware provided a personal learning space, such that students could be at various places at any given time. This was especially true as the week progressed and some students liked the content so much they were working on it away from school. Having students at different places was a hard concept for teachers at first, but since the content was an elective they let loose a bit and were able to find a harmonious shift to this multifaceted learning environment. At the end of the day, teachers pulled reports to look at together with their peers and discuss their observations. Again, with the minimal risk elective content, conversations were open and insightful about the data and what picture it was painting about individual students.

By the end of the week, most students had earned one-half elective credit. The few that had not completed the course, due to absences, did not have to stop. They were given an extension to finish the course the following week. That's the beauty of digital courseware, students do not have to be tied to arbitrary deadlines set by calendars and the students information system.

This one-week experiment of "going slow" set the stage for digital learning deployments in core classes. Now that teachers and students had a full understanding of the digital classroom, they were open to using the digital courseware in a blended learning environment in their core content classes.

A Slow Roll

After teachers and students have a full understanding of the digital learning environment, and with more experiences, they will be able to handle additional and different digital deployments. Setting the stage, by going slow to start, allows us the

> By going slow to start, allows us the ability to go faster later down the road.

ability to go faster later down the road. I've seen way too many schools that started out thinking students would go right through courseware, but were disappointed, as students failed to launch. A slow roll is much better.

Think of trying to move a large boulder. At first it is hard to even budge the boulder. Slowly you rock it back and forth, gaining momentum. Then it begins to move forward. Little by little it gains speed and you need less pushing efforts to keep it rolling forward. This is much like students in a digital learning environment. Like the boulder, they too are heavy in the traditional classroom customs. They will resist movement, rocking back and forth with comments like, "Why can't you just teach us" or "Come on, just tell us the answers." With guidance and support, students begin to take ownership of their learning in the digital courseware and won't need so much pushing to keep them rolling forward.

Set your students and staff up for success by going slow, to go fast. Start by creating learning environments that use a lot of hand holding, guidance, and support. Slowly you can open more doors with the courseware as students have a better understanding on the demand of learning digitally. As they become mature digital learners, they will be more independent with better time management skills. Allow them to grow up digitally.

Middle Grades

Young students coming out of an elementary single classroom, into the middle grades multi-classroom period schedule is a huge adjustment. Look for opportunities where digital content can enhance the learning and engage students in different learning modalities, such as:

- Blended Classrooms
- Grade Improvement / Unit Recovery
- Summer Bridge
- Semester Electives + Project Learning

Planning programs at the middle grades should begin with blended classrooms. Allow the technology to deliver low level understanding and basic skills. Then using the CIA of blended learning, teachers can provide the young students with daily guidance and support to stretch them into depth of knowledge (DoK) levels three and four. Also look for other opportunities to expand the use of courseware to support student learning when there are gaps that need filling, such as grade improvement and summer bridge.

One place to stay away from in middle grades is independent study. The maturity level of the student is still developing; thus, they are not really looking to gain conceptual understanding of course material, rather they will seek an easy out. Even the most studious students may find independent study difficult. Remember without the teacher to guide and extend learning, they are only being exposed to DoK 1-2.

At one middle school, they wanted to afford honors students the opportunity to take high school Geometry. The students were assigned courseware in an independent study format. They had access to a mathematics teacher when needed, by reaching out to their former Algebra teacher from last year. Most students passed the Geometry courseware with flying colors. And so, they should, be that it was low level instructional material. However, when taking the high-risk end-of-course exam for Geometry there was no indication that these were honors level students, as they scored near the general population.

Blended Classrooms

Digital courseware can be introduced in a blended classroom by using the CIA model of blended learning. It is an ideal way to introduce students to taking ownership of their own learning, in a nurturing environment. Students still have a structured learning environment and see their teacher five days a week. Teachers can conduct whole group introductions, set the student loose on digital courseware, while pulling small groups for tutoring, then bring everyone back together for a classroom closure. Using digital curriculum to deliver depth of knowledge (DoK) levels one and two, will open time in the traditional calendar for stretching students with thought provoking and collaborative authentic assessments.

Go back to the blended classroom chapter for more ideas on how to structure the class period. Station rotation over several days or a daily flipped lab rotation tends to work well at the middle grades. Revisit the CIA of blended learning chapter to ensure that teachers fully understand and embrace a balanced approach to 1) *digital* <u>c</u>urriculum, 2) *guided* <u>i</u>nstruction, and 3) *authentic* <u>a</u>ssessment. There are seven regions in the triple Venn diagram. Teachers need to ask themselves daily, where is my classroom today. Think of the diagram as a dart board. Have

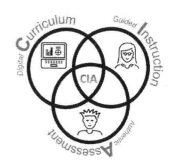

teachers chart their findings. This will help them identify if they are too heavy in one area, or too light in another.

I have seen middle grade buildings create a small school-within-a-school blended learning academy. They started with an application process for new incoming students, with a plan to roll up the academy annually into the higher grades. The next year all incoming students were blended, creating a path to a school-wide adoption. The small academy was so successful, that it sparked excitement among staff and the community. It provided a proving ground for digital learning and allowed staff to see it in action onsite, with their student population, building buy-in to this new learning modality.

Several of the one-to-one schools went school-wide adoption into blended learning. All core classroom used digital courseware to blend. Elective courses continued to use traditional learning modalities and adding in digital components. Given a school-wide learning management system helps tremendously, such that every classroom had a digital footprint.

There are many ways to plan digital programs in small bite size chunks. Some sites have targeted specific content areas with blended learning, such as math, English, or social studies. One might tackle just a single classroom. This is especially helpful with weak teachers or in a setting with a long-term substitute who need an extra support to keep students on benchmark. When buildings were looking to expand their elective offering, they brought in courseware for courses such as world languages and career technical education, like coding.

Blended classrooms provide daily support and access to a highly qualified teacher who is guiding instruction through a balance of face-to-face and online learning. It is an ideal way to start your digital learning program.

Grade Improvement

Middle grade students are still finding their way through period schedules and intense daily studies in multiple subject areas. Thus, they may find themselves in situations where they fail an exam or two. This creates an opportunity to use courseware for grade improvement. By assigning students very specific lessons, targeting their individual need in the courseware to re-learn concepts in a new and different modality opens doors to student understanding. It's a hard concept for teachers in a traditional classroom to grasp. Their fixed mindset, "I taught it. They should know it" does not take into consideration the student needs.

At one school, they were looking to adopt a grade improvement program in their mathematics department. The staff was very resistant. It was a school of high socio-economics students where the expectation was college, and prestigious colleges at that. After much debate and contemplation, the staff agreed to using digital courseware to allow students to improve failing test grades to a maximum of only sixty percent, or that of a very low 'D.' As you can imagine, the program was small, few taking advantage of these additional learning opportunities for such little reward. Even with this type of grade improvement program the need for full course credit recovery stayed consistent.

Grade improvement programs should be built on the premise of helping students to master difficult concepts. Catching student misunderstanding early, in the moment, and using digital content to rectify the situation is so much better than waiting the entire semester to see if the student can pull out a passing grade.

Credit recovery programs can be eliminated by not allowing students to fail in the first place. By providing additional supports like courseware for re-learning, plus one-on-one tutoring, where students can succeed in a course the first time around. This is the premise of competency-based education. We already know what students should know and be able to do. Now it is up to us, the educators in the room, to ensure that every student understands the material and we do whatever it takes to not let students fail. More on competency-based learning in the next chapter.

Summer Bridge

Summer is a perfect time to fill student gaps. Bridge doesn't have to be at transition years from elementary to middle grades, or middle to high school. It can happen every summer, no matter the grade level. With digital courseware you have a curriculum that can drive instruction for foundational knowledge and skill sets. If the data shows the students are weak in grade-level content, yet the student passed the class, this is an appropriate time to bring in digital courseware. Technology doesn't give grades for participation, or because you tried so hard.

With a focus on DoK levels one and two, you can build students understanding up over the summer months, to support the coming year's enrollment.

Why pay for a full year vendor contract, if you don't have plans to use it in the summer months. Okay, I get it, because there is no option for a nine or ten-month contract. So why not consider using your vendor courseware in the summer months. Look for targeted populations that would benefit with a summer bridge program. Don't let "summer slip" become a norm in your building. Open opportunities with digital curriculum and teacher guided instructional support. Go back to the chapter on summer bridge for ideas and sample deployment designs.

Semester Elective + Project Learning

Electives in middle grades are always difficult to find. Many schools have gone with an explorations model, where students rotate between topics that may or may not interest them. Typically, this is based on the expertise and desires of the staff, rather than student voice and choice. Yet, with digital curriculum, students can be given opportunities that takes students into research and project learning authentic assessment. You can still call it Exploration, but let the student determine what they want to explore.

One Semester Elective Extended

Semester A	Semester B
Blended classroom with digital courseware to set the foundations. PLUS, extended project learning to personalize the learning experience.	
A single semester elective courseware can be stretched to a full year with extended learning opportunities, using the CIA of blended learning.	

Using a semester elective course from a vendor catalog can be stretched an additional semester with in depth analysis and project learning. This will allow students to dig deeper into an area of study that they are interested in. Take Music Appreciation and Art History as an example. The student may not want to be a musician or play a band instrument, but loves music and possibly wants to digitally mix it to create their own tracks. Maybe a student loves art, but cannot draw. Why not let them immerse themselves in a range of styles and eras of art over time. This is where students and teacher can **think outside the box** together.

High School

Depending on your feeder school(s), squirrely freshmen may not have been exposed to digital learning. Again, **"go slow, to go fast."** The maturity level has increased as pre-teens become teenagers, but they still need hand holding.

All the suggestions above, continue to hold true in high school. Look for opportunities where digital content can enhance the learning and engage students in different learning modalities, such as:

- Blended Classrooms
- Grade Improvement / Unit Recovery
- Summer Bridge
- Semester Electives + Project Learning

In high school, the key is to go beyond credit recovery. That box is bound so tight it is difficult to move past it in high schools. By now, most high schools have the credit recovery design already in place. It possibly could use some fine tuning (consider grade improvement to reduce need or quarter catch-up below). It's time to move on, look elsewhere, and **think outside the box**:

- Freshman Studies
- Quarter Catch-up
- PE & Health Combo
- Digital Electives
- Nine Week Acceleration
- Advanced Placement
- Independent Study
- College Hybrid

Definitely look closely at the quarter catch-up design below, as this will reduce the need for recovery at any grade level. It can begin as early as freshman year.

Freshman Year

Freshman year is tough for many students. They were top dogs last year in their schools, now they are the low man on the totem pole again. Emotionally and socially they are still awkward teens looking to find their place, a place where they can find success. This is a brilliant time for freshman teachers to adopt a blended learning model.

Freshman Studies

When students transition to a new setting, like high school, they are often ill prepared for the new level of rigor and the mandatory requirements for graduation. Freshmen need counseling on how to make good decisions, prepare academically, deal with peer pressure, and manage stress. A freshman elective advisory program, such as Freshman Studies, is an ideal blended course to prepare students in soft and study skills when dealing with the challenges of high school.

Blending a digital elective course within the a freshman studies advisory course sets the foundations for digital learning habits that can carry students throughout schooling and into college and/or workforce. This is a great design, one that creates a "no harm, no foul" situation, such that if the student fails to complete the digital elective they will still earn the traditional semester credit for the face-to-face portion.

Again, "**go slow, to go fast.**" There is no rush to move students through the digital courseware quickly. The instructor should use this opportunity to walk students through the digital classroom and talk through the importance of note taking, even though it is a digital course and not a lecture, as well as steps to prepare for exams. That's what advisory is geared towards, helping student to succeed in their classrooms. The habits of digital classrooms, are much the same habits needed to be successful in the traditional face-to-face settings.

If you are using a summer bridge program, allow the students to start the digital elective in the summer session and carry it forward into the school year, via the Freshman Studies advisory course. See the Freshman Studies chapter for more details on possible deployment structures.

Freshman Studies

Semester One	Semester Two
Freshman Studies 0.5 credit	Freshman Studies 0.5 credit
Digital Elective 0.5 credit	Digital Elective 0.5 credit
Lay an elective online course over the top of the advisory face-to-face Freshman Studies class. Completion of the digital courseware will earn students addition high school credits.	

This is an excellent design to kick off the freshman year. In one traditional period, students can earn up to two full credits with the additional digital learning opportunities and guided instruction. What a better way to start of a student's high school career, than by becoming credit rich. As we know, it's the freshman year when students begin getting behind in credits.

Quarter Catch-up

To help students stay on track, freshman teachers should look to grade improvement as a strategy to ensure students don't fall into credit recovery situations. Statistics show that freshman core courses, like Algebra I and English 9 are some of the most failed courses. Years later, as juniors and seniors, way too many students are attempting to recover credits they failed to earn as a freshman.

If students learn how to become digital learners in their freshman studies advisory course, we can use this to our advantage. There is always a handful of students that have already fallen behind at quarter, thus they are on a path to possible credit loss. Data has shown that students can complete a digital course in nine weeks. So… if we pulled students from their failing face-to-face classrooms and have them 'start fresh' in the courseware equivalent, they could possibly be caught up with their peers by semester end.

The goal here is to not wait and "hope" a student passes the face-to-face traditional course, but to catch them early. I remember the day, clear as can be when I was sitting with an administrator, just prior to the quarter end and I asked, "What is your plan for students who have a F this first nine weeks?" He looked at me like I was crazy and replied, "What do you mean?" There was no plan. They were "hoping" that students would change their ways, start studying, ask more questions, put in more time and effort in the class - after nine weeks of bad habits. I'm not saying that they won't take those same bad habits with them in the digital classroom. This is a "no harm, no foul" design. Students were already on a path to fail, the quarter catch-up design can gave them a chance to possibly redeem the situation.

Quarter Catch-up

Quarter A	Quarter B
Traditional Core Class	Digital Courseware
Identify failing student at quarter progress reporting time.	Failing student are pulled from the face-to-face class and assigned to a digital equivalent.
When students show signs of potential course failure at the quarter progress reporting period, let them "start anew" in the digital courseware equivalent. By semester, they potentially could match peers with earning a one-half credit.	

With digital courseware students can start anew, from ground zero. And with proper support and guidance, coaching and mentoring, within a personalized digital learning environment, students just might be able to see the light at the end of the tunnel. A tunnel that was closing in on them in the traditional classroom, where the light had become dim and so far away. It creates a chance that looked nearly unobtainable moments ago.

It would be best if failing students were also given a new classroom setting, but who has time to re-level classrooms and change students' schedules. Make your student information system happy, by looking for other teachers of the same content area, that you can place the handful of students in the back of the room to work on the digital courseware.

For example, Ms. Smith has five failing students in her third period English and Mr. Gomez has four failing English students the same period. Flip the students, so they have a new environment for their fresh start. A new teacher too, who is highly qualified, in the room with peers learning English too and a teacher who is supporting their digital learning. This should <u>not</u> be an independent study setting. Ms. Smith and Mr. Gomez, must take ownership in student success in the courseware. Daily monitoring of progress and setting assignment due dates is crucial to managing student time in the digital courseware. Student-teacher quick check-ins should happen daily. And when opportune times afford themselves in the face-to-face class, such as when students are working in groups or taking a test, will open the door for one-on-one or small group intervention for the digital learners. Again, either you instruct, or you don't. This is not the time to step down from being a caring educator.

The quarter catch-up is an impressive design that crosses grade levels. It can be used in any course at any grade level. Rather than playing catch up down the line in a recovery setting, use the quarter progress grade to identify students in need, at this very moment. Rectify the situation, before students fall further behind.

Sophomore Year

By the second year of high school, students seem to have it down. They have found a peer group, a regular place in the lunchroom, and hopefully have joined a school club or sports team. Speaking of sports, this is a year to consider looking at physical education (PE) and health courses for potential digital solutions. It's also an opportune time to open some fun and engaging digital electives. The goal here is to continue to provide student with minimal risk digital learning settings so they get a feel for the digital classroom, understand the system fully, before jumping too deep into high risk core classrooms in a less structured setting - a setting that will fit perfectly in junior and senior years.

Don't get me wrong. Blended classrooms, with a balanced CIA of blended learning model, continues to be a staple adoption for any grade level. When digital content is a third of the equation, plus guided instruction where students are pushed to authentic assessment, everyone wins.

> Blended classrooms, with a balanced CIA of blended learning model, continues to be a staple adoption for any grade level.

PE & Health Combination

In the previous chapter, Innovative Designs, a six week and nine-week pull out for Health were presented. Even one with Driver Education thrown into the mix. Adding in a digital physical education course may mean less nagging students having to dress out all year long. Also consider adding Health to the traditional PE period to increases credit earning from one to one and one-half credits in a single traditional period of the day. This will open time in a student's schedule to pursue electives that peak their interest.

Digital Electives

More and more vendor courseware products are creating career education electives. Sophomore year is an excellent time to expose students to potential post-graduate workforce and career options. Also consider using the semester electives, plus project learning design as mentioned above, to allow students to take their passions to a deeper level, rich in the four Cs: critical thinking, communication, collaboration, and creativity.

Junior Year

Junior upperclassmen are more mature and are starting to think of life outside high school and what that might look like for them. This is an appropriate time to bring in acceleration and independent learning options.

Nine Week Acceleration

Some students may be looking to accelerate their studies. They may be thinking 'early graduation' or possibly just looking for opportunities to open their schedule for more electives, especially in career education preparation. Think about using a nine-week acceleration design. Data from Clark County has demonstrated that students taking original credit courses need anywhere from twenty-five to thirty hours to complete a digital course. That's about six weeks. Even in a nine-week setting, this leaves teacher plenty of time to blended and support the digital learning experience.

This is an ideal setting for alternative programs, but can be just as useful in a traditional setting, possibly in school-within-a-school program.

Nine Week Acceleration

Semester A		Semester B	
English 11 semester 1	*English 11* semester 2	*U.S. History* Semester 1	*U.S. History* Semester 1
Students spend a traditional eighteen-week semester immersed in digital courseware to complete two full courses in an expedited fashion. Semester one and two courses, in one content area, are taken consecutively in two nine-week quarters.			

In the example above, two grade level core teachers exchange students at the end of the semester, allowing students to earn two full credits in a single class period of a traditional schedule. Since grades are posted at either ninth or eighteenth week your student information system will be happy. This is much easier than adopting a rolling enrollment design.

Advanced Placement (AP)

Juniors are starting to think about college requirements and making their application as strong as possible. Advanced placement courses are an ideal solution. If your courseware catalog has AP courses, why not use them. This does not have to be difficult. Allow the digital AP students to work in the back of the room of a highly qualified instructor who is teaching a general education course of the same or similar content. My absolute favorite is AP Psychology offered in this design, as it is a high interest elective course that few high schools offer.

Layer Advanced Placement (AP) with General Ed

Semester A	Semester B
General Ed Traditional Face-to-Face	General Ed Traditional Face-to-Face
AP Digital Courseware	AP Digital Courseware
Layer a general education classroom with AP students using digital courseware with similar content in the back of the room.	

Students should be supported throughout the learning process. The digital AP content will be rigorous and challenging. The instructor will need to prepare students for the College Board AP examinations, by using time that the general education students are actively engaged, as well as creating additional study sessions before or after school. Some courseware vendors even have AP review software to prepare students for the College Board exams. The layered AP design can roll into senior year courses too, like using AP Government.

Senior Year

Senior year is our last opportunity to prepare these young adults for life beyond high school for college, careers, and citizenship. Digital courseware works well for creating environments where students must manage time and be self-disciplined.

Independent Study

Independent study programs need a level of commitment, motivation, organizational skills, and self-direction much like that required by young adults entering college. Independent study programs can be set up by simply allowing students to have a late start, early out, or 'free' period in the school day yet filled with a digital course. Though anytime you can manage a student's time, via an assigned virtual learning lab, the better.

The catalog of a digital independent study program can be limited and targeted or wide open. This will depend on how the program is staffed. Ensure the staff understands their role and the expectations when working with students from a distance. They are not just a "teacher of record" recording the grade from the digital courseware, but must understand that the grade is also reflection of their efforts, or lack of.

Establish a pacing calendar for students to keep students from procrastinating. I would suggest using an accelerated nine-week calendar. Procrastination is less likely to creep in when timelines are kept tight and simple. Regularly scheduled proctored exams will also ensure that students progress through the courseware in a timely fashion, maybe even finish early. See the Independent Study chapter for possible deployment designs.

College Hybrid

Colleges are noted for holding classes every other day, possibly even in a large lecture hall. What a better way to prepare students for college, than replicating a college experience. The college hybrid design also works well to stretch an excellent teacher to more students. The digital software provides the basic foundation, and the instructor gets to demonstrate their passion and enthusiasm for the content area. Using the CIA of blended learning, students can be pushed to higher levels of analysis and synthesis - just like a college professor might do.

College Hybrid Classroom

Monday, Wednesday, and Friday	Tuesday and Thursday
Group A in classroom with teacher Group B in lab/library digitally learning	Group B in classroom with teacher Group A in lab/library digitally learning
Double a teacher's reach. Half of the students in the classroom with the instructor and the other half in the lab/library engaging with digital courseware. Each week students flip days to balance access.	

The college hybrid design maintains a traditional master schedule, which makes the student information system happy, but attendance can be tricky.

Summary

As students mature, so should digital learning options. Remember to "**go slow, to go fast**." In the lower grades, plan for baby steps and lots of hand holding. This will help students to grasp this new learning venue. Don't skip the software orientation. Those who do, find themselves in early frustration and address more software questions than guiding instruction.

Go slow, to go fast with your staff too. They also need to feel comfortable with this new teacher aide in their classrooms. Use the courseware syllabus and outlines to help ease teacher's anxiety. Remind them that technology

> **Go slow, to go fast. Start small. Add options as students mature.**

is not replacing them, but delivering depth of knowledge one and two - skills acquisition and basic understanding. And it is their responsibility to instruct students, either in the classroom or from a distance. The teacher mindset is crucial to student success. Prepare your staff with solid professional development, surrounded within a professional community of learners growing together.

Once students become familiar with the nuances and intricacies of the software system, they can handle additional courses, as well as classes of increased difficulty. As student grow in their time management and self-motivation skills, they may need less structure, opening the door to college style hybrid designs. I know this design may scare a few people, but imagine the college readiness you are giving your students. When they enter college, they will thank your high school for preparing them for digital learning and the daily structures of college life.

Start small. Add options as students mature. Build out a digital learning environment that grows up with your students and staff. Don't feel like you must jump into the deep end. Put one toe into the water. Push past credit recovery. There are so many more opportunities that courseware can provide. You just need to **think outside the box**.

Remember, all the deployment designs in this book, did not come from one school. They came for nearly one hundred different schools who found a design that worked well for them. I challenge you to find one or two that are a good fit for your vision. Any grade level, in any subject can adopt the CIA of blended learning. That's a splendid place to start.

NEXT STEPS

Questions to Consider

1. Is your school using digital courseware beyond credit recovery? How?
2. What designs intrigue you most?
3. What will it take to adopt the CIA of blended learning, even as a pilot in your school?
4. Where can you begin to **think outside the box**?

Actions

1. Create a one, three, and five-year digital learning vision for your school.
2. Identify teachers who would be open to championing the CIA of blended learning.
3. Consider the various deployment designs and how you might adopt one or two.
4. Don't let the student information system or the four walls of the classroom stop you from thinking outside the box.

Notes

1. *Reimagining the Role of Technology in the Classroom: 2017 National Education Technology Plan Update.* (2017, January). Publication. Retrieved from U.S. Department of Education, Office of Educational Technology: https://tech.ed.gov/files/2017/01/NETP17.pdf

CHAPTER 18
DON'T LET STUDENTS FAIL

"Learning is best measured by mastery rather than time spent in the classroom."

Understanding Competency Education in K-12 (2014)[1]

As we look to revamp classrooms, consider using digital courseware to create a learning environment where teachers don't let students fail. Quarter catch-up, as noted in the previous chapter, is an excellent starting place. Students who are failing at quarter in the traditional semester classroom can start anew, from ground zero with digital courseware. With proper teacher support and guidance, coaching and mentoring, within a personalized digital learning environment, students have an opportunity to obtain the needed credit by semester end and catch up with their peers. Better yet, let's reassess the purpose of school - to educate students, no matter what it takes.

We need to rethink the one-size-fits-all, delivery of curriculum, A-F grading practices, in a seat time based system. It continues to fail our students by allowing *'passing'* students to move on to the next level with Cs and Ds at the end of the year despite the fact they have learning gaps and are ill prepared for the next more advanced level. On a recent visit to one high school the Algebra II teachers were complaining that they had students in their class who had not passed Algebra I. Not only is this unfair to staff, but extremely unjust to the poor students who are age appropriate being passed along in the time-honored system.

The traditional system is biased and inequitable among students. It is treats unfairly those born into families without a college education, that struggle financially, of color, requiring accommodations, and/or raised in homes with a non-English primary language.[2] Rather than advancing students on arbitrary grades, which may include non-academic elements such as behavior, or worse yet low expectation such as minimum Fs, we need to ensure that students reach proficiency in skills needed for college, careers, and citizenship.

If you have digital courseware, the time is ripe to transform from traditional classrooms to personalized, competency-based systems and take full advantage of the courseware in a blended learning environment. Use the CIA of blended learning, to shift teacher mindset from letter grades to meeting proficiency and mastering the course standards and expectations. Their role is to do whatever it takes to <u>not</u> let students fail. The focus is on the individual student and personalizing the learning to meet their specific needs. When the digital courseware can deliver instruction in a personalized setting, the teacher can then focus on individual needs to help master course content.

Competency-based Systems

Competency-based systems have many names; proficiency-based, mastery-based, and performance-based, yet they all have one common goal - "Don't let students fail." The educators in the classroom work with the students in a personalized learning environment that is focused solely on the individual's progress and success. Teachers guide students, ensuring that they are supported and get the individualized attention they need to meet the course standards and expectations, no matter how much time or tutoring is needed.

Digital courseware sets the bare minimum, depth of knowledge (DoK) levels one and two. By using the CIA of blended learning, the teacher scaffolds the learning, making certain that every student has met the required course content. Instructors are empowered to draw upon their professional knowledge in teaching to reach every student as they reinforce and build upon DoK 1-2 to take student learning to strategic thinking (DoK 3) in their course subject areas. Teacher-led instructional settings may be in whole or small group, and most definitely in one-on-one tutoring sessions. Let's not stop there. Teachers should stretch students by extending their thinking with authentic assessments. This means pushing students to create, design, justify and prove, by requiring students to synthesize their learning (DoK 4). This type of balanced approach to the CIA of blended learning is key to <u>not</u> letting students fail.

> Competency-based education is an educational setting that is designed to help all students reach college, career, and citizenship readiness and does <u>not</u> let students fail.

Definition of Competency-based

Let's start with a working definition of competency-based education, from Patrick and Sturgis in *Cracking the Code*.[3] It is an educational setting that is designed to help all students reach college, career, and citizenship readiness and does <u>not</u> let students fail that includes:

- Students advance upon demonstrated mastery.
- Competencies include explicit, measurable, transferable learning objectives that empower students.
- Assessment is meaningful and a positive learning experience for students. Students receive rapid, differentiated support based on their individual learning needs.
- Learning outcomes emphasize competencies that include application and creation of knowledge.
- The process of reaching learning outcomes encourages students to develop skills and dispositions important for success in college, careers, and citizenship.

From the definition, you can see how competency-based education works well with the CIA of blended learning and allows us to **think outside the box**.

Digital **C**urriculum: Given quality digital courseware, student can demonstrate mastery of measurable competencies. By using the digital courseware students are exposed to the core content learning objectives. By setting mastery minimums in the courseware system, student progression is based on minimum mastery levels.

Guided **I**nstruction: The heart-felt teacher guided instruction creates positive learning experiences in small and whole groups, with lots of one-on-one tutoring. Teachers use the data from the courseware to remediate immediately and provide differentiated instruction to meet individual learning needs. Parts one, two, and three of the definition are met.

Authentic **A**ssessment: Project learning, via authentic assessment, emphasize competencies that include application and creation of knowledge using the four Cs designed to target skills and dispositions important for success in college, careers, and citizenship.

The CIA of blended learning is ideal for designing learning environments where students are <u>not</u> allowed to fail. It surrounds students with all the needed elements to be successful in class, as well as life.

Sounds simple - right? Finding the balance between *digital* <u>c</u>urriculum, *guided* <u>i</u>nstruction, and *authentic* <u>a</u>ssessment in what sounds like a free-for-all, overly flexible, non-time framed environment can be difficult and will require a huge mind shift, for everyone - policymakers, school administration, students, parents, and classroom staff - which may include both licensed teachers and/or support staff instructional aides.

Time Honored System

Much like the definition of blended learning, pacing of curriculum tends to be the most difficult element for educators. We are rooted in time. We have a start of school, progress reports, quarters, and semesters to think about. How can we throw pace out the window? **Minimum pace** is an easier concept to accept. And given a minimum pace, teachers can group students and easily identify students in need of individualized instruction and are struggling with *'keeping pace.'*

> With a **minimum pace**, teachers can group students and easily identify students in need of individualized instruction.

By setting **minimum pace**, with check point progressions, students are afforded a calendar of due dates and teachers can intercede when students fall behind the minimum pace. Again, this is a minimum pace, so students are not prohibited from moving ahead. With a minimum pace, course mastery of specific content is scheduled. Thus the teacher can create whole class instructional environments and possible project learning opportunities based on a course timeline. This allows teachers to lesson plan (a very familiar setting) and prepare quality guided instruction situations based on student data. Even students who may have moved ahead can be supported in small group settings.

Image a secondary calendar with all the different grade reporting terms. Below is a general school year calendar. The typical eighteen-week semester has various grade checkpoints, including progress reports, quarter grades, and eventually the semester final grade posted to transcript. In Clark County, summer session is broken into two three-week terms to mimic the traditional school year by only offering semester one courses in the first term and semester two courses in the second term. Summer is commonly focused on credit recovery. Yet in a competency-based system this time could be used not to recover credits, but to allow for more time to master course material.

Traditional Grading Periods

First Semester (18 weeks)				
Progress Report	Quarter 1	Progress Report	Quarter 2	Final Grade
Second Semester (18 weeks)				
Progress Report	Quarter 3	Progress Report	Quarter 4	Final Grade
Summer Sessions (two 3-week terms)				
Progress Report	Final Grade		Progress Report	Final Grade

Grading periods tend to be more disciplinary that rewarding. Progress reports are seen as punitive, such that parents *must* be informed prior to issuing a failing grade. Some schools and districts have policies that weigh the quarter grades, like forty percent each quarter and twenty percent for the course final exam. This too is penal in nature. If a student had misunderstanding or was absent for teacher-led instruction, there was no need to go back and remedy the situation if the grade was already deemed. And mastery for the sake of a pending final exam that is nine weeks away sounds outright absurd to a teenager.

Such policies do not take into account that students are still learning and attempting to master course material. However, if a minimum pace was aligned to each grading period and teachers did everything to ensure students were "keeping pace," than mastery of course material is held to a continuum. Students, who have fallen behind could be provided additional time as needed. Learning would just pick up where one left off, even at semester or summer - until the student mastered the course.

The idea of minimum pace is much easier for blended teachers to visualize. It allows them to establish lesson plans, based on concepts that students are learning in real-time. They can set the stage with class openers or close the day with concept reviews. Build upon vocabulary and dig deeper into course content. Minimum pace, also helps students with self-discipline and time management skills. Students can work together, side-by-side, on the digital content. Peer tutoring becomes a classroom norm as students learn to communicate and collaborate among each other, about course content topics - rather than who is wearing what and did you see who is dating - okay that may still happen. However, the teacher is no longer the sole authority and questions can be posed to one another, where students may feel less intimidated when thirty other students don't see the raised hand or hear the question aloud to a teacher standing at the front of the room. The classroom becomes a community of learners focused on course content mastery. It's a mind shift for both students and teachers. Nobody gets left behind!

Finding a Balance in CIA

Setting minimum pacing and using a balance in *digital* curriculum, *guided* instruction, and *authentic* assessment is a step in the right direction towards not letting students fail, by digital curriculum providing an individualized learning environment, opening doors for targeted teacher instruction based on data, and stretching students with real-world project learning via authentic assessments.

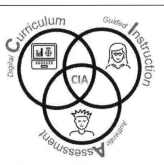

Competency-based learning should not be left to alternative school settings. Matter of fact one alternative school had a tough time with the CIA of blended learning. Even with digital courseware to support student learning, the teachers felt that they too needed an active and equal role in the classroom. So they created general lesson plans, that did not complement the digital courseware but were long established favorite lessons that *'everyone'* should know. And when it came time for students to work on the courseware, the teachers stepped aside. They let students work in isolation, sitting alone, attempting to master the basic skills of the course with no peer interaction or teacher support. It broke my heart to walk into a small classroom, with less than five students spread out in different rows and the teacher sitting behind their desk. It was forty-five minutes of teacher-led instruction, plus forty-five minutes on the computer in a completely disconnected and disjointed learning environment. There was no blending happening and students were failing miserably.

The mindset is so important in this innovative and new style of learning. Students must take control of their learning. Teachers must look for instruction that supports the digital courseware and prepares students for mastery. Everyone is focused on learning and not letting each other fail. It starts with a vision and helping the leader in the classroom, the teacher, understand their place in the CIA of blended learning. The triad of elements; *digital* curriculum, *guided* instruction, and *authentic* assessment, share equally in the success and failure of students.

Let me share a success story. A twenty-five hundred student body traditional high school created a competency-based program. They started with a small pilot of four core teachers and 150 students in grade ten. This was the first step in building a successful program. **Go slow, to go fast.** They started small, with a handful of teachers. Only the four core classes were competency-based. Students took the traditional electives offered at the school. The teachers and administration took a full year to plan, prepare, market, and recruit students for a competency-based learning experience. The program embraced digital learning, mentoring, and project learning. Excellent ingredients for the CIA of blended.

Digital learning was new to both students and teachers, as well as this new flexible learning modality. At first teachers were unclear about their role. In the beginning, some teachers sat back thinking the digital content would take the lead, but saw students struggle with pace and mastery, so they began seeking instructional opportunities - like class opening and closure that they could lead.

The digital academy classrooms were clustered together creating a family atmosphere. Each staff member was assigned a group of students to mentor and monitor progress in all classes. If a student was ahead in one subject area, yet behind in another they were excused from one class to attend to their area of need, in the classroom with the subject teacher on-hand for immediate support. Project learning opportunities extended student learning with group work. Teachers designed creative ways for students to demonstrate mastery of material. Students were afforded time to complete courses early and if needed they could take a little extra time, beyond the eighteen-week semester, to finish. With teacher guidance and all hands on deck support from everyone, nobody was allowed to fail.

Each year a new set of tenth graders were added to the program, building out the digital academy. Again, **going slow, to go fast**. They started with a pilot. Proved that it worked. Staff could view it onsite. Student excitement grew. Parents were encouraged. Recovery programs were not needed. The principal's goal is to create a school-wide competency-based program, starting with a proving ground.

Learning is best measured by mastery rather than seat time, when students and teachers, working with digital courseware, come together and agree to do everything possible to ensure that no child is left behind.

Grading Proficiency

Failure is not an option in a competency-based learning environment. Let no student slip behind the minimum pace. Teachers should target and differentiate instruction for individuals who struggle and help them to meet baseline proficiency. And for students who are excited about the subject and move more rapidly than the minimum pace, allow them to do so. Just like we don't want to leave anybody behind, we also don't want to stop another from moving ahead. So how do we equate proficiency to letter grades?

Today's student information systems and grading windows do not favor competency-based learning. Proficiency based on the depth of knowledge is one way to classify a letter grade in a competency-based implementation. With minimum pacing teachers can ensure students are making progress relative to the courseware content delivery of basic knowledge and skills at low level depth of knowledge (DoK 1-2). This would indicate be a bare minimum proficiency, or letter grade C.

I remember a conversation I had with a social studies teacher about the digital courseware gradebook. He was so upset that students could earn a high letter grade in the courseware with little analysis, comparison, and justify. This is why the teacher-led guided instruction (DoK 1-3) is important to push student beyond basic recall and understanding, into depths of knowledge three, into strategic thinking. Through teacher observation, teacher-graded assignments, and individual quick-check assessments a student's proficiency level could be brought up to an above average B letter grade.

Extended thinking, via authentic assessments, will push students to demonstrate deeper levels of mastery (DoK 4). Students can shine and excel into letter grade A when using project learning activities. Yet, keep in mind all students should be expected to partake in project learning. It should not be reserved only for students seeking a specific letter grade. Authentic assessment projects and activities should be thought of as an opportunity to solidify a student's mastery level.

Remember the CIA of blended learning triple Venn diagram. All three components are important. As you can see, each play an important part in the learner demonstrating proficiency. We cannot leave any one of the three elements out, if we want to ensure students' high-level mastery. The *digital* curriculum is not enough, nor is the isolated *guided* instruction. And without *authentic* assessment students will lack the four Cs that prepare them for college, careers, and citizenship. It is through these three elements that we find the sweet spot in the middle, a balanced approach to CIA, that learners and learning facilitators can target, to demonstrate student mastery of content.

Program Design

Like other designs in this book, competency-based learning program design should start with a problem/opportunity statement, then describe the solution, design, and considerations.

SAMPLE: Competency-Based Learning Program

Problem / Opportunity

Looking for innovative and engaging ways to blend digital content with highly effective teaching staff.

Solution

Create a flexible competency-based school-within-a-school for students who desire a different learning experience. Blended learning classrooms are provided in all core areas, offered in a digital format supported by highly qualified instructors in the classroom. Teachers extend the learning via project-based activities to engage and challenge students. Students are assigned a teacher mentor to ensure a well-rounded and supported learning environment. The schedule is flexible and free flowing to allow access to teachers, as needed, beyond the traditional slated period schedule.

Design

Dedicate a wing of the school for the competency-based school-within-a-school to allow students and staff freedom and access to move among classrooms. Utilize a digital learning platform with rigorous content and project-learning components. Select teachers with a willingness to be innovative with digital content and blended learning pedagogy. To create a balanced approach, expect teachers to plan with the CIA of blended learning: *digital* curriculum, *guided* instruction, and *authentic* assessment. Follow the start and end times of the school day, allowing students to take electives within the general population of the larger school, yet provide freedom to move among the school-within-a-school classrooms as student need arises.

Considerations:
- Digital Content Selection
- Teacher Identification and Training
- Established Teacher and Student Expectations
- Classroom Pedagogy: CIA of Blended Learning
- Competency-based Grading Practices

Share Your Program – Create a One-page Document

It's important to document your planning process. A simple outline like above with problem-solution-design-considerations, is a great place to start.

Using the information above, a school could then create a one-page document that can be shared about their digital learning program. Think of this as your elevator speech, that allows the reader to visualize your innovative instructional design. An elevator speech is a clear, brief message or "commercial" about your school. It communicates who you are, what you're doing to benefit student learning. It's typically about 30 seconds, the time it takes people to ride from the top to the bottom of a building in an elevator. A one-page document can be used for establishing marketing material, sent to local media outlets, or shared when the community members visit your school site. Below is a sample.

Global HS Competency-based Program

The high school administration and blended learning team spent an entire year planning and preparing a small competency-based school-within-a-school blended environment that individualizes student learning via digital content with supportive core teachers. The fundamental concepts of the competency-based school-within-a-school experience are:

1. Digital Courseware
2. Response to Intervention
3. Project-based Learning
4. Teachers as Mentors
5. CIA of Blended Learning

Instructional Quick Facts

Digital Content: Vendor Courseware

Staff: Core content area teachers: Math, Science, English, and Social Studies.

Location: Classrooms housed in the same wing of the school.

Target Population: Application process with approximately 100 students in each grade level. Started as 9th grade pilot, with students rolling up each year.

Model: The competency-based blended learning school-within-a-school to personalize the learning experience. All core classes are taken using digital content and have high-qualified teachers guiding instruction. Project-based activities inspire and stretch student learning. Electives are taken with the general population.

Staff

A team of teachers in all four core areas: math, science, English, and social studies, were selected for each grade level. Staff members were provided training in the digital content and learning management system. Ongoing professional development was provided in the CIA of blended learning: *digital* **C**urriculum, *guided* **I**nstruction, and *authentic* **A**ssessment. Teachers hold sixty-minute weekly site-based collaboration sessions to review student data and program progress. Teachers are assigned a cohort of students to mentor, ensuring student success.

Students

Students applied for the school-within-a-school experience. Parent informational nights were held to describe competency-based learning, where students are provided a personalized learning environment that is balanced between digital content and teacher guided instruction. Students take ownership of their learning and are free to accelerate at their own discretion. Parents were assured that teachers would continue to be a vital part of the learning experience.

Academy Daily Schedule

Students maintain the same start and end times of the regular school day and take electives outside their competency-based core content classes, scheduled with the bell schedule. However, students have a flexible curricular schedule based on their online performance, academic need, and achievement data. For example, a student may be in a math period and is progressing fine in math, but struggling in English, would be excused from the math classroom to spend time with their English teacher. Within their digital classrooms, students can work and learn on their own schedule, setting their own pace. Yet teachers set a minimum pace to ensure progression and completion by semester term. To complete a class and earn credit, students must show seventy percent mastery of one hundred percent of the content. Students are not allowed to fail. Teachers do whatever is needed to ensure that students meet mastery. Project-based learning is utilized to breed curiosity and extend learning.

FOR MORE INFORMATION CONTACT:

Global High School Principal: Mr. Jones

Summary

Digital courseware, along with the CIA of blended learning, are a step in the right direction for competency-based environments. By setting a minimum pace within the eighteen-week calendar, students have flexibility in learning with teacher guided support and scaffolding to ensure proficiency in the course content standards. It will also keep the student information system and parents in familiar territory. Teachers too.

Setting minimum pace, aligned to grading periods, helps teachers to plan and review student data. They can use the data from the courseware to evaluate student understanding and determine who needs targeted instruction, possibly in a one-on-one setting or small group. If students are moving somewhat in the same path over a four to five-week time frame, teachers can create lessons on essential, or power standards and build quality authentic project learning assessments for students to demonstrate mastery of content.

The transition to competency-based is not easy. Two key main ingredients are digital courseware and pedagogy based in the CIA of blended learning. Communication with stakeholder is essential. And it will take a lot of **thinking outside the box**.

Today, entire states, especially on the east coast,[4] and school districts are succeeding in a competency-based system.

Lindsay Unified School District is a public K-12 school district in the farm belt of central California. The entire 4,100 student body has embraced **performance-based** education. Students advance once they have demonstrated mastery of a specific content standard, regardless of their age or the time of year. Teachers bring together learners who are progressing through content as expected (minimum pace) for a quick lesson on new content. Those falling behind receive one-on-one tutoring. If learners are ahead of the game, they are given the freedom to keep going.[5]

- Video (6:48) - See QR code or the Internet Web address below:
  https://www.youtube.com/embed/CgSvFZMYuWM

Competency-based learning does not have to be difficult. It can be as simple as not letting students fail. Put the learner at the center of the learning environment, with teachers doing everything possible to ensure that failure is not an option.

NEXT STEPS

Questions to Consider

1. Is competency-based instruction an option for your school or classroom?
2. Are there policies or legislation that might hinder competency-based learning in your school or state?
3. Are there personnel on your staff that could pilot and lead competency-based learning at your school?
4. How will you prepare staff to make the mindset shift to the CIA of blended learning and setting a minimum pace in the digital courseware within a semester-based instructional setting?
5. What do you need to determine how to document grading procedures for competency-based learning?

Actions

1. Read at *Understanding Competency Education in K-12*. See Note #1 below. Consider looking at other Chris Sturgis publications listed in the Notes.
2. Review school district policies and state legislation that might help or hinder the adoption of competency-based learning.
3. Consider creating a program design one-page document you can share with others about your digital learning program.

Notes

1. *Understanding Competency Education in K-12*. (2014). Whitepaper. Retrieved from CompetencyWorks: https://www.competencyworks.org/wp-content/uploads/2014/09/CWorks-Understanding-Competency-Education.pdf
2. Sturgis, C. and Jones, A. (2017). *In Pursuit of Equality: A Framework for Equity Strategies in Competency-Based Education*. Publication. Retrieved from CompetencyWorks: https://www.competencyworks.org/wp-content/uploads/2017/06/CompetencyWorks-InPursuitOfEquality-AFrameworkForEquityStrategiesInCompetencyBasedEducation.pdf

3. Patrick, S. and Sturgis, C. (2011, July). *Cracking the Code: Synchronizing Policy and Practice to Support Personalized Learning*. Publication. Retrieved from International Association for K-12 Online Learning: https://www.inacol.org/resource/cracking-the-code-synchronizing-policy-and-practice-for-performance-based-learning/

4. Sturgis, C. (2016, October). *A Reaching the Tipping Point: Insights on Advancing Competency Education in New England*. Publication. Retrieved from International Association for K-12 Online Learning: https://www.inacol.org/resource/reaching-the-tipping-point-insights-on-advancing-competency-education-in-new-england/

5. Quattrocchi, C. (2014, June). *How Lindsay Unified Redesigned Itself from the Ground Up*. Web Article. Retrieved September 23, 2017 from: https://www.edsurge.com/news/2014-06-17-how-lindsay-unified-redesigned-itself-from-the-ground-up

CONCLUSION

If you have read this far, thank you! *Think Outside the Box* was born out of love and passion for ensuring that teachers and schools have the tools, like the CIA of blended learning, the four mindsets (online, blended, innovator, or designer), and well-crafted deployment designs to create high quality digital learning environments. The subtitle said you would get 10+ designs for secondary schools. I doubled my word. Throughout the book, we have looked at over twenty different deployment designs:

Ten Deployment Designs	Ten Innovative Designs
1. Traditional Semester-based Online	1. College Hybrid Classroom
2. Single Content Super Classrooms	2. *Mass* Hybrid Classroom
3. Credit Recovery Programs	3. Nine-week PE/Health Mix and Match[+]
4. Freshman Academy*	4. Six-week PE Pull Out
5. Independent Study Courses	5. Flipping Grade Level Core
6. Unit Recovery or Grade Improvement	6. One Semester Elective Extended[^]
7. Blended Classrooms or Academy	7. Layer AP with General Ed
8. Graduation Flex Academy	8. Freshman Studies*
9. Suspension and Homebound	9. Quarter Catch-up
10. Summer Programs	10. Competency-based Learning

[+]Add Driver Ed for Second Option
[^]Two Elective Extension Possibilities
*Similar to Freshman Academy

If you missed any of the innovative designs, don't worry, they can all be found in the appendices. For ease of locating some of the other resources in the book, like the CIA of blended learning lesson plan template and example, they too have also been placed in the appendices.

I've had the great fortune to work in a very large school district, allowing me to see a multitude of deployments, working with numerous schools to design and deploy digital learning environments. It has been my pleasure to compile and catalog them here for others to ponder and consider.

Remember to *go slow, to go fast*. Start small. Consider the seven steps in the ladder of success. It all starts with a vision. One that you can sell to others. Be clear on your expectations. Help teachers with developing a growth mindset. One that is not afraid to fail. One willing to try new things. One that is reflective and will iterate and try again, over and over.

Making the transition to blended learning and partnering with digital curriculum, is not as easy as it sounds. I've seen many programs fail because teachers were not provided the professional development needed to change classroom pedagogy. A teacher's mindset is crucial to a successful program. They must know and understand the value of all three elements in the CIA of blended learning, especially when it comes to lesson planning:

- *digital* **c**urriculum
- *guided* **i**nstruction
- *authentic* **a**ssessment

Creating a balanced approach in the classroom is key to student success. Use the CIA lesson plan template to push teachers into reviewing the digital courseware so they can support what it is asking students to know and be able to do. Then they can identify areas where students will need scaffolds, or have misconceptions, so they can guide instruction to deeper levels of knowledge. And when digital courseware is used to deliver baseline content, time is afforded for stretching students into authentic assessment opportunities, building skills for college, careers, and citizenships via the four Cs; 1) critical thinking, 2) collaboration, 3) communication, and 4) creativity.

Remember, it's a blended classroom. Just because the digital courseware has discussion posts, it doesn't stop teachers from hosting a live discussion. Or if there are projects, consider making them team projects. Create relationships within the classroom. Don't allow students to feel isolated behind a computer screen. Students and their teachers need to work together to create an environment where nobody gets left behind. Please, don't let students fail.

I challenge you to **think outside the box**.

APPENDICES

PART 1   FOUNDATIONS OF BLENDED

PART 2   TEN DEPLOYMENT DESIGNS

PART 3   PLANNING FOR SUCCESS

CIA of Blended Learning

Digital **C**urriculum - COMPUTER ACCESS

Digital curriculum can be thought of as a teacher's aide with significant advantages.

- Baseline Instruction
  - Low level Depths of Knowledge (DoK)
- Aligned to Standards
- Engaging Digital Software
- Individual Data Points

Guided **I**nstruction – TEACHER ENDEAVORS

With digital curriculum taking center stage in the learning environment, the teacher role changes.

- Extended Coaching on:
  - Power standards
  - Where students typically struggle
  - Scaffolding and extending content
- Small and Large Group, plus one-on-one Tutoring

Authentic **A**ssessments – STUDENT APPLICATIONS

In a classroom filled with digital tools students can stretch their thinking into analysis, synthesis, and creation while engaging in the Four Cs:

5. Critical Thinking
6. Communication
7. Collaboration
8. Creativity

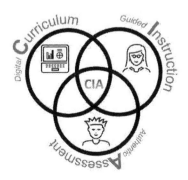

TEMPLATE: Unit Lesson Planning with the CIA of Blended Learning

 C = *Digital* **C**urriculum COMPUTER ACCESS • Engaging software • Aligned to standards • Personalized learning space • Individual data points • **DoK 1-2**	Preview the digital curriculum and identify topics and activities presented. List what students will be asked to know and do.
 I = *Guided* **I**nstruction TEACHER ENDEAVORS • Data driven • Small and whole group • Scaffold, support, stretch • Power standards • **DoK 1-3**	Determine what guided instruction is needed to support student mastery. Data will help diagnose groupings and individuals.
 A = *Authentic* **A**ssessment STUDENT APPLICATIONS • Critical thinking • Communication • Collaboration • Creativity • **DoK 3-4**	Consider how to stretch student learning with authentic assessments: working with peers, real-world applications, projects, and productions.

EXAMPLE: Unit Lesson Planning with the CIA of Blended Learning

C = *Digital **C**urriculum*
 	
COMPUTER ACCESS
• Engaging software
• Aligned to standards
• Personalized learning space
• Individual data points
• **DoK 1-2**
	Preview the digital curriculum and identify topics and activities presented. List what students will be asked to know and do.
	• Lssn 1 – What is a Polynomial + Quiz
	• Lssn 2 – Adding and Subtracting Polynomials + Quiz
	• Lssn 3 – Multiplying Binomials + Quiz
	   o Practice: Area Model
	• Lssn 4 – Multiplying Polynomials + Quiz
	   o Journal: Area Model
	• Lssn 5 – Polynomials Wrap-Up
	   o Discussion: FOILed Again
	   o Diagnostic Pre-Test
	• Computer Scored Test
	• Teacher Scored Test

 I = *Guided **I**nstruction* TEACHER ENDEAVORS • Data driven • Small and whole group • Scaffold, support, stretch • Power standards • **DoK 1-3**	Determine what guided instruction is needed to support student mastery. Data will help diagnose groupings and individuals. • Daily opener and closure • Data-driven individual tutoring and small group • SCAFFOLD: Combine like terms, Distributive property, Area of a rectangle • *Misconceptions* +/-: Identifying like terms, paying close attention to negative terms, variables remain the same • *Misconceptions* x & /: Forgetting the middle term, increased exponent of variables • GROUPWORK: Area Model and FOIL • OPTION: Jeopardy Pre-Test Prep • RESOURCE: Khan Academy: Videos + Practice https://www.khanacademy.org/math/algebra/introduction-to-polynomial-expressions
 A = *Authentic **A**ssessment* STUDENT APPLICATIONS • Critical thinking • Communication • Collaboration • Creativity • **DoK 3-4**	Consider how to stretch student learning with authentic assessments: working with peers, real-world applications, projects, and productions. • Extension – Performance Task: *Polynomial Farm* http://www.radford.edu/rumath-smpdc/Performance/src/Emily%20O'rourke%20-%20Polynomial%20Farm.pdf

Blended Models Weekly Lesson

Station Rotation Weekly Lesson Model

Monday	Tuesday	Wednesday	Thursday	Friday
Teacher-led large group instruction	One-third rotations A - Indp. online B - Peer work C - Teacher group	One-third rotations A - Peer work B - Teacher group C - Indp. online	One-third rotations A - Teacher group B - Indp. online C - Peer work	Full class digital independent learning and 1-on-1 conferences

Lab Rotation Weekly Lesson Model

Monday	Tuesday	Wednesday	Thursday	Friday
Teacher-led large group instruction	Full class digital independent learning and 1-on-1 conferences	Teacher-led large group instruction or peer pair work	Full class digital independent learning and 1-on-1 conferences	Authentic learning tasks and/or explorations

Flipped Classroom Weekly Lesson Model

	Monday	Tuesday	Wednesday	Thursday	Friday
Classroom Instruction	Teacher-led small or large group instruction	Peer-to-peer collaborative work and 1-on-1 conferences	Teacher-led small or large group instruction	Peer-to-peer collaborative work and 1-on-1 conferences	Authentic learning tasks and/or explorations
Outside Digital Instruction	Independent digital learning with data points to guide instructional needs				

Flex Weekly Lesson Model

	Monday	Tuesday	Wednesday	Thursday	Friday
Courseware	Independent digital learning in an online semester-based courseware with individual data points				
Classroom Instruction	1-on-1 conferences & tutoring	1-on-1 conferences & tutoring	Teacher small group instruction	1-on-1 conferences & tutoring	Authentic learning tasks

Four Mindset & Their Costs

Online $$$$

Too often when digital content is first introduced, the initial thought is, "I'm now an online teacher." This is a huge mind shift change. Teachers feel out-of-control when the digital content takes the lead. The courseware determines the content, the delivery modality, and even the assessment elements. When students and teacher are physically distance communication is difficult. With no bell schedule, self-motivation is essential for both the teacher and student. Lack of control creeps in when teachers don't physically see their students daily. Teachers must work hard to maintain the human touch, the caring heart, in the online classroom.

Blended $$$$

When students and teachers see each other daily, it is much easier to control the learning elements, even when introducing digital content. Consistent social dynamics among peers and with the teacher in the daily face-to-face classroom allows teachers to take control of the learning environment. The role and expectations change in this environment, however there is comfort in the traditional bell schedule and the ability to pace student learning.

Innovative $$$$

Early adopters tend to be risk takers and enjoy the thrill of trying something new. They typically can deal with change and the need for iteration. The ability to take risks with others can support teachers. By creating a peer group that openly reflects upon the changing dynamics of the classroom when digital content plays a role can sooth the anxiety of possible failure. It's learning from failures that drive this mindset.

Designer $$$$

Open educational resources (OER) and learning management systems (LMS) have created an environment where many administrators believe teachers can create their own digital learning environment. It takes a rare person, with lots of time to curate OER content, craft a digital learning environment within a LMS into units of instruction based on the components of an effective lesson, with thought-provoking assignments and quality assessments – PLUS teach. That is asking a lot!

Online Highly Qualified Teacher Self-Evaluation Rubric

Exceeds	Meets	Approaches	Needs Improvement
Classroom Preparation			
Attended a software training and feels very comfortable with interface, and supports peers as needed	Attended a software training and knows where and can access how to guides and videos	May have been trained by another on site or self-taught using how to guides and videos	Has no software training and unaware of how to guides and videos
Has thoroughly gone through the course content and identified possible areas where student might need assistance	Has looked over the course content, syllabus, and gradebook	Has previewed the course gradebook	Is not aware of the course content
Monitoring Students Progress			
Sets individual students calendar start and end dates, holds students accountable to due dates, and adjust as needed	Sets individual students calendar start and end dates, reminds students of due dates	Sets individual students calendar start and end dates	Does not set calendar start and end dates
Knows each student's progress and where they should be to date and quickly turns around teacher scored activities	Monitors student progress daily – checking computer scored activities and teacher grading	Looks for teachers graded materials to be graded, but does not monitor computer scored grades	Does not check student progress daily. Waits to post grade upon course completion
Interactions with Students			
Uses the email and course announce features to keep students informed and motivated (e.g. "shout out" to students for good scores or discussion posts)	Uses the email (e.g. welcome to class) and course announce (e.g. spring break coming) features to keep students informed	Uses the email system to speak with individual students about grades only, does not use whole class announcements	Does not email individual student nor posts whole class announcements
Has established system for student access to teacher for support and tutoring (e.g. after school, at lunch) that can be accessed or required (e.g. failing grades)	Actively identifies students who need help, directs them to resources and best practices (e.g. study guides, note taking) with process to request tutoring	Directs students to others for tutoring (e.g. lab coach, peers) or directs students to resources within the courses (e.g. study guides)	No student support or tutoring system in place

Virtual Lab Coach Self-Evaluation Rubric

Exceeds	Meets	Approaches	Needs Improvement
Monitoring Student Progress			
Greets students as they arrive and takes attendance	Takes attendance	Takes attendance	Takes attendance
Knows individual student's progress and discusses daily with student	Knows individual student's progress and discusses weekly with student	Can locate individual student's progress if prompted	Unaware of individual student's progress
Interactions with Students			
Has established classroom behavioral expectations posted in several places in room and consistently holds students to them	Has established classroom behavioral expectations posted and holds students to them	Has established shared classroom expectations with students, yet not be posted in classroom	No established classroom behavioral expectations
Actively looks for and provides immediate assistance to students who may need help to make progress (e.g. watches for lack of screen changes/page turns, sees no new assessment attempts over several days, looks over handed-in work and quiz answers)	Actively seeks out students who may need help to make progress (e.g. watches for lack of screen changes/page turns, sees no new assessment attempts over several days, looks over handed-in work and quiz answers)	Responds to students who request assistance and occasionally looks for students who may need help	Responds to students who request assistance
Communication with HQ Teachers			
Daily communication with HQ teachers to share updates and concerns regarding student progress	Weekly communication with HQ teachers to share updates and concerns regarding student progress	Limited communications with HQ teachers	Few or no communications with HQ teachers

Academic Integrity			
Vigilant proctoring of students taking computer scored assessments. Has separate testing stations away from others, with screens visible and near teacher's station	May uses highly visible marker (e.g. flag, cone) to indicate which students are testing. Ensures academic integrity (e.g. no talking, no use of cell phones, no other websites)	Proctoring consists of opening computer scored exams at student workstation. No identification as to who is testing	Proctoring consists of opening computer scored exams and may student leaves alone in the room

Online Student Self-Evaluation Rubric

Exceeds	Meets	Approaches	Needs Improvement
Daily Progress			
Completed software orientation	Completed software orientation	Aware of software orientation, but has not accessed.	Not aware of student orientation within software
Uses calendar to identify what activities need to be completed	Makes daily progress	Jumps around within the course	Has login, but may not access course
Within the Course			
Keeps a course notebook	Takes notes	Reads course material	Does not read material
Always seeks built in scaffold activities, links and print resources	Accesses built in resources to help complete assignments	Skips over work deemed "too hard." Unaware of built in resources.	Clicks around, may be on non-course content websites.
Prepared for exams prior to taking them	Accesses notes prior to taking exams	Reads questions and all choices when taking exams	Quickly guesses on exam questions
Daily monitors progress in gradebook	Access gradebook to check grades	Periodically checks grades	Unaware or avoids gradebook
Interactions with Teachers			
Verifies with lab coach that they are on pace towards completion	Review progress with lab coach to help stay on pacing	Talks to lab coach about non-academic topics	Avoids lab coach
Maintains an open dialogue with course teacher (e.g. email or verbal)	Dialogues with course teacher (e.g. email or verbal)	Knows name of course teacher, but never "spoke" to them (e.g. email or verbal)	Unaware who is the course teacher

Individualized Academic Educational Plan (IAEP)

Course	Sem.	Type	Start	End	Weeks	Grade
CORE COURSES						
Geometry	1	Original	08/14	10/13	9	
Geometry	2	Original	10/16	12/22	9	
World History	1	Original	08/14	10/13	9	
World History	2	Original	10/16	12/22	9	
English 10	1	Original	01/8	03/14	9	
English 10	2	Original	03/15	05/24	9	
Biology	1	Original	01/08	03/14	9	
Biology	2	Original	03/15	05/24	9	
ELECTIVES						
Career Planning I	1	Original	08/14	09/22	6	
Computers	1	Original	04/09	05/24	6	
Health	1	Original				
Spanish II	1	Original				
Spanish II	2	Original				
RECOVERY COURSES						
Algebra I	2	Recovery	02/20	04/06	6	
Geoscience	2	Recovery	01/08	02/16	6	
English 9	1	Recovery	09/25	11/09	6	
English 9	2	Recovery	11/13	12/22	6	
Spanish I	2	Recovery				
PE	2	Recovery				

Innovative Designs

College Hybrid Classroom

1 teacher	Monday, Wednesday, and Friday	Tuesday and Thursday
5 periods	**Group A** in classroom with teacher **Group B** in library digitally learning	**Group B** in classroom with teacher **Group A** in library digitally learning

Seventy students each period, half in the classroom with the teacher, the other half in the library engaging with digital courseware. Each week students flipped days to balance access.

Mass College Hybrid in Lecture Hall

1 teacher	Monday, Wednesday, and Friday	Tuesday and Thursday
5 periods	**Group A** in theatre with teacher **Group B** in lab digitally learning	**Group B** in theatre with teacher **Group A** in lab digitally learning

One hundred students each period, half in the front of the theatre with the teacher, the other half in the back half of the theatre (e.g. virtual lab) engaging with digital courseware. Each week students flipped days to balance access.

Nine-week PE/Health Mix and Match

Semester A		Semester B
9 weeks = Lab	9-weeks = Lab	18 weeks = Classroom
Health Online Content	*Personal Fitness* Online Content	*Physical Education* Face-to-Face

One-half of the students are pulled from PE class each semester to attend to online courses. Using an online PE course (or an equivalent), students earn one full credit in PE, along with one-half credit in Health for a total of 1.5 credits by the end of the term in a single class period.

Nine-week PE/Health/Driver Ed Mix and Match

Semester A		Semester B	
Personal Fitness, s1 Online Content	*Personal Fitness, s2* Online Content	*Health* Online Content	*Driver Education* Face-to-Face

Students spend three nine-week sessions in digital PE and Health courseware, plus a nine-week face-to-face Driver Education session to earn two full credits in a single class period of a traditional schedule.

Six-week PE Pull Out

Semester A			Semester B		
6 weeks	6 weeks	6 weeks	6 weeks	6 weeks	6 weeks
PE or Online Health (1st group)	PE or Online Health (2nd group)	PE or Online Health (3rd group)	PE or Online Health (4th group)	PE or Online Health (5th group)	PE or Online Health (6th group)
One-sixth of the students are pulled from PE class every six weeks to attend to an online Health course. At the conclusion of the term students have earned 1.5 credits.					

Flipping Grade Level Core

Semester A		Semester B	
English 10 semester 1	*English 10* semester 2	*World History* Semester 1	*World History* Semester 1
Students spend a traditional eighteen-week term immersed in digital courseware to complete two full courses (semester courses are taken consecutively each nine weeks) in an expedited fashion. An English teacher and social studies teacher exchange students at term. Students earn two full credits in a single class period of a traditional schedule.			

One Semester Elective Extended

Semester A	Semester B
Blended Classroom with Digital Courseware	Extended Project Learning and Personalization
OR	
Blended classroom with digital courseware to set the foundations. **PLUS,** extended project learning to personalize the learning experience.	
One semester courseware can be stretched to a full year with extended learning opportunities into the second semester, using the CIA of blended learning.	

Layer Advanced Placement with General Ed

Semester A	Semester B
General Ed Traditional Face-to-Face	General Ed Traditional Face-to-Face
Advanced Placement Digital Courseware	Advanced Placement Digital Courseware
Layer general education classrooms with Advanced Placement students using digital courseware in the back of the room, with immediate access to the course instructor.	

Freshman Studies

Semester One	Semester Two
Freshman Studies 0.5 credit	Freshman Studies 0.5 credit
Digital Elective 0.5 credit	Digital Elective 0.5 credit
Lay an elective online course over the top of the advisory face-to-face Freshman Studies **class**. Completion of the digital courseware will earn students addition high school credits.	

Quarter Catch-up

Quarter A	Quarter B
Traditional Core Class	Digital Courseware
Identify failing student at quarter progress reporting time.	Failing student are pulled from the face-to-face class and assigned to a digital equivalent.
When students show signs of potential course failure at the quarter progress reporting period, let them "start anew" in the digital courseware equivalent. By semester, they potentially could match peers with earning a one-half credit.	

Competency-Based Learning Program

Problem / Opportunity

Looking for innovative and engaging ways to blend digital content with highly effective teaching staff.

Solution

Create a flexible competency-based school-within-a-school for students who desire a different learning experience. Blended learning classrooms are provided in all core areas, offered in a digital format supported by highly qualified instructors in the classroom. Teachers extend the learning via project-based activities to engage and challenge students. Students are assigned a teacher mentor to ensure a well-rounded and supported learning environment. The schedule is flexible and free flowing to allow access to teachers, as needed, beyond the traditional slated period schedule.

Design

Dedicate a wing of the school for the competency-based school-within-a-school to allow students and staff freedom and access to move among classrooms. Utilize a digital learning platform with rigorous content and project-learning components. Select teachers with a willingness to be innovative with digital content and blended learning pedagogy. To create a balanced approach, expect teachers to plan with the CIA of blended learning: *digital* curriculum, *guided* instruction, and *authentic* assessment. Follow the start and end times of the school day, allowing students to take electives within the general population of the larger school, yet provide freedom to move among the school-within-a-school classrooms as student need arises.

Considerations:
- Digital Content Selection
- Teacher Identification and Training
- Established Teacher and Student Expectations
- Classroom Pedagogy: CIA of Blended Learning
- Competency-based Grading Practices

Global HS Competency-based Program

The high school administration and blended learning team spent an entire year planning and preparing a small competency-based school-within-a-school blended environment that individualizes student learning via digital content with supportive core teachers. The fundamental concepts of the competency-based school-within-a-school experience are:

6. Digital Courseware
7. Response to Intervention
8. Project-based Learning
9. Teachers as Mentors
10. CIA of Blended Learning

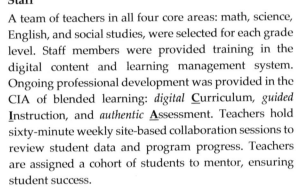

Instructional Quick Facts

Digital Content: Vendor Courseware

Staff: Core content area teachers: Math, Science, English, and Social Studies.

Location: Classrooms housed in the same wing of the school.

Target Population: Application process with approximately 100 students in each grade level. Started as 9th grade pilot, with students rolling up each year.

Model: The competency-based blended learning school-within-a-school to personalize the learning experience. All core classes are taken using digital content and have high-qualified teachers guiding instruction. Project-based activities inspire and stretch student learning. Electives are taken with the general population.

Staff

A team of teachers in all four core areas: math, science, English, and social studies, were selected for each grade level. Staff members were provided training in the digital content and learning management system. Ongoing professional development was provided in the CIA of blended learning: *digital* **C**urriculum, *guided* **I**nstruction, and *authentic* **A**ssessment. Teachers hold sixty-minute weekly site-based collaboration sessions to review student data and program progress. Teachers are assigned a cohort of students to mentor, ensuring student success.

Students

Students applied for the school-within-a-school experience. Parent informational nights were held to describe competency-based learning, where students are provided a personalized learning environment that is balanced between digital content and teacher guided instruction. Students take ownership of their learning and are free to accelerate at their own discretion. Parents were assured that teachers would continue to be a vital part of the learning experience.

Academy Daily Schedule

Students maintain the same start and end times of the regular school day and take electives outside their competency-based core content classes, scheduled with the bell schedule. However, students have a flexible curricular schedule based on their online performance, academic need, and achievement data. For example, a student may be in a math period and is progressing fine in math, but struggling in English, would be excused from the math classroom to spend time with their English teacher. Within their digital classrooms, students can work and learn on their own schedule, setting their own pace. Yet teachers set a minimum pace to ensure progression and completion by semester term. To complete a class and earn credit, students must show seventy percent mastery of one hundred percent of the content. Students are not allowed to fail. Teachers do whatever is needed to ensure that students meet mastery. Project-based learning is utilized to breed curiosity and extend learning.

FOR MORE INFORMATION CONTACT:

Global High School Principal: Mr. Jones

BRING KIM LOOMIS
TO YOUR SCHOOL OR DISTRICT

Kim Loomis is available for digital learning program design consultation. She can provide empowering keynotes and professional development workshops, plus offer insight to online course development and strategy. Having served at a variety of levels as an educator and administrator, Kim shares her personal experience and wisdom to equip educators and leaders to take risks that result in innovative learning opportunities for today's youth. Her insightful combination of research, personal stories, and practical advice for online and blended learning helps others to **think outside the box.**

Popular Messages from Kim Loomis

Although her presentations can be tailored to your specific needs,
here's a sample of keynote presentations that Kim has previously done:

Blended Learning Models

The CIA of Blended Learning

Crafting a Roadmap for Digital Learning

Growing Up Digital in High Schools

10 Design Models for Deploying Courseware

ABC's of Developing Online Content

Connect with Kim Loomis

Connect with Kim Loomis for more information about bringing her to
your school or district:

 Kim@i3DigitalPD.com

 @LoomisKim

 Kim Loomis

ABOUT THE AUTHOR

Kim Loomis is a leading educator in the area of innovative program design for digital learning environments. She is the Director for K-12 Online and Blended Learning in Nevada's Clark County School District, the fifth largest district in the nation. Kim supports hundreds of schools and thousands of teachers in the deployment of digital content. She has a background rich in digital learning systems, professional development, and innovative program design, from digital instruction, course development, vendor contracting and set-up to implementation and refinement. Kim is a former high school mathematics teacher, building administrator, curriculum coordinator, high school reform and innovative projects manager. She has a well-rounded background for blended learning program design and has shared her passion for digital learning across the nation in various speaking engagements and at national conferences. She is also the founder of i3DigitalPD.com a consulting and professional development firm that helps schools and districts create meaningful digital learning opportunities for students. Her family, which includes two tech-savvy teenage daughters, enjoys soccer, traveling, and hiking.

Photo by Michele Nelson

Think Outside the Box

Made in the USA
San Bernardino, CA
23 December 2018